Praise for This Book

"An important text guiding the reader through the important and necessary changes to be made for ethnographic research to keep pace with the growth and pace of the digital world."

—Kareema J. Gray, Johnson C. Smith University

"This text is definitely one all researchers and PhD candidate mentors have to have in this day of digital communication."

—Lois McFadyen Christensen, UAB School of Education

"*Hybrid Ethnography* provides practical approaches to conducting both online and face-to-face ethnographic research. Readers will find a detailed step-by-step methodology, with clear ethical guidelines, that supports cutting-edge interdisciplinary studies."

—Monica Prendergast, University of Victoria

"The author has developed a book which is highly engaging whilst being a very pragmatic and helpful guide for the novice researcher to undertake hybrid ethnographic research. The author takes the novice researcher by the hand and guides them with a flowing narrative through a very practical approach so they can fully grasp the research process."

—Elaine Haycock-Stuart, The University of Edinburgh

"Today's cultures span physical & virtual spaces. This is an important book that will teach tomorrow's ethnographers how to navigate effectively across these multiple and distributed spaces."

—Nick V. Flor, University of New Mexico

"*Hybrid Ethnography* is an important and cutting-edge text and a must-read for serious students of ethnography as well as researchers and scholars in fields such as literacy, teacher education, educational leadership, English education, and pop culture. This book is an excellent companion text to classics in ethnography."

—Margaret-Mary Sulentic Dowell, Louisiana State University

Qualitative Research Methods Series

Series Editor: David L. Morgan, *Portland State University*

The ***Qualitative Research Methods Series*** currently consists of 58 volumes that address essential aspects of using qualitative methods across social and behavioral sciences. These widely used books provide valuable resources for a broad range of scholars, researchers, teachers, students, and community-based researchers.

The series publishes volumes that

- Address topics of current interest to the field of qualitative research
- Provide practical guidance and assistance with collecting and analyzing qualitative data
- Highlight essential issues in qualitative research, including strategies to address those issues
- Add new voices to the field of qualitative research

A key characteristic of the Qualitative Research Methods Series is an emphasis on both a *"why to"* and a *"how-to"* perspective, so that readers will understand the purposes and motivations behind a method, as well as the practical and technical aspects of using that method. These relatively short and inexpensive books rely on a cross-disciplinary approach, and they typically include examples from practice; tables, boxes, and figures; discussion questions; application activities; and further reading sources.

New and forthcoming volumes in the series include the following:

Qualitative Instrument Design: A Guide for the Novice Researcher
Felice D. Billups

How to Write a Phenomenological Dissertation
Katarzyna Peoples

Reflexive Narrative: Self-Inquiry Toward Self-Realization and Its Performance
Christopher Johns

Photovoice for Social Justice: Image Capturing in Action

For information on how to submit a proposal for the series, please contact

- David L. Morgan, Series Editor: morgand@pdx.edu
- Leah Fargotstein, Acquisitions Editor, SAGE: leah.fargotstein@sagepub.com

Hybrid Ethnography

To Gaspé

Hybrid Ethnography

Online, Offline, and In Between

Liz Przybylski

University of California, Riverside

Los Angeles | London | New Delhi
Singapore | Washington DC | Melbourne

FOR INFORMATION:

SAGE Publications, Inc.
2455 Teller Road
Thousand Oaks, California 91320
E-mail: order@sagepub.com

SAGE Publications Ltd.
1 Oliver's Yard
55 City Road
London, EC1Y 1SP
United Kingdom

SAGE Publications India Pvt. Ltd.
B 1/I 1 Mohan Cooperative Industrial Area
Mathura Road, New Delhi 110 044
India

SAGE Publications Asia-Pacific Pte. Ltd.
18 Cross Street #10-10/11/12
China Square Central
Singapore 048423

Printed in the United States of America

ISBN: 978-1-5443-2032-8 (pbk)

This book is printed on acid-free paper.

20 21 22 23 24 10 9 8 7 6 5 4 3 2 1

Acquisitions Editor: Leah Fargotstein
Editorial Assistant: Sam Diaz
Production Editor: Gagan Mahindra
Copy Editor: Karin Rathert
Typesetter: Hurix Digital
Proofreader: Barbara Coster
Indexer: Wendy Allex
Cover Designer: Dally Verghese
Marketing Manager: Shari Countryman

BRIEF CONTENTS

DETAILED CONTENTS

PREFACE

This book was inspired by a need. When I began doing ethnographic research, not only was there no established methodology for hybrid digital and physical ethnography, but the academy had yet to grapple with the reality of the research field that was both on and offline. This acknowledgment required thorough theorization on my part before I was able to put together the framework for research, which I articulate in this book. *Hybrid Ethnography* represents years of reading, consultation with established faculty in a variety of disciplines in the humanities, arts, and social sciences, and trial and error in the field. I successfully completed a dissertation project using this methodology and have since been employing it for my ongoing professional research projects with popular musicians and fans whose artistic lives unfold in what I have productively theorized as the hybrid online/offline sphere. When I teach ethnographic methods, I find that there is no concise source that has yet worked through the hybrid reality of much contemporary fieldwork, so I offer this volume.

Hybrid Ethnography provides the roadmap that I so desperately craved early in my career. It exists alongside traditional ethnographic methods books. What this book adds is an important clarification: many ethnographic fieldsites, notably those in expressive culture, exist across digital and physical spaces. In these pages, you will learn how to design, carry out, and analyze ethnographic research that situates itself in this type of hybrid fieldsite. This research-focused volume pays particular attention to media, including images, audio, and video that are part of contemporary research into expressive culture. Intentionally a small volume, it should be easy to read before starting a new research project and then handy to revisit sections as a step-by-step guide. References to relevant scholarship are offered throughout.

HOW TO USE THIS BOOK

The volume is an actionable supplementary text that is designed to be actively used by researchers during the design and completion of research studies. It synthesizes a new methodology for interacting with participants in increasingly integrated online/offline fields. *Hybrid Ethnography* pays special attention to research in expressive culture because so many fieldsites in this area require an accounting of more than just physical or digital spaces. Creating, cataloging, annotating, and analyzing photos, audio recordings, and videos are particularly important for expressive culture research, and so they are covered in detail here. Researchers in other disciplines may also find the method useful.

Making sense of researcher positionality is crucial for ethnographic research; my own background and vantage point have influenced how I synthesized and developed a methodology for hybrid ethnography. My experience lies in doing ethnographic research in expressive culture that exists between online and offline fields as well as actively participating as a musician and performance maker. My training in ethnomusicology, musicology, performance studies, gender studies, and Indigenous studies is evident in my writing. So too is an interdisciplinary approach that has long guided my research. The method is informed by the style I have developed as a practitioner and scholar—I come with a critical ear, listen for what makes sense, and adapt and connect what can be productive in other contexts. This interdisciplinary, asset-based attitude means that my scholarly approach to hybrid ethnography is flexible for research in a variety of contexts.

As a researcher, I have been lucky to be faced with a scene that required me to adapt to the field as it was, not as I was trained to expect it would be. This methodological problem—how to handle hybrid fieldwork theoretically and practically—has become a bit of an obsession. It intersects, augments, and works through my research and teaching. I've talked with fellow researchers, participants, students, and media professionals about issues that arise in this kind of work, and I've learned from all of them. Our dialogues have produced new ideas. Here, I synthesize strategies from fieldwork practice—mine and others—and literature that speaks to the scholarly practice of contemporary ethnography. I've read and listened widely to inform my method, and you will encounter ideas from anthropology, ethnomusicology, dance studies, performance studies, cultural studies, sociology, and interdisciplinary scholarship in expressive culture—including theatre, music, dance, and other types of performance. I've refined the methodology of hybrid ethnography over multiple projects, and I offer you here strategies that make the work possible and productive.

Recently, I was discussing a book on online ethnography with a graduate student. She had expressed some frustration about being unable to understand the authors' method based on what she felt was a limited description from the text. I offered a series of open-ended questions, which brought her to the crux of the matter: She couldn't grasp how it was possible to understand the sociality of a particular scene either by doing face-to-face participant observation or by logging on to relevant social media sites as an internet user. And how indeed? Either strategy would cut out key players and venues of interaction. So we went through an example together, creating a visual map of key players and locations in the hybrid scene and discussing how different kinds of connections across the online/offline divide informed the sociality of the scene, not as it has been conceived of in scholarship but as it really exists. This mapping exercise is described in detail in Chapter 5 of this book. I offer this and other exercises that have been useful for me and my students and mentees for you and your students to use and adapt for your particular situations.

My research has required innovation, and I offer you this methodology as a flexible format for adaptation. Online interaction is constantly changing, as are peoples' attitudes toward internet-based technologies. Apprehension, excitement, and creativity vis-à-vis integrating online communication technologies in our lives is uneven across groups and individuals, and even a single person changes the way they fold technology into their daily life over time. This book is a guide, and like all guides, it is best used as a starting point for the user and adapted to their individual projects. I've written with points of opening and choice on purpose, knowing that you can make this into what you require for your own research.

The COVID-19 pandemic has greatly affected lives and research, and it will continue to do so. When I began research for this book, adapting to the hybrid field was in some ways a choice; now many people must incorporate online activity for our ethnographies, and for our daily lives. Realistically, some blending of online and physical face-to-face research will be a viable option for most people. Aspects of this methodology that expand into the online parts of field sites are crucial for many projects due to the pandemic. I started working on this methodological research because the musicians I work with blend their offline and online worlds so seamlessly that talking about spaces as separate is largely inaccurate. Due to global pandemic, bridging offline research to online research became uncomfortably timely. But with this discomfort comes some possibility. While equal access to internet connectivity and hardware is a concern, many more people can log on to hear D-Nice on Club Quarantine than would get to be live at an in-person event with him and his guests, who have included Alicia Keys and Michelle Obama. With so many people and so many kinds of activities moving online, we experience layers of intimacies and pseudo-intimacies. We stare at other people's posters and home decor over Zoom, and read confessional posts about how Taylor Mac and possibly everyone else is also listening emotively to Fiona Apple's new album. Even with the frustration and loss that come with pandemic-related changes to research, the tools offered in this book can help researchers be flexible even in times of crisis.

THE HYBRID RESEARCH PROCESS

Over ten concise chapters, this volume will proceed as a research process typically does, from site selection to data collection to analysis and presentation. As research often moves back and forth as aspects of each step are refined, non-linear reading is also invited. To start, Chapter 1 introduces a hybrid example from fieldwork and offers a starting point for identifying your own hybrid fieldsite and research question. It describes the primary practical and theoretical concerns that hybrid ethnography addresses. It provides strategies for developing a hybrid ethnographic project that productively draws on relevant aspects of physical and digital ethnographic work. Chapter 2 begins an ongoing discussion of research ethics in hybrid research. It outlines specific project design guidance for an application to an institutional review board, research ethics panel or board, or other oversight board. Further, the chapter delves into professional standards that are not expressly covered by these bodies. This chapter approaches ethical questions at the design phase. Professional ethics appear throughout the book as related to subsequent research phases: reflective and responsible interactions in Chapter 3, ethics for documentation in Chapter 6, those guiding interviews and surveys in Chapter 7, and for sharing results in Chapter 9. Introducing the selection of a research site and pre-fieldwork preparation, Chapter 3 helps the reader ask and answer the questions, "Where are you?" and "Who are you?" grounding the researcher in reflexive practice. This chapter begins a strategy used throughout the volume, in which exercises will help you to focus on your particular research project as you plan and conduct your fieldwork.

Moving into the active research phase, Chapter 4 introduces strategies for collecting data across online and face-to-face aspects of your fieldsite and cataloging multiple kinds of media. Chapter 5 addresses interpreting your initial experience and refining your questions as you continue in the field. This includes creating a lexicon for your particular online platform and making information you encounter online mutually understandable with what you are learning across all aspects of your site. The chapter also prepares you for dialogic ethnography in the hybrid field. Chapter 6 attends specifically to expressive culture, describing how to use photo, audio, and video documentation. The chapter describes researcher-created and dialogic recording techniques and then identifies how the hybrid ethnographer makes sense of media made exclusively by participants. As a whole, the chapter prepares the ethnographer to create and use materials by the researcher and collaborators in the hybrid field. In Chapter 7, you will learn strategies for conducting interviews in a variety of settings, as well as ways to conduct qualitative online surveys. Chapter 8 provides strategies for analyzing your ethnographic information, and then illustrates these with step-by-step insights from a field research example. Chapter 9 outlines the writing process that takes you from analysis through presenting your findings. This section offers approaches for sharing your research results in academic publications as well as in venues with a wide public audience. You will discern what to publish—and not publish—and navigate multiple formats for communicating through written text and media. Finally, Chapter 10 concludes with tools for becoming adaptable as fieldwork continues to change. Reflective and also future oriented, the chapter reconnects you as a reader back to your thoughts from the beginning of the project described in Chapter 1, refined through the research process.

This book is designed as a practical guide for the researcher. This does not aim to replace the vast literature on field methods, but it does outline a specific method for integrated online/offline research. I aim to be clear and even conversational when explaining the methodology, and I know that you are a sophisticated reader. I speak to you as someone who already has some knowledge of ethnography. You might be a seasoned researcher who is adding hybrid ethnography to your fieldwork plan or a student completing coursework or getting started on a new research project. This book provides focused further reading so you can follow up on topics of particular interest. *Hybrid Ethnography* can also be used as part of a course on fieldwork methods. I have used some activities outlined in the book as graded assignments for graduate students in field methods classes, and others I have offered to mentees needing to hone particular aspects of their projects. The book in its entirety could comprise a course section dedicated explicitly to hybrid ethnography, or the chapters could each be read alongside related material thematically throughout the semester or quarter. The activities, while designed for the individual researcher, can also be given as assignments to students and then discussed together. If you use this volume in your classroom, you might also try challenging your students to keep finding new examples in their field to extend the case studies I cite in the book. As more researchers thoughtfully and carefully research across an online/offline divide, there will be an increasing variety of studies published as articles, websites, presentations, documentaries, and in forms we may not yet have imagined. Perhaps subsequent editions of this book will reference your own hybrid ethnographic research.

ACKNOWLEDGMENTS

I could not have completed this project—nor can any ethnographer successfully undertake any project—without the meaningful support, dialogue, and engagement of fellow participants. I am grateful to far more people than I could name in this regard. This book reflects back on many research projects undertaken over years. I have been lucky to learn from and with Cindy Soto, Lori Faber, Negwes White, Jordan Gurneau, April Tsosie, Raven Roberts, Mary Tucker, Josie Dykas, Mahli Saunders, and Kitty Alfonso Gurneau, and all the hip hop show participants. Thank you to Sherry Farrell Racette, Niigaanwewidam Sinclair, and all the inspired crowd-media makers who took part in Idle No More. I recognize Jared McKetiak, Michael Elves, and the radio community at UMFM. Thank you to the many music and language teachers I have learned alongside over the years. I extend much appreciation to artists and arts professionals who are trying new forms of collaboration and have invited me into the process, notably Andrew Balfour, Lindsay Knight, Mel Braun, Sandy Mielitz, and everyone who has experimented alongside you.

Every time I advise research projects or teach ethnographic methods, I learn from my students. Thank you all for learning with me. Special thanks to Lindsay Rapport, Chun Chia Tai, Nattapol Wisuttipat, Jessica Margarita Gutierrez Masini, Stella Chan, and Kevin Sliwoski. Much appreciation to my colleagues at the University of California, Riverside: to fellow faculty members, especially Deborah Wong, as well as to library specialists who advised on resources, especially Bergis Jules and Robin Katz. I appreciate my many scholarly mentors, including Drew Davies and Ramón Rivera-Servera, for offering thoughtful advice as I faced, and then sought strategically to join, the online and offline aspects of one of my first fieldsites. René Lysloff, I have been inspired by your writing, and then usefully challenged by our dialogues about the changing nature of online participation. Nasim Niknafs, thank you for being a generous research collaborator. Erin Nathalie Edwards, your clear vision of how I could explain this methodology in clear language—and belief that it was worth doing—drove this entire book.

My research for this project was supported by a Fulbright Fellowship, a Hellman Fellowship, and grant funding from the University of California,

Riverside Academic Senate. I thank the selection committees for seeing potential in the research projects I present here, and recognize that it takes material support to make scholarship move forward.

I extend deep appreciation to Leah Fargotstein and the entire editing and production team at SAGE Publications for seeing the relevance of this book and working to make it a reality. Thank you for taking a leap with me into a new direction in research methods. Alongside SAGE, I recognize the following reviewers for their feedback throughout the review process for this book:

Andrew J. Brown, Western Washington University
Lois McFadyen Christensen, University of Alabama at Birmingham
Robert L. Dahlgren, SUNY Fredonia
Paula Dawidowicz, Walden University
Teresa Delfín, Whittier College
Kris Erickson, Ryerson University
Nick V. Flor, University of New Mexico
Kimberley Garth-James, Notre Dame de Namur University
Kareema J. Gray, Johnson C. Smith University
Elaine Haycock-Stuart, The University of Edinburgh
Jocelyn Hermoso, San Francisco State University
Hosu Kim, College of Staten Island
Amanda Licastro, Stevenson University
Eve C. Pinsker, University of Illinois at Chicago
Monica Prendergast, University of Victoria
Andrew Spieldenner, California State University San Marcos
Margaret-Mary Sulentic Dowell, Louisiana State University
Jasmine Ulmer, Wayne State University

Finally, I thank my family: you sustain me. You are so patient as I dedicate time and energy to research and writing. This work would not be possible without all the big and small ways you support me along the way.

AUTHOR BIO

Liz Przybylski (BA, Bard College, MA and PhD, Northwestern University) is an Assistant Professor of Ethnomusicology at the University of California, Riverside where she specializes in hip hop performance practices. As an ethnographer whose research sites exist between the online and offline in hybrid fields, her interdisciplinary popular music research moves with performers, industry professionals, and audiences, responding to changes in technology and communication strategies.

Dr. Przybylski was awarded a Fulbright Fellowship to conduct research with hip hop artists and music broadcasters in Winnipeg. Her research in both popular music pedagogy and Indigenous hip hop appears in *Ethnomusicology, Journal of Borderlands Studies*, and *IASPM Journal,* among others. She has presented her findings internationally, including at the Society for Ethnomusicology, Native American and Indigenous Studies Association, Feminist Theory and Music, International Association for the Study of Popular Music, and International Council for Traditional Music World Conferences. She also shares ideas from her research projects in free and open access articles, blog posts, and online commentary. As part of her ongoing project to present her work in multimedia formats, Dr. Przybylski hosted the world music show "Continental Drift," on WNUR in the Chicago area, and has conducted interviews with musicians for programs, including "At the Edge of Canada: Indigenous Research," on CJUM in Winnipeg. Also working with new media and web-based sources, she served as the Media Reviews editor for the journal *American Music.*

Committed to linking research with pedagogy, Dr. Przybylski's teaching works in tandem with the interdisciplinary nature of her scholarship. She regularly teaches ethnographic methods at the graduate level, and other courses are often cross-listed in fields including anthropology, gender and sexuality studies, and ethnic studies. She has also taught adult and pre-college learners at the American Indian Center in Chicago and the Concordia Language Villages program of Concordia College. In professional leadership, her elected positions include serving as the president of the Society for Ethnomusicology, Southern California and Hawaii Chapters, and serving on the Society for Ethnomusicology Council.

INTRODUCTION TO HYBRID ETHNOGRAPHY

It's a chilly October afternoon. I am walking slowly through the streets of Winnipeg, which, at that time, was still known as the most dangerous city in Canada. I am in the city's North End—the neighborhood best known for its diverse population of Indigenous people and immigrant Canadians, concentration of social service organizations, legacy of missing and murdered women, and the hot bannock bread distributed to hungry people by a local organizer from her own truck.

On this particular day, the neighborhood is pulsing with a different kind of energy. Not only am I walking very slowly, but I am also walking to a beat. And I am not alone. A small crowd has gathered, and our rhythm has a purpose.

Idle No More, a Canadian-born grassroots movement for global Indigenous rights and environmental activism, has brought us to a public event where we are walking in solidarity with the Elsipogtog Mi'kmaq First Nation. During our medicine walk, a small group begins singing and playing hand drums. We pause, and people take turns speaking into a megaphone. Participants talk about fractured and resilient communities, police violence, and the dwindling natural resources on Canadian reserves. Indeed, First Nations reserves just outside Winnipeg function on a boil-advisory for their tap water.

As in previous public North End gatherings, news cameras are filming. And again this time, official video and audio feeds are not the only forms of media being collected and distributed. From the megaphone, one participant urges us all to "be our own media." We use our phones to document and to share the images, sounds, and words of the event beyond the street where we have gathered.

People can—and have—expressed much about the reasons participants might prefer to disseminate their own media rather than rely on mainstream news sources. Taking out cell phones and going online during a physical gathering helps to share images and sounds with their own networks, removes the need to rely on outside sources to tell their stories, and allows them to tell the stories that matter most to them. It also allows participants to send personalized invitations and encouragement for friends to come join the rally in the street, completing the circuit from the physical to the digital and back to the physical again.

In the moment I just shared, I am most struck by the interconnectedness of this circuit. When rally attendees were encouraged to "be our own media," the only question was whether we *would*, not whether we could. Cell phones and other mobile devices with microphones, cameras, and internet access make the ability to record and share information widely available. While equal access continues to be a real concern, it is no longer just official broadcasters who can record and tell stories. In the world of the academy, it is no longer just the ethnographer who can do so, either.

How can we as ethnographers conduct fieldwork that responds to the very real technological changes that continue to alter the ways in which we communicate? The ethnographer has long had an important role as an observer, analyst, and storyteller. As Clifford Geertz wrote in 1973, "The ethnographer 'inscribes' social discourse; *he writes it down*" (Geertz, 1973, p. 19). This is hardly the whole of the ethnographer's work. The process is relational; texts, understandings, and records already exist through performance, embodied knowledge, and writing. Further, the researcher uses all of these sources to contextualize and analyze, ultimately making the (hopefully) elegant leap from the specific to the general that allows her conclusions to be relevant beyond the specific community in which she lives and works. This is the process by which, ideally, "understanding a people's culture exposes their normalness without reducing their particularity" (Geertz, 1973, p. 14). But before any of that is possible, the ethnographer has to "write it down."

But not anymore. In the 21st century, many participants are documenting themselves. This is true with video, audio, photos, and the commentary that individuals create during live events. It is also true of the plethora of media and text that participants share online. No longer is it a privileged role to be the only one documenting an event, choosing what to record, and sharing details with others. It is true now, as it was in the 19th century and earlier, that ethnographers interpret the meaning of the speaking in writing it down. Added now to this function of inscribing discourse is an additional responsibility linked to this profusion of media: Even as we continue to create our own records, what can be learned from interacting with so many other participants' recordings of discourse?

When Frances Densmore began researching Native American music in the first decade of the 20th century, she traveled with heavy and expensive equipment to make recordings. She secured funding from the Bureau of American

Ethnology to help shoulder the costs. A now-famous photograph of her research from 1914 depicts Densmore and a Dakota interlocutor, Mountain Chief, both facing a large gramophone, which sits squatly on a sturdy case. Densmore took on the task of inscribing quite literally, etching recordings that have preserved the sound of her collaborators' songs. She was working with sound recording machines and film cameras that were hard to come by; choices made during her research have determined what is preserved—and what is not—of the sound and images she encountered (Densmore, 1918).

Now that a typical cell phone can take photos and record audio, the ethnographer is not the only person capable of documentation. Yet choosing what to record and conducting a high-quality documentation process requires expertise. An ethnographer must also sift through a large quantity of digital and physical information, a skill set that neither Densmore's nor Geertz's contemporaries experienced as it exists today. Now, it also requires a critical skill set to tell an analytical story that makes sense of all of the documents, data, and experiences available to ethnographers. This means having a strong methodology that cuts across both digital and physical field spaces. Because—if you take one thing away from this introduction, let it be this—very rarely will ethnographers today find a space to be purely one or the other. As data collection, management, and sharing continue to change, ethnographers need to nimbly organize and understand multiple streams of data from changing sources. Today's research landscape requires an updated set of analytical skills to tell the story of how and why people are interacting with contemporary culture and to understand how we make meaning from our interactions with expressive culture. This book outlines the process in an explicit manner in order to support hybrid research that is responsive to contemporary realities.

OVERVIEW

In hybrid fieldwork, like physical and online work from which it germinates, the researcher engages in cultural practices as a participant while simultaneously observing the field with critical ears and eyes, all the while making it known to others in the scene that participant-observation is part of an overt research process. Fieldwork is often defined as a highly personal aspect of research in expressive culture. Helen Myers describes fieldwork as the process that reveals the "human face" of the research (Myers, 1992, p. 21); Bruno Nettl calls fieldwork "the most personal part of the job" (1983, p. 136). These ethnographers' humanizing tone here is notable: Ethnography is about relationships between people. Crucially, even during moments in which technology mediates faces, this kind of research is still about seeing, hearing, and knowing each other. As in physical and online studies, cultural meanings are experienced and expressed through the body.

The emergence of the hybrid field offers a contemporary parallel to a shift away from so-called armchair ethnography that was practiced in the late 19th and early 20th centuries. No longer just relying on data collected by another person, anthropology embraced the idea of a researcher going alone or in pairs to other places to learn about foreign cultural practices. As practiced in anthropology, as well as in later-emerging disciplines of ethnomusicology, dance studies, performance studies, and related fields, ethnography expanded to include research in a scholar's home, as well as across multiple sites. This research relies on in-depth, personal knowledge of people and groups (Marcus, 1998, addresses the intimate nature of this engagement). Some scholarship suggests that online ethnography is a kind of shortcut to accessing lots of data (Kozinets, 2006) or that it facilitates *non*-participant observation (Snodgrass, 2014). Hybrid ethnography is emphatically not a return to the armchair approach. Truly integrating one's self into multiple aspects of one's fieldsite does involve online work that we can do at home or remotely via a smartphone in many places. Yet thinking of hybrid fieldwork as any kind of shortcut means you are missing the point: Your research site has many aspects, and it takes dedicated time and attention to become an active, culturally aware participant across all of them. In the hybrid field, "face-to-face" communications may take place across a table or through video chatting. The focus on the personal aspect of this kind of research is maintained from the offline to the online and in-between.

Since the beginning of online ethnography, a distinction has been made between "virtual" and "physical" worlds, which carries into much contemporary work (Boellstorff, Nardi, Pearce, & Taylor, 2012; Markham & Baym, 2009; Miller & Slater, 2000). Online ethnographers frequently take advantage of digital tools (Murthy, 2008). Networked tools do indeed offer strategies for, for example, taking fieldnotes in new mediums. However, there is more to be accounted for than simply jotting traditional fieldnotes in an online format: The hybrid field requires a conceptual shift in ethnography.

As online connectivity has become more integrated into many people's lives, the idea of true connection online has gone from being met with suspicion (Rheingold, 1998) to making a self-conscious argument for itself (Lysloff & Gay, 2003) to being largely accepted as a manner in which people can connect (Nardi, 2010; Pink et al., 2016). Groundbreaking work on how identity formation has changed in the online sphere (Turkle, 1997) can now be connected back through the hybrid scenes in which we live and work. Online spaces offer possibilities for connection, exchange, and mutual support. And today they are increasingly integrated into daily life.

Conducting research in a manner that accounts for the hybrid field responds to the contemporary reality in which fully online and fully offline methodologies offer useful—but not sufficient—tools. Current strategies for ethnography show their limitations precisely where fields overlap. Picture a pair of ethnographers who enter a media lab in a library or a cybercafé in a place where computer access is far from universal. Participants come to the space as physical bodies, and their individual lives impact the relationships in the room. If the ethnographers stay offline, they can learn about the dynamics of the lab, but they have no insight into participants' interactions with each other through internet-mediated communication or beyond the room at all. Should the ethnographers instead choose an online ethnography, they could participate in what is happening online, but they lack context that comes from seeing the physical space in which participants produce their communication online. While it is rarely pragmatic or even possible to be everywhere that individuals are interacting when they engage with networked communications, seeing only a single part of the space precludes the researchers' abilities to analyze sociality in participants' full, lived environments.

In response to the limitations of other methods, hybrid ethnography accounts for a shift in not just what researchers do but how all participants approach the field. In your scene, you may encounter different degrees of involvement in an online or offline portion of a hybrid fieldsite. Yet in all online research situations, autonomous, unique people have created and continue to update the online platform and participate together. These individuals are already part of physical lives and scenes. This also has implications from the online to the offline. When interacting in a primarily online space, we benefit from considering the different experiences and structures in which people participated before they moved online or between which they move when they are not on the internet; when we look at physical spaces, we should account for the direct and indirect ways that people have formed their creative processes previously. For example, members of a laptop ensemble who improvise together may also be informed by one individual member who also plays with a jazz combo on a different night of the week—for a researcher, not knowing this information leaves a crucial gap in knowledge about how improvisation works in this context.

HYBRID ETHNOGRAPHY: THEORETICAL AND PRACTICAL SHIFTS

Fieldsites that span digital, physical, and digital-physical spaces require more than an additive methodology; the hybrid field requires *a conceptual shift* in conducting research. In hybrid research, the conception of space and the related positioning in time, the delimitation of the material of research, and the way individuals and groups are implicated all shift in qualitative ways.

The "What" and "Who" of Hybrid Research

The "what" and "who" of the research change in multiple ways. As described in the first part of this chapter, hybrid ethnographers must prepare for a role change in which we are not the only people who record social interaction; this involves a conceptual shift. When interpreting media in the hybrid field, researchers contend with content that was made by participants, including ourselves. The line between producers and consumers, which is relevant particularly for expressive culture research wherein audience/artist divisions are important aspects of performance, can become indistinct. When at a live concert, an individual may make and share a video from the audience, in that moment acting as audience, content maker, and distributor, all at once.[1] We must interpret individual actors in multiple roles—as artists/content makers, audience members, readers—in ways that change based on time, location, and purpose.

This hybrid method accounts for the way the "what" of the research shifts. We still inscribe discourse, in person, and sometimes do so online as well. Yet we also interact with large amounts of discourse that is already pinned down—and we need tools to organize and analyze this discourse. With the proliferation of information available, the researcher's role expands further into analysis of great quantities of data, including our own observations, recordings, surveys, and interviews; website and social media data; and recordings, photos, posts, and other texts created and distributed by participants. We must make sense of data that comes from many sources and viewpoints that circulate for multiple purposes. As will be detailed in Chapter 6, identifying

[1]Take a moment to think about how this manifests in your own scene: perhaps in the way fans make response videos, viewers learn dances from online videos that they then perform for other audiences, or artists create social media posts related to their branding that are not exclusively showcasing their primary artistic content.

who is making the media, why they choose to create and circulate it, and for what gain—financial or otherwise—impacts how the researcher interprets the data in context. Data profusion places pragmatic limits on research: These can inform what the researcher considers. In other words, it might be germane to ask about the performance background of everyone participating in a scene but not germane or possible to attempt to know everything about all aspects of those same participants' lives. Researchers must make choices about what to investigate—which necessarily involves choosing what not to investigate. The structures in which we work, and our place in them, impact what we choose to include, what we do not, and why. These concerns fall under the umbrella of positionality, a key concept in hybrid fieldwork that will be explored in the following chapter.

The hybrid field offers more information and spaces of interaction than a fully online or fully offline field—and more analytical tools as well. The core of ethnography remains the patient observation of and participation in interactions between researcher(s) and fellow scene members. Just as researchers now reach beyond inscribing social discourse, we also now have tools that allow for multiple levels of analysis. Research software allows us to sort through vast amounts of information feasibly, catalog it in a manner that can be searched and displayed easily, and enumerate some types of results very quickly. These possibilities in no way preclude the use of techniques that are central to in-person fieldwork. Rather, they help us to account for the massive amount of data that is available and offer possibilities for doing multiple layers of research simultaneously. We can thus extend the focused work of participant observation by filtering through relevant data—text on websites or social media platforms, tags on photos, words in emails—to get a more detailed contextual picture of our field.

In hybrid ethnography, the "who" of the project becomes complex. As being active online becomes a common characteristic in many places, researchers encounter individuals whose daily life moves between—and may aim to integrate—multiple aspects of ourselves. This internal multiplicity is amplified by the 21st situation phenomenon in which many people live and move across social media spaces, but the idea that the self comprises multiple identities rather than a single coherent one was first productively theorized in a wholly offline context (Stets & Serpe, 2016). Because life and work involve aggregating many aspects of our identities, a fieldwork model needs to stretch to make sense of the many aspects of ourselves and each other. Even if we may know that each individual has multiple aspects of themselves that they show in different times and places, field methods typically encourage us to identify participants by relevant descriptors and use these categories to form conclusions: What differences in attitude do we hear based on age categories? Are men and women and nonbinary people cast in the same roles in the ritual under study? In the hybrid field, we're asked to hold our community members in their multiplicity. Instead of explaining ruptures away, we let them help us think through the core research questions.

An intersectional approach helps to account for the complexities of the self and fellow participants in the hybrid field. As will be detailed in Chapter 3, the researcher's position in relationship to the field and to fellow participants is mutually informed by multiple aspects of one's identity. Carefully analyzing how you understand yourself, how fellow participants understand themselves, and how you are read by others reveals much about the various perspectives that are at play. This kind of analysis also makes you aware of how power operates across various parts of the scene. Engaging in intersectional analysis often provides insight into how you will approach the praxis of research. Because of the increased interconnection between researcher and participants in hybrid ethnography, the theory/praxis divide erodes, and the researcher needs to thoughtfully and reflexively address the practical concerns of fellow participants.

The "When" and "Where" of Hybrid Research

Hybrid ethnography responds to a reality in which the "where" of the field has changed. This is a shift that started with the advent of online or "virtual" ethnography.[2] As Rene Lysloff points out in his study of online electronic music making, his experience of the field changed when he chose to study an online community (Lysloff, 2003). Shifting to an online ethnographic approach makes sense because Lysloff examined the ways in which musicians share ideas and create new music through digital channels. Yet when working with this online community, Lysloff's relationship with place changed in character. In physical ethnography, Lysloff conducted research in West Central Java and analyzed the way narrative performances are consciously interrupted for dramatic purposes (Lysloff, 1993). Place in physical ethnography is tied to regional cultural practices. The place-specific conceptions of narrative frame the situated use of chaos in the dramas about which Lysloff learned. The experience of the ethnographer in a physical scene was experienced immediately

[2] I do not find the term "virtual" entirely productive, as its colloquial use suggests that it is a stand-in-for or a pseudo-ethnography. Online ethnography is real ethnography, but it is ethnography that has a different fieldsite and different rules from physical ethnography. Hence, I use the term "online" ethnography, except when quoting other sources that use the term "virtual."

through the body; Lysloff writes of his visceral experiences of Java, from "driving my motorcycle on dusty and dangerous two-lane highways filled with chaotic traffic" to "drinking hot, sweet jasmine tea" (Lysloff, 2003, p. 235). In his online work, however, participants in the electronic modular music scene come from across the globe and interact without leaving their home locations. As a result, they bring a variety of regionally distinct attitudes toward composition and sociality to the interaction. In contrast to the physical immediacy of face-to-face ethnography, Lysloff identifies how he is seated in a chair in his home.[3] When he mentions "'traveling' the far corners of cyberspace" (Lysloff, 2003), "traveling" is in scare quotes: One "travels," yes, but to different "kinds" of social space (p. 236).

Interrogating the way physical locations are discursively brought into being through research has also been a pursuit of scholars active in physical research since the reflexive turn in ethnography. One clear example of this problematizing comes from feminist anthropology: Troubled by a contrast between an unmarked researcher and marked other, scholars noted that this bifurcation created an assumed geographic distance between researcher and researched, which in turn implied a temporal distance locating those who research in the present and those who are researched in the past (D'Amico-Samuels, 1991). Revealing how assumed marked and unmarked categories are indeed all socially situated, scholars worked to close the distance between researcher and researched. Bringing these ideas forward into contemporary research, we continue to be informed by a conceptual change that questions the distance in space and the assumed distance in time between field and researcher as well as field and the academy. Present studies, then, should take seriously shifts that have already occurred in research and placemaking; the researcher must account for the ongoing negotiations that hybrid online/offline spaces require.

Conceptualizing the "where" of the field requires the researcher to develop an understanding of "when" as well. As will be explored in Chapter 4, for some hybrid scenes, participation gains richness if you and your collaborators are online at the same time. This allows for immediate chat responses, multi-player games, online jam sessions, and other activities that thrive on instant responses. Yet for many kinds of activity on the web, there is a lag time between one participant posting information and others responding to it, whether that information be a video file on a sharing site or

[3]Sensory details can lead to revelations across all aspects of the hybrid field—see Chapter 4 for more.

a short update to social media. Researchers might enter mid-conversation, reading a series of messages and responses before adding their own. Taking the ethnography in the cybercafé as an illustrative example, the researcher interacts face-to-face and online in encounters with specific start and end times and face-to-face in spaces with known geographies. There are also moments of face-to-face interaction in a particular place that involve interaction with websites or platforms; the participants who make and interact with these forums may or may not be participating at same time as the participants gathered in the physical café. As a result, the hybrid field involves integrated use of synchronous and asynchronous communication styles.

Online ethnography readied the researcher for widespread asynchronous communication, though this was not a completely new phenomenon.[4] Online aspects of the hybrid field, like a relevant social media site, require the skills and mental framework for understanding and engaging in asynchronous communication. Simultaneously, hybrid field researchers engage in synchronous communication. When you get to rehearsal, how do conversations unfold if some—but not all—participants have already read and responded to a post about your group's last performance? What about when someone reads a post on their phone during an in-person meeting and is suddenly up to speed in both the social media site and physical meeting room at the same time? The circuits that online fieldwork began now expand multidimensionally to include physical interaction, including physical interaction with internet-mediated spaces and devices.

Physically going to and coming back from the field and having an experience bounded by geography and time is common in many kinds of research: An education researcher may go to work at a school for a semester or an anthropologist may spend years studying a culture in a geographic location far from home. Though the idea of a fieldsite that is always "on" came regularly into scholarly literature with the advent of online fieldwork (see, for example, Meizel, Cooley, & Syed, 2008), always being connected to the field was not new to ethnography, just to certain ethnographers. Constant potential access and no predetermined end date for fieldwork was only new to ethnographers who traveled to a physical fieldsite for a specific length of time; researchers working in their home communities have long faced this scenario.

In hybrid fieldwork, a feeling of constant activity extends further, as the researcher must navigate physical, virtual, and blended aspects of the site. Across all aspects of the field, it can feel like there is always something

[4] Asynchronous communication exists in the offline field in the form of voicemails, letters, photographs, reports, and so forth.

happening. In my own research, I have found that I can almost always interact with new communications if I refresh social media, scroll through the websites in my scene, read user-shared video comments, or connect with users online. Paired with regular activity in concerts, rehearsals, social spaces, and media distributors, the only moments of pause are those that I create. Practically, this means maintaining a schedule for interaction across multiple areas of the fieldsite that are always potentially active, observing potential variance across the field, and dialoguing directly with fellow participants about the way they interact with various parts of the field.

The possibility of constant connectivity requires carefully navigating one's roles. Across locations in the hybrid field, one's position can shift: You may have many markers of insider belonging in an expressive culture group yet be a relative newcomer to the most used social media presence among members. This is an expansion of the fieldwork phenomenon in which all of us navigate degrees of insider and outsider status across our researcher–participant roles. Given the multivalent nature of the hybrid field, this flux in status is compounded. Reflections on degrees of the insider researcher position are helpful here, and though they only speak to a physical field, Durham (2014) and Burnim (1985) are good starting points. Because of the potential for ongoing access, at least to the online portions of the field and potentially to some physical parts of the site as well, "leaving" the hybrid field follows the precedent for "leaving" insider fieldwork. It presents not so much the end of the relationship with fellow participants but another role shift away from active new research toward a less formal manner of interaction.

Sharing Hybrid Research

Because hybrid ethnographers interact in a field that has online and offline aspects, we are well positioned to explore innovative ways of sharing information. Many researchers share more than a printed paper essay to convey our meaning to audiences. Multimedia research projects offer the potential for multivocal products that incorporate and re-present perspectives and voices of multiple researchers and co-participants. Because we already work in hybrid spaces, some options for communicating with multiple publics are logical outputs of the process itself. This is an exciting opportunity for research and its relevant dissemination to many audiences.

In the hybrid field, there is an increasing interrelationship between researcher(s) and participants. This change is due in part to the greater research landscape. After the reflexive turn, academics across disciplines changed research practices from masking the position of a falsely assumed objective researcher. In the 21st century, we are experiencing increasing attention to power dynamics and decolonizing methodologies. In a related move, the academy is opening to calls for community-based research and social responsibility. As anthropologist Bea Medicine summarizes, "As with any human relationship, reciprocity, responsiveness, and responsibility are essential" (Medicine, 2001, p. 5). This increasing interrelationship is also due to changes in technology. Increased internet access and a proliferation of sharing platforms make it possible for research findings to reach more people in more ways; these possibilities invite researchers to think expansively and collectively about ways of sharing that are both possible and desirable.

WHAT YOU NEED TO BEGIN

This guide is designed to facilitate the planning and implementation of a hybrid research strategy. In order to get the most out of it, it is recommended that you iron out the following details before beginning.

Select Your Area of Study

The area of study may be any aspect of expressive culture, including music, dance, film, theatre, or other types of performance—including performance that is part of daily life. This book is most helpful once you have developed working knowledge of your area, including general topics in research, specific concerns in research related to your sub-specialty, and any specific technical proficiency required for your scene. If you are an experienced researcher adding hybrid ethnographic methodology to your research, this will already be clear. If not, develop your bibliography and working knowledge of the ideas it covers.

The amount of time it takes to acclimate to your scene as an active participant and researcher will vary, based largely on whether your work is at the exploratory stage or you are already an established professional in your area and what kinds of participation you have already pursued. No matter how you are already established in your field, anticipate that beginning a new ethnographic project will require negotiation as you establish a new role in the scene. Established researchers may still have much to learn as performers; cultural workers with years of experience renegotiate their roles when taking on the mantle of researcher. Anticipate sharing information about yourself and your work with fellow participants in a way that lets people know what roles you would like to take on: student, co-teacher, archivist, media specialist, culture bearer, learner. You will also be interpreted and assigned roles in ways that are beyond your control. The cultural scene existed before your entrance, as did participants' ideas of what it is to do research; you are stepping into a moving stream.

Identify Your Physical Fieldwork Site

This book will help you conduct ethnographic work in a cultural community in which you are a participant. You will build on rapport you have established and work on navigating your role(s) in the scene. Whether you dance with a troupe, sing in a band, intern at a radio station, teach acting, work for a film festival, or learn sitar, your experience as a participant will guide the research process. With an understanding of thresholds informed by queer theory, Fairn herising (2005) finds power in the in-between state of the researcher. As scholars, we can ask productive questions about our role vis-à-vis our research community; questioning how we address gaps between ourselves and other participants and how we navigate space between participants is applicable regardless of the degree to which we are already part of the community.

If you have started exploratory work but have not yet clarified your scene and guiding question, two key points can help you focus this process: interest and logistics. Interest is perhaps the most obvious first source of impact on a scene selection process. The kinds of films, music, dance, theatre, and other performance that you make and of which you are an active fan is often the first place to start. Questions you have as a researcher build on this interest: When you have been active in making or observing a performance or other cultural activity, what has made you stop and wonder what exactly is going on or why? This helps focus a general area into one that is more specific. Professional interest is germane. Consider goals you have as a researcher and/or applied professional and consider what aspect(s) of your scene could help you work toward your goals. Paired with this are the goals you have for the scene in which you take part. Are there applied problems or questions whose answers would benefit your scene? Look for those areas about which you are passionate and toward which you can reasonably contribute. Finally, consider relevance. How might working on a particular aspect of a scene help to answer an intellectual question that is not in the literature or that needs to be revised or updated? How can focusing on part of your scene address a concern held by members of the group that participates in it? What seems so relevant and interesting that it calls for time, energy, skills, and resources to be poured into it?

Logistics follow interest. Within an interest area, consider access. Where are groups meeting? If you are already active in some but not others, is it logistically possible for you to expand your participation? If you are relatively new to the scene, what connections do you already have to the area, and where do you need to develop more links? Talk with existing point people. Call or meet with people whose expertise would be relevant, or contact them via social media or other web presences if they are more active online. If you are hoping to move into a related but somewhat separate scene, start by working with participants who you do know and ask if they might be willing to put you in touch with friends or colleagues. Taking an asset-based approach can be productive: Focus on where you already are active and build additional rapport there. This may be through a university, by way of clubs or groups, via physical spaces in your neighborhood, or starting with relevant online communities. Questions of feasibility may also include some special considerations. For example, if you anticipate working with children or doing research from within an institution that has its own protocols, plan for additional conversations to make sure that you will be able to do the work and allow additional time to respectfully and completely follow required procedures. Finally, consider the frequency and timing of events. Are there frequent enough rehearsals, concerts, film screenings, meetings, and so forth for you to interact as much as you need to when you need to? Can you make events time-wise? Can you get to them geographically? Chapter 3 delves more specifically into planning your schedule and sites around where participants are active.

Generate a Working Research Question

The design for the research will flow from this question. Your research question should define the scope of the project, articulate its relevance, and relate to previous research in your field. If this is still in development, take time to refine it now. Herndon and McLeod outline a step-by-step method by which to formulate such a question (1983, pp. 9–15). As you formulate the question, consider the following: Whom does the research serve? What inspires your interest in the aspect of your research question that you plan to investigate? With whom will you need to collaborate to address the question? Mutua and Swander offer ways to think through these questions (2004, pp. 1–23). Throughout this book, you will be invited to select the way in which hybrid ethnography is most relevant to your particular question. Use this adaptability to create a process that fits your needs. Once you have identified your area of study, fieldsite, and working research question, you are ready to get started.

SUMMARY

This chapter introduced the theoretical and methodological shifts in ethnography that hybrid research addresses. It identified changes in technology and attitudes that alter the skills necessary for contemporary fieldwork. Rather than just inscribing social discourse experienced in a physical field, the ethnographer must also sift through large quantities of data and media. No longer one of the few participants with access to recording, photography, publishing, and distribution, the ethnographer fills a shifting role as many participants document and share their own participation. Over the next chapters, you will be able to use this book as a solid point of departure. The material here can be adapted to your specific scene as you use it, and it can and should be added to as new ideas emerge, as technologies change, and as peoples' attitudes toward and use of networked systems shift. Starting from a scene in which you are or will soon act as a participant, you have honed in on an area of study, a site, and a research question. Your work will proceed from this base, moving with fellow participants through the hybrid research space.

FURTHER READING

Burnim, M. (1985). Culture bearer and tradition bearer. *Ethnomusicology, 29*(3), 432–447.

D'Amico-Samuels, D. (1991). Undoing fieldwork. In F. Harrison (Ed.), *Decolonizing anthropology*. Washington, DC: Association of Black Anthropologists and the American Anthropological Association.

Durham, A. (2014). *Home with hip hop feminism*. New York: Peter Lang.

Geertz, C. (1973). *The interpretation of cultures*. New York: Basic Books.

Herndon, M., & McLeod, N. (1983). *Field manual for ethnomusicology*. Norwood, PA: Norwood Editions.

herising, F. (2005). Interrupting positions: Critical thresholds and queer pro/positions. In L. Brown & S. Strega (Eds.). *Research as resistance* (pp. 127–151). Toronto: Canadian Scholars' Press.

Lysloff, R. T. A. (1993). A wrinkle in time: The comic interlude in the Javanese puppet theater of Banyumas (West Central Java). *Asian Theatre Journal, 10*(1), 49–80.

Lysloff, R. T. A., & Gay, L. C. (Eds.). (2003). *Music and technoculture.* Middletown, CT: Wesleyan University Press.

Medicine, B. (2001). *Learning to be an anthropologist and remaining native.* S.-E. Jacobs (Ed.). Urbana, IL: University of Illinois Press.

Mutua, K., & Swander, B. B. (Eds.). (2004). *Decolonial research in cross-cultural contexts: Critical personal narratives.* Albany: State University of New York Press.

Turkle, S. (1997). *Life on the screen.* New York: Touchstone.

2 ETHICS

Like its offline and online counterparts, hybrid ethnography must be undertaken with careful attention to ethical behavior. This chapter outlines ethical concerns at the design stage, offers guidance for applying for ethics board clearance, and provides opportunities to think through professional and community standards of responsibility. You will deepen your approach to tailored aspects of your ethical research in subsequent chapters. Ethnographic research comes with guiding principles that are applicable across disciplines. Researchers are first expected to do no harm. We are expected to communicate honestly with participants about the research, which includes letting people know when we are conducting research and obtaining informed consent from anyone who takes part in research activity. We expect each other to put the needs of the community of research first and to avoid letting our own personal or professional desires supersede those of the community. Whether or not it is framed explicitly as applied research, fieldwork should be undertaken with an awareness of community needs, and these needs should fit in with the research project. In general, research results should be made accessible to community members so that it can be of use. At the same time, personal or sensitive information should be safeguarded; researchers are expected not to share materials in a way that is inconsistent with the permissions given by people who shared it. We access guidance on specific ethical concerns, such as how recordings are treated, through professional associations whose members' research interacts with artifacts, recordings, and other data.

IRBs, ETHICS BOARDS, AND RESEARCH DESIGN

At its best, working with your institution's board or group that oversees research ethics is one of many tools to help you conduct an ethical research process.[1] If you are experienced with this process, skip directly to the next section on unique challenges that hybrid research can pose for ethics board review in "Concerns for Partially Online Fieldsites."

University-Based Review Boards

An institutional review board (IRB), research ethics board (REB), or similar group is charged with holding university-based research projects to standards that protect research participants and safeguard your institution from legal liability. Members of the IRB or ethics team will review your research plan, subject recruitment strategy, interview and survey protocols, and other relevant portions of your research project. While their language is legalistic, these boards are in place for a very good reason: Participants should be treated with respect, and your research project should not harm your collaborators.[2]

To prepare for ethics review, read your institution's documents for researchers and start a list of questions that you have about the process. If possible, attend an information session or meet with a staff member early on to get a sense of university-specific rules, forms, and timelines. Work at the planning stage helps to avoid delays later. Even if you have completed ethics reviews in the past, be aware that rules and best practices can change. For example, U.S.-based researchers were affected by a change to the Common Rule that went into effect January 1, 2019. Flip forward to Chapter 6 in this book for more information on the ethics of working with recordings and to Chapter 7 for work with surveys and interviews. If your fieldwork receives external funding, verify the rules to which you assent by accepting funding and review any deliverables expected of your work. When you complete the positionality exercise later in this chapter, consider the way constraints of

[1]Working with an ethics board is a reality of doing research with people. It may be helpful in some ways, and it may feel like a hindrance in others. These boards tend to have conservative approaches to research, and, as is the case with many types of bureaucracy, they do not change quickly, even when updates could be helpful. A critique of the conservative nature of IRBs and an explanation of how this can burden qualitative researchers is found in Lincoln (2005).

[2]Research review boards help to prevent abuses that have been perpetrated in the name of research in the past, such as the infamous Tuskegee Syphilis Study, in which African American men were studied but not treated or informed about the disease. The U.S. public health service disguised research as healthcare, and the men did not receive a medically sound treatment that could have improved their health and even saved lives (Reverby, 2009). This well-known case is worth revisiting: It demonstrates the dangers of othering research participants and of failing to take ethical considerations seriously.

funding or priorities of funders may impact you as a researcher. For more on seeking funding and the ethical implications of accepting funding, consult Cheek (2005).

Additional Oversight Boards

In addition to a university oversight board, some groups have their own review boards or procedures for researchers. Schools, Indigenous Nations, religious institutions, and other groups may require an additional formalized review process. Take time early in your design phase to learn about appropriate documentation for review so that you can follow these processes if applicable. It is useful to familiarize yourself with the standards to which your university or other institution will be holding your project and to learn about the standards held by the group with whom you will be working, as described above. These exist in balance with your professional and personal ethical standards.

PERSONAL AND PROFESSIONAL ETHICS

A review process addresses the minimum standard of consent, privacy protections, risk level, standards of compensation, and related aspects of a qualitative research study. Yet the permissions granted by an IRB, REB, or similar body do not take the place of ethical decision-making on the part of the researcher or research team. Working with other people carries ethical implications. Sharing information gained through participant observation, too, has moral resonances. The importance of ethical decisions is compounded across differences in status or position, hence the focus on positionality in hybrid ethnography. Expressive culture research does not carry the same risks as biomedical or psychological research, yet the way we understand ourselves and each other carries implications of value, which impact how people treat each other in material terms.

As researchers, we may find that some standards to which we hold ourselves are more stringent than those required by ethics boards. For example, in the United States, data published in public forums on the internet is often considered by IRBs not to require an ethics protocol because the information is considered public (Buchanan & Ess, 2008). Yet should you choose to use such data, you might consider the potential risks to naming contributors or quoting directly from public forums, particularly if your research question touches on potentially sensitive topics. Additionally, consent is often best understood as a process, not a one-time procedure. Simply obtaining a signed consent form to share results from an interview, for instance, does not impel you to share all of the information therein. Should a participant share information that is not widely known, you might check back in with that person to see whether or with whom they wish for the information to be shared, a practice I have found helpful in my own research. Finally, IRBs respond to culturally situated norms of behavior: those of the institution in which they are housed. In a particular fieldsite, guidelines for how to gather information, what information can be shared, and how, may be very different—and potentially more stringent.

A practical example of navigating varying standards of appropriateness is found in the work of Erin Debenport. The anthropologist worked with Pueblo communities on Indigenous language reclamation. Her collaborators in the Rio Grande valley began to write down a tribal language that had previously only been orally transmitted. This transition brought potential aids for learning and also risks for material that was previously internally controlled. As Debenport explains, "Tribal members are at once eager to innovate, producing written materials to aid language learning, yet wary of the possible risks involved with writing Keiwa. Potential hazards include the inappropriate circulation of cultural knowledge, language standardization, and damage to the religious system" (Debenport, 2015, p. 5). Eventually, the group chose to return to oral-only language teaching and learning. Due to concerns about making information public, Debenport uses a pseudonym for both the language and the community with which she worked.[3] She uses pseudonyms for her collaborators—a decision that she notes was her own—"in order to reflect the importance that is placed on the careful circulation of cultural knowledge and the centrality of inference and avoidance in this community" (Debenport, 2015, p. 8). In other words, it is her reading of culturally relevant standards of information transmission—and not the external imposition by a university or tribal-based governance board—that impacted the level of detail she included in her writing. Her interlocutors directly impacted her decision not to share certain facets of the language: She "omitted tokens of the Keiwa language in this book or any other of my publicly available materials, a decision made in collaboration with tribal members" (Debenport, 2015, p. 8). She is able to share insights about language use, transmission, and community interactions around Indigenous language without actually revealing details about

[3]Keiwa, the term she uses in her book, is her pseudonym for the language of San Ramón, the pseudonym for the region in which she worked. Her 2015 book details how she chose these pseudonyms, a useful model for research with sensitive cultural information.

the community or the language, a stance that allows her work to enter into dialogue with linguistic anthropology without sharing information about the language that should, as her colleagues helped her understand, remain secret.

Adapting to Changing Standards

Internet-based communications and the way people interact with them in the hybrid field are constantly changing. Publications cannot anticipate all of the specific ways that these changes may occur. Following the spirit of the ethical research standards that guide qualitative inquiry for your field is good practice, as the specifics of regulations and work-arounds may be out-of-date. Checking in regularly with fellow researchers, your fieldwork community, and yourself is no less important to ethical research than it is to meet required research standards.

Some basic rules of thumb include the following:

- Consider collaborative and/or community-based research methods, if appropriate.
- Be transparent that you are conducting research.
- Respect your group and its members.
    - This includes respecting the group's decision if they determine it's not a good place for research.
- Proceed only with permission.
- Listen and watch for other people's comfort.
- Ensure that everyone has a real choice to not participate if they do not want to.
- Dialogue early on about how research products will be shared in ways that are productive and accessible for scene participants.
- Ask for permission before recording.
- Check back in regularly for other people's opinions and thoughts.
- Give credit to your fellow participants in a way that is consistent with how they have asked to be identified.
- Make yourself consistently available for questions, and answer honestly.

Professional associations help to clarify ethical expectations. The American Anthropological Association (AAA; 2007) distills ethical behavior into seven central activities for research: avoiding harm, behaving honestly, obtaining consent, weighing competing interests, making results accessible, protecting your records, and maintaining respectful relationships (American Anthropological Association, 2012). Key points are described with a specific bibliography for each section on the AAA Ethics Forum (blog). Your disciplinary association may be able to help you develop appropriate ethical protocols. The International Sociological Association (2001), National Communication Association (1999), American Psychological Association (2017), and the Society for Ethnomusicology (1998) all offer support; links are in this chapter's Further Reading. You may also have community protocols or even an additional formal review process in order to comply with best practices (Tuhiwai Smith, 2012). Discipline-specific codes are sometimes available in published volumes (such as Robben & Sluka, 2007), yet the online versions from professional associations are often the most up-to-date. Some, like the AAA, mentioned above, also maintain an ethics blog for professional discussion. If your discipline or subdiscipline does not yet have a formalized research ethics code, start with one of these and consider joining or starting a working group or conversation at your association conference to discuss ethical concerns.

While professional organizations offer guidance, these standards should be considered a minimum for professional responsibility. Because of the rapid pace of changes in communication technologies, it may be necessary to think beyond the existing guidance for online interactions, data access, and the current realities of privacy concerns. Contemplate your own perspective as a researcher and empathetically consider the position of your fellow research participants as you add additional safeguards that are relevant to your scene. The following exercise can help you develop an ethical approach appropriate to your specific project.

EXERCISE 2.1

Locate the most recent version of your professional society's ethics statement or, absent a specific code, one in your nearest discipline.

Then, find two to three others in related fields.

Read these carefully, and then jot down your responses to the following questions in your research notebook:

- How is online activity addressed or absent in each code?
- What guidance is offered about the ethics of data management, storage, and privacy?

- Read the code for assumptions about what constitutes a fieldsite and what qualifies as research activity. If there are aspects of your hybrid field that exceed the boundaries of the ethics statement, what are these?
- How are ethical and legal requirements that differ across national borders or geocultural areas addressed in the statement? Consider how your own project's regional or cultural specificity may require additional guidance.
- To what other standards might researchers in your field hold themselves?
- To what other standards might you be held by participants?

Jot down your responses, writing in detail or discussing these with members of your research team as fits your situation. Your own personal ethical standards for research will also be influenced by your position in the field, as is detailed later in this chapter and in Chapter 3.

Balancing Multiple Ethics Standards

Arriving at consent to share information and deciding what to share with whom involves juggling the multiple sets of standards described in the previous sections. These are seen clearly in an example from participant observation. In an ethnographic study with people who post regularly on Wikipedia, Christian Pentzold first reviewed the standard for what insiders consider to be an appropriate level of confidentiality. Community expectations in a specific field are a central measure of ethical behavior. In the case with which Pentzold was working, these expectations were published within Wikipedia, and though not strictly enforceable, they informed the spirit of his ethical approach. He cites discipline-specific and interdisciplinary research guidelines, which in his case are the standards of the International Communication Association and the American Sociological Association as well as the Association of Internet Researchers (Pentzold, 2017, p. 144). The detailed ethics guidelines articulated by the AoIR working group offer questions and answers, as well as narrative examples and sample guidelines for researchers (Ess & AoIR Ethics Working Committee, 2002). This pragmatic document provides a starting point for questions that are best addressed through online research. While, as Pentzold notes, it is limited in the specific technology that it can address due to the quickly dated nature of specific guidelines for internet-based communication, the 2012 version provides a relevant reboot

(Markham & Buchanan, 2012). This later document specifically articulates guidelines, not a specific code of rules, "so that ethical research can remain flexible, be responsive to diverse contexts, and be adaptable to continually changing technologies" (p. 5). Indeed, researchers must be flexible not just within a single guiding document but when applying multiple standards of ethical behaviors that apply in a given field context.

Combining insider expectations, professional ethics guidelines, and specific research on areas of concern creates a study that is responsive to multiple stakeholders. Information deemed sensitive or private, in Pentzold's case, did help the researcher in his own analysis, but it was not shared with others. His informed consent process was more than a one-time assent on the part of platform editors. Rather, he gained informed consent when pragmatic and adopted a policy that applied to the reality of his field. He writes, "While it seemed advisable to gain informed consent in all episodes and for all stations, it was mandatory or at least appropriate in observing interactions and collecting documents from episodes and stations that were treated as being private or limitedly private and which contained information thought to be sensitive or limitedly sensitive" (Pentzold, 2017, p. 151). Open or non-sensitive materials were not subject to consent, but the researcher "considered it compulsory for episodes and stations which Wikipedians treated as being more private and secluded from public view" (Pentzold, 2017, p. 152). He chose to use the platform to make his scholarly affiliations and name accessible to other users, publishing details about himself on his user page and always logging in when he participated.

This example of an online ethnography offers useful take-aways for the hybrid researcher. Informed consent is a process, not a one-time yes/no response. However, it can be more complicated than an ethics procedure that assumes simple face-to-face interaction. Platform-specific ethical guidelines are best used to navigate consent; these should take into account how publicly (or privately) information is made available, the closeness of the researcher's relationship with participants, the sensitivity of the information they share, and how necessary the information is to the research question. Disclosing researcher status with participants is crucial. Not everything the ethnographer learns must be published.

CONCERNS FOR PARTIALLY ONLINE FIELDSITES

For the hybrid ethnography researcher, important ethical concerns of online fieldwork are accuracy and transparency, which are commonly discussed in digital ethnography as well. Past research in online fieldwork offers useful lessons in representing the scene accurately. While initially applied to online-only research, these can be pragmatically adapted for the hybrid field. One concern that some researchers have about working online is the verifiability of information (Walther, 2002). Interestingly, this is also a concern when speaking with people face-to-face: One cannot know immediately if a participant is attempting to share small untruths, which typically are only revealed over time and with input from multiple individuals. There are, admittedly, some kinds of deception that are more common on the internet (perhaps so common so as not to always be considered deception). For example, frequent Reddit commenters may create multiple accounts; this is understood on the platform as within the range of expected behaviors. A single participant creating multiple personas is much more difficult—and more socially stigmatized—in a physical setting. In the hybrid scene, the researcher's imperative not to perpetuate false information continues, yet we have additional tools in this area: When working with the same individuals on- and offline, we have additional data points from which to discern how individuals are crafting their personas and how they choose to present themselves in overlapping internet-mediated and physical worlds.

As a method that is grounded in interacting with fellow humans, ethnography accounts for a range of beliefs and opinions. It also helps the researcher make meaning from our situated observation of behaviors. In hybrid work, we account for a variety of perspectives on actions we observe and also hold ourselves to relate what we learn as accurately as possible. Reading observations alongside each other, we operate across online and on-the-ground communications in order to come to useful conclusions. An example starting with offline ethnography demonstrates how this can work. Watching audience members interact in a dance performance, it is possible to read how engaged they look by watching them. Carefully observe behavior and take cues from body language. Talking with dancers afterward about how they felt creates opportunities for conversation that checks the way the researcher has observed behavior and also gives insight when self-reported and observed behaviors seem to be at odds with each other. Online, how do you do firsthand readings? Certainly it is possible to do a first-hand reading of text; other signifiers layer on more information. One can look at the frequency of participation, wording, capitalization, spelling, and learn to "read" other kinds of discourse. That is, one can read for norms and see when participants are fitting with them and also observe for behaviors that show enthusiasm, detachment, anger, or other emotions. More on interpreting norms across the hybrid field—including in internet-mediated communication—is detailed in Chapter 5.

In fully online research, it is possible to observe without contributing to a site, platform, or discussion. This presents an ethical quandary for the researcher around potentially avoiding disclosure, which is a pitfall for transparency. The hybrid field ethnographer should not be tempted to hide one's participation; being communicative in-person about how one is also active online deepens communication with fellow participants and helps build trust (Bruckman, 2002). While less commonly treated in methods literature, possible non-participant observation also extends to others reading online communications. That is, people other than the researcher and those commenting may be observing what happens on a site without their presence being publicly known. Hosts of sites may be able to access information on who is viewing but not actively commenting through logs of IP addresses and/or geographic information for visitors. However, especially for sites not operated by the researcher, this information can be harder to access. Navigating the possibility of users who avoid direct engagement is addressed in Chapter 9. The hybrid site again offers a strength here; talk with people you know in person about potential risks of disclosing sensitive information and discuss what is—and is not—possible to learn about who is reading online content and whether privacy limits are prudent for certain kinds of sharing.

Researcher Safety and Privacy

Ethics boards are charged only with protecting external research participants—not the researchers themselves. Reflective scholarship by ethnographers details the scope and type of risks that academics face when conducting participant observation, including risks to reputation, harassment, physical threats, and violence, including sexual violence (Berry, Argüelles, Cordis, Ihmoud, & Velasquez Estrada, 2017). Hybrid research intensifies these concerns. As a researcher, you make some information about yourself public as part of establishing trust. This is the case in face-to-face communications, as well as online. It is possible for a fellow participant or someone who is not a participant but learns about you and your work to threaten or harass you, including through trolling or online harassment.

BOX 2.1

Berry et al. (2017) describe each individual anthropologist's experience in the field and how she responds to threats and/or violence. These reports, each from a researcher who is situated differently within global power structures, call attention to the importance of safeguarding the researcher as well as fellow participants. They also address a concern that is a theme in this book: Each combination of researcher(s) and research situation requires context-specific reflection, navigation, and adaptation. Because of the power dynamics in which research takes place, attending to these contextual differences can require adjustment at the design level. Claudia Chávez Argüelles writes that the listening postures she was taught to assume as a general best practice for fieldwork were misinterpreted when she was interviewing male leaders in a mountainous area of southeast Mexico. In this case, "best practice" listening postures may work well for a male researcher, particularly a foreign male researcher, but Chávez Argüelles' experience pushes us to consider when alternative listening practices are required to create clear limits for safety reasons.

Ethics boards and professional organizations suggest best practices for protecting fellow participants from harassment; we can and should ask our institutions and professional organizations to also safeguard researchers. Structural change can be slow, so it makes sense to come up with strategies for individual safety as well. When you as researcher-participant are likely to face more than a minimal risk, ask colleagues, advisers, or community members for help employing strategies to mitigate threats. Ask yourself the following questions: What information about me needs to be publicly available? Should I limit some kinds of personal data, like my personal address or exact movements, to a smaller or more private group? Are there situations in which it would be helpful to have members of a research team with me or other fellow participants I trust available, for safety? Identify trusted colleagues you can read in should you or members of your team be threatened online or in person.

The platforms you use in the hybrid field also introduce unknowns in the realm of researcher safety and privacy. An IRB might reasonably want to know if we are asking people questions about sensitive political topics. At present, they typically do not investigate how sensitive data can be shared when people do not disclose it directly. However, this can come up in hybrid ethnography. When scene members use an app, they provide certain information to the operator or parent company. It is possible that this could be information that users would rather keep private. For example, some communication apps track location data. Others make certain kinds of message content available to companies that purchase it or government entities that acquire it. Whether or not a professional ethics board requires it, it is worth investigating what we can learn about data sharing, expressing caution for those platforms that do not meet participants' standards for privacy and looking for alternate communication mediums, if available. Ethical concerns of online data sharing are further explored in Chapter 9. As a rule, when thinking about participant safety and privacy, ask which provisions should also extend to the researcher. We are working with fellow participants to generate new understandings of relevant scenes and pressing research questions; our searches do not need to place our fellow participants or ourselves at significant risk of harm.

POSITIONALITY

Qualitative research offers opportunities to work collaboratively and comes with responsibilities for accurately representing the scene in which one works. The power dynamics between you and your fellow participants impact the way you navigate ethical questions. Additionally, your position may have specific ramifications for what you can and cannot access. For example, your perceived gender might impact whether or how you may participate in gendered events (Kisliuk, 1998). Other aspects of your personal background, such as your religious affiliation, might help you integrate yourself into your scene, or you may find yourself conflicted about how much you share if your beliefs differ from those of your scene members (Koskoff, 2014). Just as

EXERCISE 2.2

In your fieldnotes, jot down your responses to the following:

- What aspects of your identity as a researcher and as a person are likely to be foregrounded in your scene?
- How do you perceive these aspects of your identity? How might your friends and family? Your colleagues?
- How do these aspects overlap—or fail to do so—with various members of your scene?
- How might these degrees of overlap come into play during your research?

your knowledge of yourself influences how you act in the field, the knowledge others have of themselves influences how they behave in your scene. Using a reflexive approach, it is imperative to recognize how your situated position and those of your fellow participants impact perception in your scene.

Research context affects the aspects of participants' identities that come to the fore. If your research question addresses depictions of racial difference on film, anticipate that the way fellow participants perceive your racial identity will impact the encounters you have. Your position also influences power dynamics in the scene. In hybrid research, if you have a significant degree of familiarity with the online platform on which participants communicate, this may give you some prestige and act as one power differential in the field. The technical fluency aspect of your identity could provide an opportunity to take an active role, perhaps in the group's media sharing strategy. Continue reading and reflecting as you prepare for the field. For sources on the responsibilities of representation, the writings of Dwight Conquergood and Soyini Madison offer points of departure (Conquergood, 1991; Madison, 2005). This chapter's Further Reading offers additional reading on positionality and includes case studies in which authors navigate their position in the field. These topics will be explored further in Chapter 3 as well. After completing the initial steps outlined here to prepare your research ethics for your project design, you are ready to start practical pre-field hybrid ethnographic work.

SUMMARY

Building from how past scholarship wrestled with ethical issues online, the chapter has detailed concerns and suggested practical protocols for maintaining research integrity in the hybrid field. Given multiple standards of ethics and shades of gray that are likely to emerge, thoughtfully balancing many perspectives is required, and some degree of ambiguity is likely to remain. As you proceed, communicate carefully in order to set realistic expectations of privacy with participants, given the realities of online archiving and the potential for security concerns with online data. It is crucial to follow best practices for maintaining appropriate privacy safeguards. Taking care to abide by your research community's ethical standards, your discipline's professional code, your institution's research ethics standards, and your own ethical barometer will help you proceed with a research design that is personally and professionally sound.

FURTHER READING

American Anthropological Association. (2012). *Statement on ethics: Principles of professional responsibilities*. Arlington, VA: American Anthropological Association. Retrieved from www.aaanet.org/profdev/ethics/upload/Statement-on-Ethics-Principles-of-Professional-Responsibility.pdf

American Anthropological Association. (n.d.). AAA ethics forum [blog]. Retrieved from http://ethics.americananthro.org/

American Psychological Association. (2017). *Ethical principles of psychologists and code of conduct*. Retrieved from http://www.apa.org/ethics/code/

Berry, M. J., Argüelles, C. C., Cordis, S., Ihmoud, S., & Velasquez Estrada, E. (2017). Toward a fugitive anthropology: Gender, race, and violence in the field. *Cultural Anthropology, 32*(4), 537–565.

Cheek, J. (2005). The practice and politics of funded qualitative research. In N. K. Denzin & Y. S. Lincoln (Eds.), *The SAGE handbook of qualitative research* (3rd ed.). Thousand Oaks, CA: Sage.

Conquergood, D. (1991). Rethinking ethnography. *Communication Monographs, 58*, 179–194.

Debenport, E. (2015). *Fixing the books: Secrecy, literacy, and perfectibility in Indigenous New Mexico*. Santa Fe, NM: School for Advanced Research Press.

Ess, C., & AoIR Ethics Working Committee. (2002). *Ethical decision-making and internet research: Recommendations from the AoIR Ethics Working Committee*. Retrieved from http://aoir.org/reports/ethics.pdf

International Sociological Association. (2001). *Code of ethics*. Retrieved from https://www.isa-sociology.org/en/about-isa/code-of-ethics/

Koskoff, E. (2014). *A feminist ethnomusicology: Writings on music and gender*. Urbana: University of Illinois Press.

Lincoln, Y. S. (2005). Institutional review boards and methodological conservatism: The challenge to and from phenomenological paradigms. In N. K. Denzin & Y. S. Lincoln (Eds.), *The SAGE handbook of qualitative research* (3rd ed., pp. 165–181). Thousand Oaks, CA: Sage.

Madison, D. S. (2005). *Critical ethnography: Method, ethics, and performance.* London: Sage.

Markham, A. N. (2004). Representation in online ethnographies: A matter of context sensitivity. In M. D. Johns, S.-L. S. Chen, & G. J. Hall (Eds.), *Online social research: Methods, issues, & ethics* (pp. 141–155). New York: Peter Lang.

National Communication Association. (1999). *NCA credo for ethical communication.* Retrieved from https://www.natcom.org/sites/default/files/pages/1999_Public_Statements_NCA_Credo_for_Ethical_Communication_November.pdf

Pentzold, C. (2017). "What are these researchers doing in my Wikipedia?": Ethical premises and practical judgment in internet-based ethnography. *Ethics and Information Technology, 19*(2), 143–155.

Reverby, S. M. (2009). *Examining Tuskegee: The infamous syphilis study and its legacy.* Chapel Hill: University of North Carolina Press.

Society for Ethnomusicology. (1998). *Position statement on ethics.* Retrieved from https://www.ethnomusicology.org/? EthicsStatement

Tuhiwai Smith, L. (2012). *Decolonizing methodologies: Research and Indigenous peoples.* London: Zed Books.

GROUNDING

Research Reflexivity and Connectivity

A singer nods her head in time with the beat. From the inside of a recording studio sound booth, she sings into a microphone. Her rich R & B vocals repeat the chorus again, lamenting the hard knocks she faces in life. The singer, Karla, builds up the emotion that simmered in the verse of the rapper whose words preceded hers. Her metaphor of bumpy roads brings together all of the hardships that the rapper has just described in his narration. Then the visuals shift. The camera cuts from the studio to an urban scene, showing a city from above. Karla's fluid singing continues. She glides from note to note as the camera follows her. Now she walks through a cemetery on a literal bumpy road, winding past white crosses that mark graves. Her voice fades out as she walks away, the camera at her back fades to black and silence descends.

After the video ends, I ask what everyone thinks. We're in a community center, in a combination meeting room that holds toys for kids. The assembled group of teenagers and young adults is working to put together a hip hop show—but not just any hip hop show: The youth group at a local American Indian Center wants to showcase intertribal Native American culture in a hip hop-based community event. The idea came from a group discussion and was carefully written on a large piece of paper in the room: "Native dance with hip hop music." And so we were listening to hear what other people have done like this. We've gathered to discuss the aesthetic and ethical implications of combining traditional and popular music and dance. Karla's is the third music video we've watched this afternoon.

Responses to the music videos are diverse. Some people appreciated the pictures that are intercut into the video, particularly the combination of shots in the studio and outside. These, a young woman says, help the music video sound like a story. A group leader responds to the music, observing that he likes the beat one MC raps over and that the woman singing the hook sounds talented. But what, if anything, could we learn from the videos?

For the group to put on their own show, they could try to tell a story like one MC did or use a hand drum as was heard in another video. There is consensus to avoid falling into the trap of being "cheesy," a criticism of one of the videos we watched. Group members offer ideas, listening though they sometimes disagree with each other. Then, one young man brings up the question of respect. What about the performer who did a hip hop jingle dress dance, he asks? Didn't she get in trouble? To settle the question of what exactly happened and if it would be disrespectful, another member looks up the dance video on YouTube. He presses play, and we all quiet down to listen.

This moment marked two turning points. First, for the group, watching the performance on streaming video sparked the serious—and pragmatic—conversation on combining powwow and hip hop music and dance. Second, it indicated that I would need to pay careful attention to online videos dedicated to this kind of performance, and it demonstrated how this media was already integrated into my neighborhood offline fieldsite. It was my on-the-ground interactions that helped me select the relevant online areas; participating in the room in which the online/offline circuit was once again completed immersed me into the hybrid fieldsite.

RESEARCHER AND FIELD

The ethnographer's "self" forms a central piece of fieldwork in hybrid research. Particularly when doing research with an artistic or cultural group of which you are a part, asking questions about your roles, including why certain potential research questions draw your attention, is a crucial early step. Reflect regularly on how you fit into the scene. How do various others perceive you, and how do you perceive yourself? Just as your knowledge of yourself influences how you act in the field, the knowledge others have of themselves influences how they behave in the hybrid research sphere.

We and our collaborators juggle professional selves, family selves, artistic selves, Twitter selves, Instagram selves, and so forth, and we often make—or aim to make—coherent if multivalent identities that incorporate them all. For example, an artist I know from my fieldwork appears to me as a physical person with identifiable qualities. I get to see and hear his stage persona as well, which differs in degree from his quotidian self-presentation. Further, he has a professional social media persona, which has overlapping and non-overlapping qualities with those I see face-to-face. He has a personal online presence that too has overlapping and non-overlapping qualities with his two other entities, the professional online presence and the in-person presence. Researchers in the hybrid field must make a conceptual shift when working to understand fellow participants. Each participant—including the researcher themself—exists as a cluster, which includes a physical body that moves in space and one or more online selves that the physical body reflects through online communication.

Positionality and Power

Part of preparing for fieldwork is preparing one's self for the research. As with wholly physical or wholly virtual fieldwork, it is crucial to take stock of one's position in the research landscape. To make sense of how positionality is negotiated in the hybrid scene, start by considering the following: How do aspects of your identity, such as your gender expression, race, ethnicity, sexual orientation, education level, native language(s), and class, interact with identity markers of other participants in your field? You and your fellow participants are likely to respond to these in direct and indirect ways. Aspects of various members' identities impact social standing, access to information, and behavior expectations. Roles and social positions are actively negotiated, as in other types of ethnography. In the hybrid field in particular, these may shift across mediums that are more and less internet-mediated. Write regularly in your field journal about how you and others express and negotiate positionality, starting even before you begin the formal field work process.

Power is attributed to differential identity characteristics in social scenes. Critical ethnographic work requires analyzing one's own position as well as probing the power dynamics of the ethnographic scene (Madison, 2005). Power and social relationships are articulated in and through language. As Temple and Young articulate, "The perspective of one language-using community on another is rarely neutral and the perceived status of languages rarely equivalent" (2004, p. 167). Working in a multilingual scene, you and your fellow participants navigate social and political boundaries through language use. You also have practical decisions to face about when to use which languages and how a research team with wide linguistic competency could be helpful, which will be taken up in Chapter 7. With fellow scene members as collaborators, you are invited to think through situations in which the language of research and the language of sharing results differ.

In your field journal, take time to reflect on your own positionality. Guiding questions are designed to facilitate your writing:

EXERCISE 3.1

- What kinds of power are ascribed to various identity categories in your scene?
- How are positions of power distributed, formally or informally?
- What characteristics help a participant to be taken more seriously and by whom?
- What characteristics might make it more likely for a participant to be second-guessed?
- How do types of positionality shift based on different levels of internet mediation in your specific hybrid scene?
- How are these roles negotiated and renegotiated—for example, over time and in various aspects of the scene?

Power operates in multiple domains. Use your responses to examine how it operates interpersonally. That is, how does power operate between yourself and your fellow scene members in various parts of your field? These direct interactions manifest when, for example, you post to the same social media page, make decisions at a rehearsal, or watch a video clip together for new ideas. People will play various roles and encounter a range of responses based on types of prestige, an idea explored later in this chapter. Your larger research question will involve interactions with disciplinary power. How do rules apply to participants based on aspects of their own social positions? You will also encounter structural power—that is, power at the institutional and organizational level. How do the rules and operations of established entities involved in your field—for example, arts organizations, educational institutions, and media outlets—impact participants' experiences? Expressive culture research investigates cultural power. This is immediately apparent in distinctions between how media sources depict expressive culture and how participants feel and describe it. What messages are media sources invested in portraying, how do these relate to each other, and how do they compare to what you learn or hear from participants? For more on these dynamics, consult Chapter 6.

Hybrid ethnography is a dynamic framework. Critical reflection may point you toward other strategies for your scene and positionality. Knowing how you fit into your scene is not the same as placing your own experience at the center of your research design. The guidelines in this chapter help you develop a functional awareness of power and positionality, which is crucial for all hybrid fieldwork. Your approach may additionally be informed sensory ethnography, autoethnography, visual ethnography, or other relevant strategies. If these exercises suggest that your research question will benefit from reflecting upon your personal situated knowledge, consider adapting strategies from autoethnography. Robin Boylorn learned from reading ethnography how "to capture the essence of an experience and invite the reader into your thoughts" and determined that these thoughts "inevitably include your history and standpoints" (Boylorn & Orbe, 2014, p. 13). Defining autoethnography as "cultural analysis through personal narrative" (p. 17), Boylorn and Orbe identify that this is a research method as well as a way of writing about the relationship between personal experiences and culture. This requires analyzing one's own experiences within their cultural context. As such, autoethnography requires a personal critique as well as a cultural one. This kind of writing is detailed, critical, and personal. Consult sources in this chapter's Further Reading, such as Denzin (2013), to incorporate this method into your research design.

Intersectionality

The identity categories that impact your position do not operate independently; they mutually inform each other. A rich literature on intersectionality demonstrates how identity categories co-construct each other, how power dynamics influenced by these operate, and how these translate to community-based projects (Driskill, Finley, Gilley, & Morgensen, 2011; Gressgård, 2008; McCall, 2005; Yuval-Davis, 2006). In short, intersectionality offers an approach to academic research and praxis. Introduced by legal scholar Kimberlé Crenshaw (Crenshaw, 1991) as an effective manner of approaching the legal concerns facing African American women, intersectionality is an adaptable analytical tool. This approach to scholarly and community concerns offers what Collins and Bilge call its core insight, "namely, that major axes of social divisions in a given society at a given time, for example, race, class, gender, sexuality, disability, and age operate not as mutually exclusive entities, but build on each other and work together" (Collins & Bilge, 2016, p. 4). One image that helps make sense of how intersectionality operates is that of a person at a crossroads. Imagine, for example, that one road is gender, one road is race, one road is

BOX 3.1

Crenshaw offers an intersectional analysis of the prosecution of the group 2 Live Crew. The rap group—comprised of Black men—was prosecuted for obscenity in 1990 for the album *As Nasty as They Wanna Be.* In the obscenity trial, the court considered whether the album was parody or incitement to violence. Yet Crenshaw argues that this is more than an either-or situation. Violent and misogynist rhetoric had been expressed by white and other non-Black musicians in a wide variety of genres long before this album. In this case, the court did not recognize legitimate kinds of artistic expression, such as signifying, that are part of African American musical traditions. Separating race and gender as analytical categories closes off important discussions about how practices can be both deeply culturally rooted and expressed in a way that condones misogyny. Analyzing the way people talk about issues like this rap album can illuminate culturally linked ideas of gender, race, and sexual behavior and how ideas of race, gender, and sex build upon each other. In this case, an intersectional analysis helps the researcher ask compelling questions: Why was this group the first to be prosecuted for obscenity? How does lyrical content impact violent behavior in the real world? What can—and cannot—be redressed by legal challenges? These questions bring together scholarship and praxis, a central tenet of applied research. While Crenshaw's approach shows how axes of identity construction interact, her use of the analytic leverages these interactions in order to ask and explore relevant research questions.

sexual orientation, and the way a person moves through the world is impacted by all of these things. An analysis that is more than just additive but that opens into how these different roads impact each helps to reveal how power and positionality affect research and practice across scenes.

Navigating Multifaceted Identities and Increasing Interrelationships

Relationships are complex: Individuals may fall in some privileged categories—for example, be part of an advantaged social class—and simultaneously fall into some disadvantaged categories—for example, be part of an ethnic minority that experiences discrimination. Positionality includes both characteristics over which an individual does not have control and those over which one does. This largely follows from physical ethnography; work on navigating social location in the physical sphere offers a foundation for further reading.

Hybrid ethnography accounts for new categories of socially situated power. For scenes in which online activity is prominent, technical facility with a platform or tool is a social advantage. Further, there are more ways of acknowledging social advantage. This is explicit in some platforms, such as Twitter, in which an influencer has social capital because of their large number of followers. A participant can experience varying degrees of social advantage across the scene—for example, having an acknowledged leader role in a physical venue—but be a relative newbie to the same organization's online presence. Keep track of these many kinds of power within participants' identities as you analyze interactions and work to understand your own roles in the scene. Once you begin formal research (see Chapter 4), notice if your self-perception or how others perceive you is shifting and record this regularly in fieldnotes. Recall that your social location may be understood differently across the hybrid field, with various aspects coming more into focus as you move across all parts of your field.

Of particular relevance to hybrid ethnography is how personal descriptive information is accessed differently online. The emphasis is on "differently" here: Gender, race, and other identity markers are not absent online. They do need to be understood in medium-specific ways. Of course, in physical spaces, people make judgments about aspects of a person's identity based on dress, body language, physical features, possessions, speech patterns, and other characteristics. Online, these signifiers take different forms. Screen names, profile photos, avatars, followers, and writing style, among other markers, can provide indications of gender, class, race, national origin, ethnic identity, and other characteristics.

Some online ethnographers dedicate time attempting to determine whether online aspects of a participant's identity are "real." This typically means whether or not the researcher perceives that the identity that a participant expresses online—for example, being gendered female—is the same as the identity the researcher would perceive offline. As many of the people you work with online you also work with offline, you will have overlapping data sets. You can thus develop a rich understanding of participants' positionality as you interpret information they present in person and also the things they write online, share on social media, and reveal through the composition of their friend networks across the field. Focus on observable behaviors. In physical spaces as well, we choose how we dress, what we say and do, and may even alter the way we speak, consciously or unconsciously, based on the situation in which we find ourselves.

Researchers and fellow participants navigate multifaceted identities in interrelated ways. Across the hybrid sphere, scene members present themselves and are read by others. User interactions allow for a rich identity work on social networking sites (Evans-Cowley, 2010). The cultivation of a public face online develops (it does not simply "reveal") aspects of yourself and scene participants. The kinds of stories a person posts on social media can show affiliation with political leanings. Liking and sharing music, film, and other media allow the poster to link themselves with the characteristics associated with particular genres and stars. This identity work is a process that takes place among overlapping publics—closed social media groups, public pages, and official websites, to name a few. Hybrid ethnographers engage in self-presentation, participate in group dynamics, and come to know others across all of these, in addition to face-to-face parts of the scene.

Honing a Position-Specific Research Question

Determining a research question was addressed in Chapter 1. Before you start conducting research, consider whom your question serves and how you plan to share information from your participant observation. Your question will be further informed by your positionality vis-à-vis the scene in which you participate. In other words, consider the social position that you occupy and think carefully about the power relationships that will be at play between yourself and your fellow participants (LeCompte & Schensul, 2010). Use the information from your reflection on power and positionality to inform the honing of your research question.

Reciprocity is key for ethnographic research. What information does your project have the potential to generate and how can it be productive for you as researcher and your creative community of participants? Applied and collaborative ethnographic research strategies make this connection clear from the design stage. Applied research shares knowledge in a way that is applicable beyond the university, a topic that will be taken up in Chapter 9.

Collaborative and applied approaches place the scholar as engaged researcher. Applied ethnographic research has been described as "an approach to the approach" and "a state of mind" that informs the researcher's actions (Sheehy, 1992, p. 323). If ethnographic fieldwork allows you to analyze expressive culture by immersing yourself in it, then applied ethnographic research sets a frame by which you consciously focus on the applicability of your research for solving problems while doing so. Social responsibility is one of the guiding factors to consider when designing and carrying out an applied research project, which allows you to deepen academic knowledge and apply this knowledge to solve a problem (Harrison, Pettan, & Mackinlay, 2010). A healthy body of research suggests that there need be no clear division between academic and applied research (Hofman, 2010; Seeger, 2008). The problem or issue that applied research serves can vary widely.

Questions of teaching and learning form an area in which applied research in expressive culture can find relevance (Newsome, 2008; Stock, 2008). For example, one project I undertook was based in questions around minority language and culture learning through popular music. I began by working with rappers who were learning their own heritage Indigenous languages and using hip hop to do so. Then, because Indigenous language learning is an increasingly central goal for many communities, the project expanded to address a bigger question: How can popular music function as part of Indigenous language revitalization projects? This framing encouraged me to speak with teachers as well as musicians and to focus my inquiry on concrete strategies that were and were not working for learners. Listen for questions or problems that arise in your own research context and consider whether your project would be well suited to seek applied solutions while also increasing academic knowledge.

COORDINATING HYBRID FIELDWORK: PRE-FIELD RESEARCH DESIGN

Designing fieldwork with adequate time spent across your hybrid site requires coordination. To design a model of participant observation, it is helpful to begin with a snapshot of your current interactions. Complete the following exercise to identify how you currently use online sites, tools, and activities.

EXERCISE 3.2

Over the course of 24 hours, keep a log of your own use of relevant internet forums. Keep track of when you use networked sites and how long you are connected.

Make note of the following:

- Start and stop times.
  - Note when you start and stop doing a specific online activity. It's equally as important to record where you are *not* using networked sites as when you are.
- The device you are using.
  - Record whether you are on a phone, computer, tablet, or other device.

- Activity.
  - What is the general goal of what you are doing online—for example, reading the news, posting photos, messaging contacts, listening to music, and so forth?
- Sites visited.
  - Keep a log of sites where you spend time. You may opt to limit this log to those that are potentially research relevant.
  - Identify if you are on a specific platform (e.g., Twitter, Facebook, Snapchat).
- Active time or passive time?
  - Are you mostly focused on your internet use? This would include, for example, when you are actively reading a blog. Or are you multitasking—for example, periodically checking a map application as you walk, posting photos from time to time during an event, or using streaming audio at a social event? If this is passive time, note the other activities you are completing.

The following chart is a model for recording this information.

Time	Start/Stop	Device	Activity	Sites	Active/ Passive
7:00 a.m.					
8:00 a.m.					
9:00 a.m.					
10:00 a.m.					
11:00 a.m.					
Noon					
1:00 p.m.					
2:00 p.m.					
3:00 p.m.					
4:00 p.m.					
5:00 p.m.					

(Continued)

(Continued)

Time	Start/Stop	Device	Activity	Sites	Active/ Passive
6:00 p.m.					
7:00 p.m.					
8:00 p.m.					
9:00 p.m.					
10:00 p.m.					
11:00 p.m.					
Midnight					
1:00 a.m.					
2:00 a.m.					
3:00 a.m.					
4:00 a.m.					
5:00 a.m.					
6:00 a.m.					

Use the chart and your notes to create an autoethnographic snapshot of yourself as a user of virtual/physical space. For how much time do you feel fully online? When are you interacting in physical and virtual space? Are there times when you are fully offline? What device do you use most for online and/or hybrid activities? Reflect on how much time and what time of day you spend in each of these three categories in order to design your fieldsite interactions. Make note of your device usage to plan for where you need to be to connect.

Then, review your activities. How do these connect to sites and platforms? Group these into categories—for example, sites used for music listening, for messaging, for information-gathering, for sharing photos, and so forth. Afterward, do a more detailed review of the sites you use. Consider which of these are research relevant. The sites you already use to listen, watch, read about, or discuss media can form the basis for your list of possible research sites in the following section.

How do the sites you use correspond to times of day? For example, are you on Facebook during your evening commute because this is when you see the most posts from your contacts? Are you always on Twitter so you don't miss the latest updates?

Next, consider your active/passive time. Dig deeper into this category to understand the impact of an online/offline circuit. This may take the form of making audio or video recordings and sharing them during an event, looking up information during an in-person conversation, or sharing a new song via streaming audio with a friend as you drive. If you had trouble identifying exactly when you start and stop using the internet in the first category, this indicates that you may already be spending much of your time in your hybrid field.

Finally, diagnose. What is already working well for you in your use of relevant online sites? If you consulted very few or no sites connected to your proposed research topic, this is an area you will need to focus on in the next segment. Start thinking about the time of day in which you are most active on sites that could be research relevant. In the next section, you will have a chance to more fully consider how and when it makes sense to be online, whether actively or passively. If you are rarely active in areas related to research or are online when few other participants are, consider changes you could make to put yourself in communication with others.

The constant presence of the online in many people's daily lives—and in fact the lack of distinction between online and offline activities in many cases—is a core concept in hybrid ethnography. Stella Chan developed new awareness of how this plays out in her research by methodically documenting her activities. Chan finds that YouTube is a crucial research-relevant platform; its history feature also helps bolster her own record keeping of her listening history. Though at the time of writing she felt more comfortable with face-to-face interaction, she finds that internet-based communication is an integral part of her scene. She writes about being unconsciously online—that is, constantly having a connection to internet-based networks, though she was previously unaware of the perpetual presence of these networks in her daily life. She reflects that she is surprised to realize that she is completely "offline" only when asleep. She finds, "There are lots of in and out interactive moments between physical and virtual space which sometimes make me feel there is a blurry boundary between the two spaces" (Stella Chan, personal communication, February 18, 2019). Chan's use of networked tools—notably her laptop, iPad, and phone—mark daily activity. Her phone is "always connected with Wi-Fi or mobile data even though I am not using it" (Stella Chan, personal communication, February 18, 2019). Her use of a smartphone as a research

Example: A Researcher's Reflection on Online Activity

Time	Start/Stop	Device	Activity	Sites	Platforms	Active/Passive
7:00 a.m. ~ 8:00 a.m.	Sleeping, completely offline (turn off my laptop, my phone is on but disconnected with Wi-Fi/mobile data)					
9:00 a.m. ~ 10:30 a.m.	Start around 9:30 a.m.	Phone	Reading news, checking email, browsing Facebook and Instagram	Yahoo HK, my personal Facebook and Instagram sites	Facebook, Instagram, WhatsApp	Active: Only when I am reading the news. Multitasking: Checking Facebook and Instagram while I am preparing and eating breakfast.
10:30 a.m. ~ 12:30 p.m.		Laptop, phone	Laptop: For checking dictionary	Dictionary website	Online dictionary	Laptop Passive: I am reading book (hardcopy); I use the laptop only when I need to check dictionary. Phone Passive: My phone is connected with Wi-Fi, but I am not using it unless I hear a notification sound.

12:30 p.m.		Laptop, phone	Laptop: For playing music	YouTube Autoplay starts from 1990s pop songs in Hong Kong Phone: Message app, email	YouTube (autoplay)	<u>Laptop</u> Multitasking: I am listening to music while preparing for my lunch. <u>Phone</u> Passive: My phone is connected with Wi-Fi, but I am not using it unless I hear a notification sound.
1:00 p.m. ~ 1:45 p.m.		Laptop, phone	Laptop: For playing cartoons	YouTube cartoon site Phone: Message app, email	YouTube	<u>Laptop</u> Multitasking: I am watching cartoons during my lunch. <u>Phone</u> Passive: My phone is connected with Wi-Fi, but I am not using it unless I hear a notification sound.
1: 45 p.m. ~ 3:00 p.m.		Phone	Checking bus schedule	RTA bus schedule	RTA webpage	Passive: Checking my phone for the bus schedule a few times while I am shopping for groceries, have to see when will be the next bus.
3:00 p.m. ~ 3:30 p.m.		Phone				Passive: Just turn on the mobile data, on my way home.

(Continued)

Example: A Researcher's Reflection on Online Activity (Continued)

Time	Start/Stop	Device	Activity	Sites	Platforms	Active/Passive
3:30 p.m. ~ 4:15 p.m.		Laptop, phone	Laptop: For playing music	YouTube, message app, email	YouTube (autoplay)	Laptop Multitasking: I am listening to music while doing housework. Phone Passive: my phone is connected with Wi-Fi, but I am not using it unless I hear a notification sound.
4:15 p.m. ~ 6:30 p.m.		Laptop, phone	Laptop: For checking dictionary, iLearn	Course website Phone: Message app, email	Online dictionary, iLearn	Laptop Passive: I read book for a while, and then do Japanese homework and check homework answers on iLearn. Phone Passive: My phone is connected with Wi-Fi, but I am not using it unless I hear a notification sound.
6:30 p.m. ~ 7:15 p.m.		Laptop, phone	Laptop: For playing music	YouTube, message app, email	YouTube (autoplay)	Laptop Multitasking: I am listening to music while preparing for my dinner. Phone Passive: My phone is connected with Wi-Fi, but I am not using it unless I hear a notification sound.

7:15 p.m. ~ 8:00 p.m.		iPad, phone	iPad: For watching Japanese drama	iPad: Qianzun App Phone: Message app, email	Japanese drama site	<u>IPad</u> Multitasking: I am watching Japanese drama while eating dinner. <u>Phone</u> Passive: My phone is connected with Wi-Fi, but I am not using it unless I hear a notification sound.
8:00 p.m. ~ 9:00 p.m.		Laptop, phone	Laptop: For playing music Phone: Video-calling with my family in Hong Kong	Laptop: YouTube Phone: WhatsApp, call with family	Laptop: YouTube (autoplay) Phone: WhatsApp	<u>Laptop</u> Passive: For the purpose of background music only. <u>Phone</u> Active: Video chatting is my primary activity.
9:00 p.m. ~ 10:00 p.m.		Laptop, phone	Laptop: For playing music	Laptop: YouTube Phone: Message app, email	Laptop: YouTube (autoplay)	<u>Laptop</u> Mulitasking: I am washing dishes and doing some cleaning jobs, at the same time listening to the music. <u>Phone</u> Passive: My phone is connected with Wi-Fi, but I am not using it unless I hear a notification sound.

(Continued)

Example: A Researcher's Reflection on Online Activity (Continued)

Time	Start/Stop	Device	Activity	Sites	Platforms	Active/Passive
10:00 p.m. ~ 11:30 p.m.		Laptop, phone	Laptop: For checking dictionary	Dictionary site Phone: message app, email	Online dictionary	Laptop Passive: I am reading book (hardcopy), I use the laptop only when I need to check dictionary. Phone Passive: My phone is connected with Wi-Fi, but I am not using it unless I hear a notification sound.
11:30 p.m. ~ Midnight		Phone		Message app, email		Passive: I am taking a shower, my phone is connected with Wi-Fi, but I am not using it unless I hear a notification sound.
Midnight ~ 12:45 a.m.		Phone	Browsing Facebook and Instagram	Personal Facebook and Instagram pages	Facebook, Instagram, WhatsApp	Active: Switching between different platforms for updated posts.
12:45 a.m. ~ 6:00 a.m.	Sleeping, completely offline (turn off my laptop, my phone is on but disconnected with Wi-Fi/mobile data)					

Courtesy of Stella Chan

and communication tool makes her aware of her responsiveness to alerts that ping through her phone or appear on the locked screen. This troubles the idea of really ever being fully "offline," even when she is not actively paying attention to emails, Facebook, Instagram posts, and WhatsApp communications. Without even noticing at first, her consciousness is active in a hybrid space between the online and offline.

NAVIGATING THE ONLINE PORTION OF YOUR FIELDSITE

Though it may at first seem counterintuitive, one of the best resources for online strategy happens offline. By participating in an in-person discussion, I learned which YouTube videos people were using to discuss music and dance in ways that informed my research question. This led me to analyze video comments and locate response videos that users made to express their opinions about the video that we had watched together. I also continued to talk offline with participants about these videos, completing the circle. Listen to your interlocutors and pay attention to what you hear. When you are in your physical fieldsite, what apps do people use? Where do your friends and colleagues find relevant media? Share their own? What social media sites do people use to post photos? To send invites? What sites come up in live conversation, either because people are talking about them or because they are using them? Listen to these cues to figure out where you need to participate online.

Make a list of sites that members of your research community have used or discussed in offline communications. Then, consult the list of sites you created during your 24-hour internet-journaling exercise. Consider overlap and relevance in order to put together a preliminary list of active spaces.

Moving from a preliminary list to a research list requires careful observation. This period of preparatory research will shape the initial fieldsite. For many topics, the possibilities are vast. As a result, you are likely to be actively choosing your sites rather than discovering the only possible venues in which your topic can be addressed (Burrell, 2009). As a researcher, you choose relevant aspects of your scene based on sites that are

1. Relevant
2. Actively maintained
3. Media-rich

Keep in mind that your scene may change over time if one site becomes inactive or another emerges as relevant.

A preliminary list of active spaces may contain about 6 to 12 sites, depending on the community. These might include commercial sites, newsgroups, and sites maintained by individuals. To build a balanced initial list, consider whether any of the following types of sites could be relevant to your topic:

- Sites associated with a performance venue
- Arts news pages or event calendars
- Festival web pages
- Fan pages
- Commercial school pages
- Record label or film studio pages
- Artists' personal pages
- Media personalities' pages
- Media outlets' pages, such as a radio or television station
- Message boards
- Newsgroups
- Wiki pages
- Channels on video sharing sites such as YouTube
- Pages on photo sharing sites such as Tumblr
- Blogs dedicated to your research community or topic

These pages will largely fall into two categories: sites that primarily disseminate information and sites that encourage active participation. The former includes pages whose primary audience will read them in order to learn relevant information. These are likely to include pages maintained by an artist's management company or a website for a performance venue. They are often media rich and helpful for connecting to on-the-ground events. Read these critically to analyze how an individual, group, or company presents itself to the public. The latter category includes sites in which you can actively participate. These include sites with upload and comment features, like user-generated media sharing sites, and sites whose main function is group communication, like message boards and social media. Plan to consult and participate on these types of sites. You may find that these categories are not always neatly divided. For example, a news site may also make it possible for readers to comment on stories. Staying present with types from each category and those that blend both creates useful variety.

Select two times of day to consult the sites on the preliminary list. Consider times in which you are generally active online, as identified in the 24-hour internet-journaling exercise. Each time you consult a site, document and annotate. In your fieldnotes, document what has been newly posted, identify media or information relevant to your research topic, and jot down your own responses to the material. Finally, take a screen shot of the site. At the end of the week, review each site for the following criteria:

1. Relevant

   Does the site provide information that is directly related to your research topic? For sites with active participation, do discussions or comments address aspects of your topic that you find important?

2. Actively maintained

   Information disseminating sites

   How often is new information posted? Are calendars up to date? Does the site generate new content or repost from other avenues?

   Active participation sites

   How often do participants post text, media, or comments? How many active members does a site or group have? How regularly do members interact with each other? Are comments substantively linked to each other?

3. Media-rich

   A study of expressive culture requires more than a study of words. Does the site offer images, sound, and video, and can you also post your own media as relevant? Depending on your specific topic, you may want to post your own videos or audio files, listen to those posted by others, comment and read others' comments on videos, or share photos from performances.

From your preliminary list, immediately remove any sites that do not meet the first criterion. If a site is not actively maintained, remove it from your list of sites to check regularly. If it is still relevant, move it to a list of sites to check semi-regularly, for example weekly, depending on how often it is maintained. Not all useful sites will be media rich, but make sure to keep on your list some that are.

Now observe your winnowed-down list. For each site you have kept, determine how often it will be helpful to check the page. Was one time of day more active than the other? Were there significant changes twice a day? Daily? Were there so many changes that checking only twice a day made each observation hard to keep up with? Use this information to decide how many times a day and when to consult the sites for each one on your list. Write this information into a list, calendar, or set of reminders for yourself in your preferred organizational format. Sites may become more or less dynamic over time; adjust your calendar as needed. This calendar will form your initial online research site strategy, which you will put into action in the next chapter.

Working With Websites and Social Media

As in active participation sites, social media sites generally are most effective when you read, comment, and share regularly. The exact definition of "regularly" is dependent upon the norms for the group in which you are active. If chatting or other real-time communication is common, you will want to be actively participating at peak times. How much does synchronous communication matter in your group? For example, do band members use a social media page's messenger function to chat, or are people more likely to post a question that collects responses throughout the day? If the former is the case, prioritize participating at high-traffic times. If the latter is the norm, asynchronous communication may work for your site.

Set a schedule for your social media use. For some people, it works to be passively "on" for large stretches of time—for example, by setting your cell phone to alert you when new messages are posted on the platform you and your fellow participants use. Other researchers prefer to check in at regular intervals. If you are already making timing choices based on when other people are active online, let this guide you. If not, think about when you tend to be online, per your 24-hour internet-journaling exercise. Add a few more daily check-in times at moments when you tend to be online, adjusting these over time to make sure you are keeping up and participating at relevant moments. If you are already in the habit of checking multiple times in a day, you need only to formalize your interactions to make sure you don't miss information. Times at which participants are active, alongside constraints imposed by your own availability, determine your schedule. As with the website process above, write down your preliminary schedule and start your notes and documentation accordingly.

Integrating Online and Offline Communications

Solidifying the online portion of your fieldsite takes time, and it's important to consistently reconnect with your in-person fieldsite as you do so. Doing the following will keep you involved across the hybrid site:

- Link yourself online to the people you interact with offline.
    - Social media platforms are often relevant to hybrid fieldsites. Take time to connect with everyone you work with who participates on your platform.
- Don't be afraid to reference your online communications when you are in-person.
    - Ask a bandmate about the article she tweeted. Tell a fellow performer what you liked about the video he posted. Ask the festival organizers when the rest of the line-up will be announced to the public. These kinds of interactions foster your 21st-century research relationship.
- Remember that online communications often treat offline topics.
    - For example, the messaging app you use may be the primary form of communication for arranging meetings or rehearsals. This is at the core of working in a hybrid fieldsite.
- Keep listening offline.
    - Be aware that communication changes can be rapid; you may need to add other methods of communication to maintain relevance.

SUMMARY

At this point, you have had the opportunity to analyze your own position as researcher and participant in relationship to your scene. This will form the foundation for the research that you will soon undertake. An example of intersectional analysis demonstrated how a probing situated power reveals mutually constitutive identity constructions. Crenshaw's approach to the 2 Live Crew obscenity case also shows how intersectionality leads to productive outcomes in terms of content. By examining various types of power at play in your field, you can not only situate yourself but also begin to craft increasingly relevant lines of inquiry that relate to your guiding research question. Finally, you now have an active and diverse set of online sites that extend your physical field locations. In the next chapter, you will put your research plan into action.

FURTHER READING

Boylorn, R. M., & Orbe, M. P. (Eds.). (2014). *Critical autoethnography: Intersecting cultural identities in everyday life.* Walnut Creek, CA: Left Coast Press.

Burrell, J. (2009). The field site as a network. *Field Methods, 21*(2), 181–199.

Collins, P. H., & Bilge, S. (2016). *Intersectionality.* Malden, MA: Polity Press.

Crenshaw, K. (1991). Mapping the margins: Intersectionality, identity politics, and violence against women of color. *Stanford Law Review, 43*(6), 1241–1299.

Denzin, N. K. (2013). *Interpretive autoethnography.* Thousand Oaks, CA: Sage.

Driskill, Q.-L., Finley, C., Gilley, B. J., & Morgensen, S. L. (2011). *Queer Indigenous studies: Critical interventions in theory, politics, and literature.* Tucson: University of Arizona Press.

Evans-Cowley, J. S. (2010). Planning in the age of Facebook: The role of social networking in planning processes. *GeoJournal: Spatially Integrated Social Sciences and Humanities, 75*(5), 407–420.

Newsome, J. K. (2008). From researched to centrestage: A case study. *Muzikoloski Zbornik Musicological Annual, XLIV*(1), 31–49.

Seeger, A. (2008). Theories forged in the crucible of action: The joys, dangers, and potentials of advocacy and fieldwork. In G. Barz & T. J. Cooley (Eds.), *Shadows in the field: New perspectives for fieldwork in ethnomusicology* (2nd ed., pp. 271–288). Oxford, UK: Oxford University, Press.

Temple, B., & Young, A. (2004). Qualitative research and translation dilemmas. *Qualitative Research, 4*, 161–178.

4 COLLECTING AND ORGANIZING YOUR DATA

During the first three chapters, you undertook pre-field planning. For this chapter and the three that follow, you will do in-field ethnographic research. This "doing" requires participation, observation, record keeping, and interpretation before you move into the last stage of ethnography. Through previous research or methods coursework, you have likely encountered multiple strategies for collecting and organizing data in a physical fieldsite. At its most basic, the process is outlined as follows: To attempt to get a better understanding of a specific aspect of culture, researchers participate in the field. We document our observations about the events and our participation. This step involves taking our own notes and also acquiring relevant media, like video and audio recordings that we make. It also includes conducting interviews and surveys. Finally, we use these notes, alongside other documentation we collect and preexisting research, to conduct an analysis that addresses the research question. Research guides for the physical field typically suggest that you write down your observations, code them for themes, and then use notes to reflect. More recent scholarship in online research recommends a data collection and organizational strategy that encompasses notetaking, storage of data files, and collecting data into a single location. One typical strategy is to take notes on the general online scene, writing down what you read across several sites. Then, save data from posts and threads in the form of images, text, or HTML files. Finally, collect all of your files together in a large word processing file, where it is ready for analysis (Clifford & Marcus, 1986; Kozinets, 2010; Van Maanen, 1988).

These principles form the foundation of ethnographic research that occurs in a hybrid field. Each set has limitations, however, as the first set assumes your research is exclusively offline and the second fully online. Even with all of the data from what you read on websites or save from posts and conversation threads, this online strategy deals only with text, not with media-rich information that the ethnographer of expressive culture will encounter. In 2005, Dicks, Mason, Coffey, and Atkinson argued, "Data overload is just around the corner" (2005, p. 120). Now, it has arrived. How is it possible to collect and analyze data when you are researching across the hybrid field without losing track of all of your interactions? And is it worth the effort?

First, a note about why it matters to keep and organize notes and other records of fieldwork activities. Fieldnotes, photographs, videos, and other recordings are not simply records. In documenting the field and our participation in it, we come to understand the scene in which we are embedded. Documentation works like journaling. You get to experience the field three times: first, when you are actively part of an event, then when you write about it, and a third time when you review your writing and associated materials. Collecting and organizing fieldwork documentation thus form critical steps in ethnographic inquiry.

It is indeed possible to keep records of fieldwork participation across the hybrid field while staying balanced, and this requires a plan. In the previous chapter, you arrived at a plan for interacting with the online portion of your fieldsite and consistently reconnecting it to your physical fieldwork. In this chapter, you will grow your online presence as part of your hybrid field, develop a strategy for notes, documentation, and write-ups, and explore tools that facilitate data organization.

CONTEXT

As recently as the first decade of the 21st century, research methods scholarship concluded that researchers are in positions of privilege because we have "ready access to audio, video, photographic, and computer equipment" necessary for documentation (Post, 2006, p. 7). As was described in the introduction, this access to equipment is far less exclusive now than it ever has been. Heed warnings from the realm of physical fieldwork by carefully considering how you represent your collaborators, and take seriously the privileges that you are afforded, as described in the first three chapters of this volume. Simultaneously, it is important to hone your skills as a reader of large quantities of media precisely because researchers are not the only ones engaged in documentation.

While scholarship often uses words like "data" and "information," it is important to recall that ethnographic research places the researcher in a relationship with participants in a dialogic process. This qualitative process does not involve ferreting out buried facts, but rather it is a collaborative manner of producing understanding.

As information technology changes over time, options for storing, organizing, and maneuvering information gathered during fieldwork shift. The widening impact of computers on ethnography has been theorized for decades and will continue to transform available tools (Houtman & Zeitlyn, 1996). This chapter encourages you to create a nimble, thorough, and internally consistent archive of your data. Setting up in this manner will make it easier for you to take full advantage of a wide range of technological tools, which should both save you time and encourage you to think about your data in a networked manner.

FIELD LOG

To begin active research across the digital and physical aspects of your field, take stock of what you are planning to do each day and when you will budget time for each activity. An activity log helps to organize fieldwork time. Keep a general plan of what you intend to do every day and when you plan to do various activities. This involves relevant web-based activity, which you scheduled in Chapter 3, and in-person meetings and events. Then, record what you actually did during the time scheduled. A paper calendar or an electronic app can be a helpful way to keep this information accessible as you go about your day and invites you to record your actual activities as you do them.

Anchor your calendar with key activities: rehearsal times for your group, concerts by artists you work with, festivals, and other events that have a regular schedule come first. Then, insert any obligations of a personal or professional nature of yours that occur at specific times. Now you have a skeleton around which you can plan other research activities. Select one or more times daily to engage with the online portion of your fieldsite and mark off time for daily fieldnotes. Then, observe when you have time for other research activities: informal interactions with other participants in your scene, planned interviews, and simply spending time in a location, on-the-ground or online, with people in your scene. Pay special attention to activities with multiple steps, like planning first to meet with potential collaborators in a social or work setting, attending an event to get to know more about their work, and then asking for and conducting an interview.

PARTICIPATION AND DOCUMENTATION IN THE HYBRID FIELD

A regular plan for posting, commenting, and sharing, as well as reading and cataloging information, keeps hybrid ethnography manageable. Regular documentation can save time and help produce useful analysis later. After several months of fieldwork, I was reflecting on a pattern I had observed.

Increasingly, rappers and other popular musicians were responding to violence against Indigenous women and girls. I knew that a specific response had been organized through community concerts, and I was also listening for anti-violence efforts in recorded music and public statements by musicians. As I was going back through my notes and documentation to analyze the type and timing of these responses, I noticed a gap: I remembered reading a tweet from a rapper I follow in which he urged fellow rappers to participate in anti-violence efforts, but I could not find a record of it in my notes. In this case, I had a work-around because I recalled that he used the hashtag #MMIW to call attention to the cause of missing and murdered Indigenous women. I used the hashtag as a search term, located the tweet, and could then review his exact phrasing. This was a time-consuming process, however. I had not documented this in my own notes, so I had to go back to the artist's Twitter page and find the tweet there. This information would have been totally lost to me had I relied on a web page that had since been altered or deleted. While I was fortunately able to recover the information, this gap in my documentation plan cost me much more time later than it would have to record the information as the communication initially occurred.

This incident points to the not-uncommon problem of too much data. Researchers often reflect back on something a participant said in a conversation or shared on social media and then need to find the exact wording or timing to make sense of how it fits into the scene. If you cannot remember exactly what day it was said or which page it was posted to, it can be difficult to find the specific remark and your notes about it unless you work for a searchable and organized documentation archive. Even more importantly, because the same participants interact online and on-the-ground, it is essential to be able to connect your communications that span the hybrid site in order to develop a full picture of the scene.

ONLINE INTERACTIONS IN THE HYBRID FIELD

As you begin your fieldwork, you will develop your social media interactions on platform(s) you identified as relevant with face-to-face collaborators. Some researchers use existing profiles and adapt what they share and privacy settings as they connect to more people. Others create new profiles just for research in order to maintain boundaries. Determining where lines are drawn between one's personal and research life has long been a topic of heightened concentration for ethnographers, and it is exacerbated in hybrid research. This is a personal decision, one that is contingent upon the dynamics of your particular scene and one that will likely be drawn and redrawn over time. As described in Chapters 2 and 3, as researchers, we need to pay attention to our own safety, and the purity of intentions of those with whom we interact cannot be assumed. In hybrid fieldwork, we have the benefit of interacting with the same scene members in person and across online portions of the field. Fellow members can help determine if someone's behavior is disingenuous or if a risk is being posed. Open communication and collaboration with participants and research team members go a long way toward participant and researcher safety.

Developing Your Profile

As you prepare, flesh out your online profile. If you are starting on a new platform or creating a new profile for research, fill in required information and start posting on topics of interest. Whether working with an established or newer presence, focus your online attention on your research field. Share articles relevant to the performance you study, offer videos by the artists you appreciate, or post news related to your scene. Pay attention to the conventions of the platform and your social group as you do so. Adjust your privacy settings in a way that balances your own security with your ability to connect with group members, and think carefully about information that you post online: Even if your photos or information are not set to be shared with everyone, anything you post might be shared widely.

Growing Your Network

As you post, pay attention to reactions to your posts. People who know your contacts may retweet your tweets, comment on your videos, download your audio files, or request to follow you. Read the comments and profiles of these interested parties and, if they seem relevant to your area of interest, consider connecting with them as well. Contacts of members of your network form another possible set of interested parties. As you post more, you will have increasing opportunities to connect with people whose interests you share. Avoid the temptation to grow your network as big as possible, however. You are looking to engage meaningfully about a particular cultural practice, so social media users who share that interest are the ones with whom you will have the most engaging interactions. When working with a closed group or network, be cautious about who is given access; some closed group administrators choose to only add people they or their fellow members know and trust personally.

Posting

In Chapter 3, you zeroed in on sites and platforms that are active and observed for times of day when members of your group are online. Use this timing to select the times of day that you make sure to be active online. During each session, read, interact, and post on the sites and platforms that you have identified. Some of this online time may well be "deep hanging out" (Clifford, 1988; Geertz, 1998), during which you listen to music on sites, watch relevant videos, read posts, and perhaps interact casually with comment sections. As in the physical field, take time to observe site-specific behaviors and participate in a way that engages with what your fellow group members are doing. You will also want to post regularly. Gauge this for the specific site: If you are observing changes on an official web page, like a record label, arts festival, or individual artist, there will likely be fewer opportunities for direct engagement, so observation and an occasional comment section may be the bulk of your interaction. For blogs and social media sites, posting, responding to posts, and sharing items with your own network is the norm. Recognizing that online work connects directly to on-the-ground aspects of your site, pay attention to notices about shows and other events of interest for your participation.

Your posting strategy will differ based on how integrated you already are into the online platform or site, but key similarities stretch across both. If you are interacting on a site that is already familiar to you, continue to interact as you would with your group, with one exception: You now take on a keener observational role. Take note of your experience as a participant as well as how your posts are received by those around you. If you are building up your interaction in the online portion of your fieldsite, make a special effort to post regularly. Some platforms have specific written codes of conduct or expectations for participants; familiarize yourself with these. Researchers are expected to meet standards for appropriate behavior on a platform. If members—intentionally or unintentionally—violate expectations, it can be instructive to attend to how others respond and discuss these incidents with fellow participants.

Following the norms of your particular group, you can share articles, photos, news, reactions to live shows, or to video and audio online. You and your fellow participants are all finding your own balance of sharing your thoughts, managing the online "face" you show to the world, and keeping enough personal information private to try to minimize the risk involved in public communication. Write about how you balance this in your fieldnotes, read others' online communications with this juggling in mind, and talk to fellow participants about it as well. As in the physical field, you may find that you contribute more as your interactions deepen over time. Combine sharing what others have posted, reposting or liking things you find interesting, and posting your own content. Be alert for potential scamming and trolling and talk directly with your fellow participants, online or face-to-face, if such activity starts. Refer also to "Researcher Safety and Privacy" (Chapter 2) for more on this topic. Record and detail your experience as described in the following section.

If you need to set a schedule so that you interact, put posts in your calendar and follow though. A good rule of thumb is to respond to content and post things that you find genuinely interesting. After all, you are interacting with people who participate in the same kind of music, dance, or other performance that interests you, so letting yourself interact according to your existing interests is a solid strategy. Do pay attention to what encourages discussion, likes, and sharing, both in terms of your interactions and those by your fellow group members. Pay attention to any negative reactions as well. Jot down notes of this and be ready to observe if the same topics or ways of instigating discourse are similarly engaging offline. Do particular topics invite discussion? Are people more likely to engage when comments are phrased in the form of a debate? Observing who reacts, when, and how offers insight into the dynamics of your scene in the hybrid field.

BOX 4.1

Griefing, or offending others on purpose, is common enough to have earned its own term as long ago as the late 1990s. As Julian Dibbell explains, irritating others brings amusement to some participants: "Not that griefers don't like online games. It's just that what they most enjoy about those games is making other players not enjoy them" (Dibbell, 2008). Instances of participants purposefully offending others can be found across social media and on comment sections for videos, music, and articles. While this is sometimes general in nature and may be simply annoying, it can become personal and even threatening. Because you know participants across the hybrid field, the anonymity that typically accompanies griefing is lessened or removed. Still, disparaging and even threatening commentary is sometimes part of the social reality of online communication. Researchers or fellow participants may have personal information made public as part of an online threat. Information about and strategies to prevent doxxing can be found in Cox (2015). Seek assistance from fellow researchers, team members, or university personnel to address these unfortunate—and legitimate—concerns that can arise in online communication. Document suspicious interactions as soon as you notice them; use this history should you or a fellow participant need to seek support from the authorities.

DATA COLLECTION AND MANAGEMENT

Organized information gathering is feasible if you follow a plan. Your collection should be

Structured

Archived

Reliable

Anchored

First, your interaction should be structured. This should flow easily from the work you completed in Chapter 3. To begin interacting in the online portion of the hybrid sphere, develop a regular plan for data collection. Start by going online the same times every day for a set period. Also include multitasking or passive time in your schedule. Interact with each of the sites and platforms you identified as relevant at the times of day you determined were active in the pre-field exercise.

Second, your interaction should be archived. Create an organized system of folders on your computer to store relevant data. One solid option is to start with a project folder named for your hybrid ethnographic research project (Figure 4.1). In that folder, save your central document in which you describe all of your interactions and refer out to other media. Then, create an internal folder for each subunit of work organized by time (a week, for example) or type (each platform, for example). As you interact, take screenshots of the layout and images you see and record relevant data as text. For text, you can copy and paste your text into your word processor or software of choice or use your browser's functionality to save a web page as text. Save your screenshots and text files with the same format for naming each time. I like to use the following formula:

PlatformUserDateTime

As long as you are consistent, vary this for your needs and preferences.

In your central document, make a note of each image you record and give a brief snippet about it. If you are working in a basic layout, like a word processing document, comments can provide this information. Alternative options include the internal logic of a qualitative analysis program. These notes should also include other media you encounter. Jot down the names of songs or other audio that play on sites, as well as videos or other media that are incorporated. You may want to capture the audio or video in your archive, details for which are included in Chapter 6.

FIGURE 4.1 Sample File Organization System

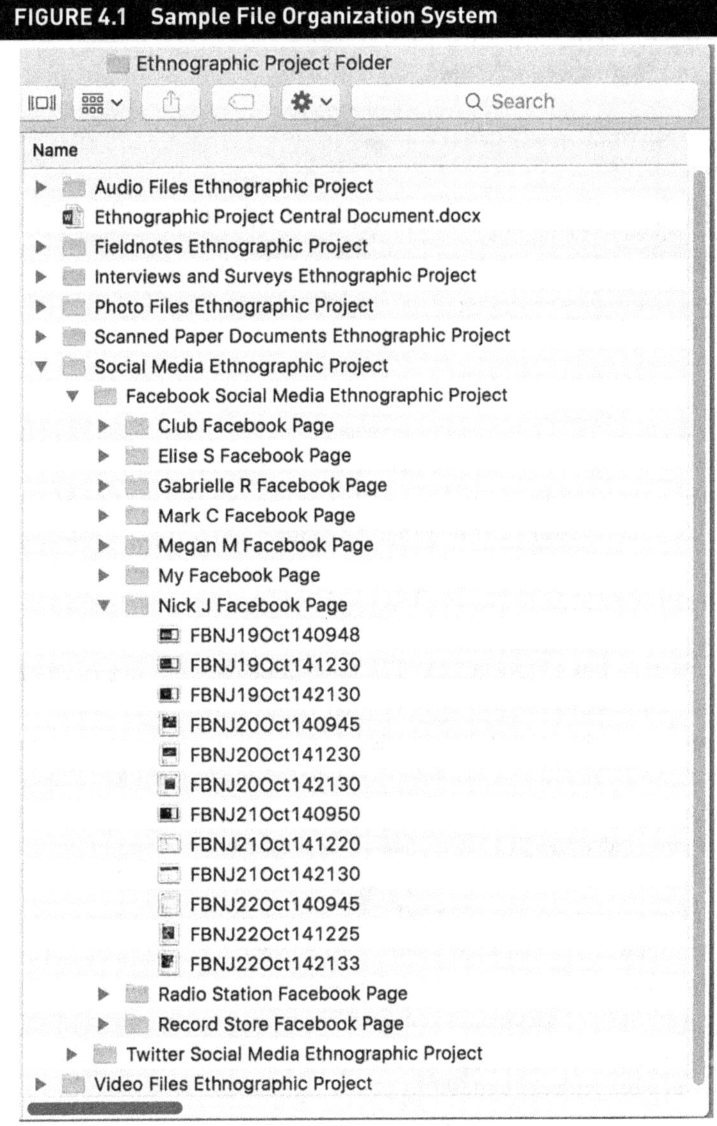

Start each session with a new section in your word processing software or a new segment in another program you choose using the exercise at the end of this chapter (Figure 4.2). Record the date and time and catalog each site and platform you use. Include the URL for any additional links or sites you visit. Take a screen shot of each site or platform to begin, or use a software

FIGURE 4.2 Sample Note Taking System

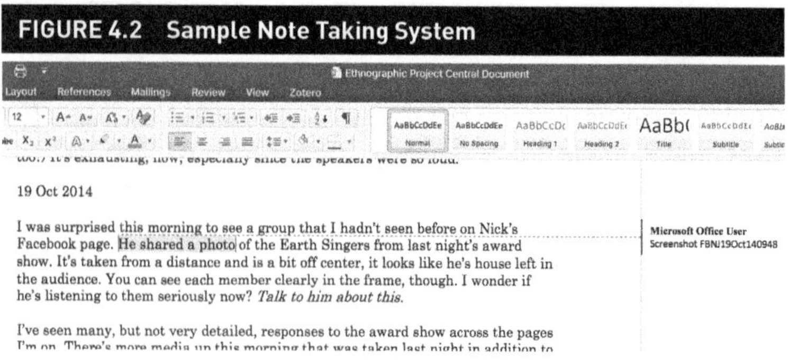

19 Oct 2014

I was surprised this morning to see a group that I hadn't seen before on Nick's Facebook page. He shared a photo of the Earth Singers from last night's award show. It's taken from a distance and is a bit off center, it looks like he's house left in the audience. You can see each member clearly in the frame, though. I wonder if he's listening to them seriously now? *Talk to him about this.*

Microsoft Office User
Screenshot FBNJ19Oct140948

I've seen many, but not very detailed, responses to the award show across the pages

capture program. If real-time interactivity is central to your project, you could use full-motion screen capture software, but this is not necessary for basic interactions on social media. You could choose to save web pages as HTML, which allows for searchability within the contents of the page. If not using a searchable format, copy and paste, if online, or type out, if verbal, key quotations so they are searchable later. If you are working with specific software, use the internal organizing logic.

Back up this archive. This follows for your online work and also for the notes you take in the hybrid field. After taking handwritten notes, use a scanner or mobile app to record these. Collate the images with the appropriate write-up. It is also helpful to keep the original paper notes while you are still engaged in the research process. This gives you a physical copy for reference and works as a safety measure against data loss. I am in the habit of regularly backing up all of my data to my external hard drive and also keeping a copy on my computer. I keep separate file folders for jotted fieldnotes, show flyers, and other objects that enter into the research. Chapter 6 goes into more detail on managing audio, video, and images; get into the habit now of backing up your own archive and storing materials in an organized manner so you can easily incorporate all of your media when you start to work with recordings.

Third, your documentation needs to be reliable. In order to move fluidly between all of your forms of documentation, establish a codebook for how you will refer to individuals, themes, and media. If you have not used a codebook in the past, a good resource is Saldaña (2016). Either within your chosen software or as a separate list or spreadsheet, determine how you will refer to keywords that encapsulate specific types of information. The code also identifies participants across platforms. As you create and use your themes, keep in mind that information and experience can fall into multiple thematic categories. Because we and our collaborators engage in meaning making across the hybrid physical/digital space, it is necessary to make online information mutually understandable with offline information. For hybrid ethnography, key items in a codebook are the following:

- Names: Create a code for participants with whom you interact in person and online and record an abbreviation to use every time you document interaction with that person. This ensures that you can connect your online and offline interactions with the same individual. Recall that some individuals may have multiple online personas, so variant endings on the same name stem (e.g., Christy1, Christy2) could be necessary. If using a software program, these can be coded with the same umbrella name or case so that they can be compiled easily.
- Themes: Start with the major themes in your research question and identify an abbreviation for each. When you refer to a theme in your jottings or encounter an example in your interactions, use the code to identify this in your notes. This will likely grow and refine over time as new themes emerge.

When taking notes on paper, get into the habit of using your code. This saves time, as you can use abbreviations for the names of key collaborators and mark ideas to which you know you will want to return. After taking handwritten notes when you are on the phone, online, or in the physical field, it's helpful to preserve these, as mentioned above. Typing these up is a helpful way to revisit your information, fill in details, and also to create a searchable archive. Using the same key words and abbreviations in all of your notes creates consistency across the hybrid field.

Finally, make sure your documentation is anchored. Your central document is the spine that supports all of your notes and media. As you work, take screenshots of interactions or posts that seem significant to you, including your own posts. Pay attention to audio that plays on sites, videos posted by users, and other media exchanged by your fellow participants. Keep a careful record of what additional documents you collect, including screenshots, HTML files, images, audio, and video. In the anchoring document, write notes with a brief summary of each, as well as thoughts you have as you encounter them. Save images, audio, and video to the appropriate project folder for future use.

NOTETAKING

The hybrid site mirrors the offline or online-only fieldsite in that ethnography requires the regular jotting of fieldnotes. The basics are clear: Jot down reminders when events occur, take time regularly to write up your experience, and use this information as you transition to analysis. Strangely, the details of what scholars actually record in fieldnotes can be hard to come by. Anthropologist Jean E. Jackson takes this on directly, interviewing researchers about the contents of their fieldnotes, as this important practice sometimes takes on an air of mystery (Jackson, 1990). Jackson cuts through what she calls the "fieldnotes mystique" (p. 24) to offer a variety of types of notes that different researchers find useful: notes researchers record as annotation on physical material, notes we take in the field as events occur, notes collaborators make during fieldwork, and notes or diaries recorded at one specific moment during the day when we are removed from direct interaction. Jottings and reflections are likely to be helpful to most researchers; collaborative notetaking and notes on or about physical material, including an archive of show flyers, programs, or the like that you collect, will depend on the particular project. Even if you do not ask other participants to take notes, the process is collaborative. Questions you ask of participants are refocused by their responses; events of significance are signaled by the interest that your fellow participants show for them.

When writing down notes as you participate, give yourself reminders that will help you fill in details. First, mark down names and specific descriptions of the scene that may escape you later. Second, write down statements your fellow participants make about significant events, quoting directly when possible. Third, make notes about your own responses. You will see that these three categories mirror the three categories for writing up your notes afterward. Also at the notetaking stage, recall that you are making a record of observable events and behavior. Do your best to avoid value judgments or making globalized remarks at this stage. Focus on what you observe with your senses. Much of hybrid fieldwork notetaking extends

BOX 4.2

For expressive culture, research notes record performance gestures. Excellent examples of strategies for documenting you and your fellow participants' bodies in space come from dance research. These are relevant beyond dance studies. Buckland (1999) and Schloss (2009) offer examples of texted and visual notes that catalog movement for later analysis.

from notetaking strategies in physical research. Use your expertise from this area or consult the reliable guide by Emerson, Fretz, and Shaw for more details (2011).

In the hybrid field, balance participating and observing: When you are participating in a scene, look for moments where notetaking does not interrupt the flow of activities, and maintain sensitivity to social norms about where and when writing things down is appropriate. When you are part of a group, be it a performing ensemble, a production crew, or a casual group that improvises together, you perform your part as researcher when you take notes. This can solidify your role as the person who helps to record important information, and it can emphasize a kind of distance, as you are likely the only person both participating and formally observing. Choose the time of your notetaking sensitively to account for these two responses. If you are taking notes when interacting with a collaborator in the field, keep in mind that your recording habits carry meaning. When you scribble or type furiously, your fellow participants recognize that what they say interests you. If you stop jotting down notes, it may convey that you are uninterested or that the topic treated or opinion offered is no longer important. Making regular notes can help smooth this over; you may later revisit information that at first seemed peripheral. Avoid the temptation not to take notes when your participation is largely online. Yes, there is a record of what has been typed, who has posted what, and even timestamps on many platforms recording when these occur. Yet your observations as researcher should be more than simply recording a series of events, so this data does not replace the richness that your notes offer for understanding your milieu.

Physical fieldwork guides often suggest that taking notes during activities is likely to be socially anomalous or may feel "odd or awkward" (Emerson, Fretz, & Shaw, 2011, p. 37). However, in the hybrid field, many participants are frequently engaged with cell phones and other devices even while participating in on-the-ground events. This can be a convenient way to jot down notes without losing the flow of the activity. If you are comfortable with texting, you may also find that common text abbreviations work as well—or better—for you than traditional shorthand. Use this to your advantage. When I attended a show during a preliminary research visit, I was nearly inundated with the wealth of details in the concert venue. I used my cell phone to jot down details; these later helped me recall specifics when writing up my notes. I never had to pull away from the show, and in that space, it was extremely common to be interacting with a cell phone while also interacting in the room.

When sitting behind a computer screen, this possibility to participate while taking notes expands. In many scenarios, like scrolling through

BOX 4.3

Asking yourself to be fully participatory and also have the time and mental space to document and analyze as a researcher is akin to taking on two full time jobs at once. As a researcher and human, you will shift your concentration to different aspects of observation and participation throughout fieldwork. Karen O'Reilly writes of the "participant observation oxymoron" (2005, p. 101), in which the practical concerns of only being able to be in one place at a time—physically and mentally—rubs up against the idea that a researcher can constantly act as both. Keisha Green (2014) models how the researcher navigates participating and observing in "Doing Double Dutch Methodology: Playing With the Practice of Participant Observer." Both of these sources are listed in the chapter Further Reading.

social media or listening to streaming audio, it is actually the norm to be doing multiple activities simultaneously. Of course, there are some activities, like collaborating on video edits remotely or engaging on a detailed chat session with another participant, that take a significant amount of concentration in order to keep up. For a multitasking environment, options for simultaneous notetaking abound. Possibilities include using a second device, like a laptop computer or tablet, or a second open window in the same computer, to jot down notes while engaged online in another window. As you interact, type notes on this window or, if you enjoy writing with pen and paper, write in a notebook set up next to your work station. Complement your notetaking with other documentation in the form of screenshots and recording.

Overall, in the hybrid field as in any other field, work to balance fully participating in the activity with creating enough space to record what is happening. This challenge warrants continual work. In hybrid sites, seek appropriate opportunities to photograph, take videos, and make audio recordings. Just as you would if the field were entirely offline, balance documentation that gives a scope of the field as a whole with documentation of key people, events, and unusual occurrences. To get a sense of how technologies operate in your hybrid field, try documenting how participants interact with technologies by jotting down when computers and tablets are used in your scene or by taking photos of how people use phones and other devices. This documentation can anchor your follow-up work. For example, if many people take photos at a show or a performer encourages live tweeting, check the pages you follow for photos and read the Twitter feed that uses the show's hashtag.

WRITING UP AFTER PARTICIPANT OBSERVATION

The jottings you make in the field are already interpretive in that you choose what to write down and your notes show your perspective as an observer. Writing up extends this process, as the ethnographer selects and develops some notes for analysis and presents a selection to readers. Writing your notes into descriptions involves scholarly interpretation. As H. L. Bud Goodall puts it, "Descriptions of the outward world come from deep inside of us. Because each of us has been shaped and informed by different deeply personal experiences, our descriptions of the same facts are likely to be as distinctive as they are personal" (2000, p. 95). Reflect as you write, paying attention to the choices you make and what these say about the field and your place in it.

After you participate in an event, write up your observations and reactions. As with all entries into your log, carefully note the date, time, and location. If you are traveling to and from a physical fieldsite, this will be after the event or interaction; if you are doing research in your home fieldsite, this occurs at a break between activities. If you are writing up after a gap, make note of how much time has passed for your reference. Some of the best advice from my methods training is to write out notes as soon as possible and—this is key—before discussing the interaction with anyone else. Write fluidly without censoring and try not to categorize your experience just yet. Technology can help you get this information from your memory and onto the page. Voice memo apps and voice recognition software programs are fallible, but they have increased in utility. As long as you review the transcription directly after you record it, these programs can save time. Try having your jottings in front of you and then narrate the recollections they spark into a voice recognition program. Practice to get the hang of verbal cues (speaking punctuation aloud, for example). Then, go back immediately over your text, correcting mistranscriptions. If you type out your notes, follow a similar pattern: Type out your long-form observations and then check for errors. Recall that technology can also bring on a new set of potential issues, though these can be easily mitigated: Verify your text for mistakes introduced through an autocorrect or spell check function. Using software or apps is helpful because you need to record a lot of data: You will want to get out all of the memories and thoughts that come to you. Then, you can focus on adding detail to events of significance.

First, record a basic accounting of people, situations, and events. Give a description of your location and first impressions. Note names and brief descriptions of people with whom you interact, describe the features of the fieldwork location, and detail events that occur. It's better to be overly detailed than to wish later that you had information that you have since forgotten. For researchers of expressive culture, it is particularly relevant to take notes about media. This is helpful in log format—for example, write down the set list for a live concert, make note of what pieces your group practices at a rehearsal every week, or record the name of a video that participants share over social media. Also, pay attention to qualitative information about this media. Is a show consistently high energy? Is your group struggling to master new choreography? Does the video that participants share relate to a current political concern? Over time, your jottings about people and places will start to convey a logic of your scene. If a rehearsal most often follows a particular format, your notes after each rehearsal convey this general logic. Noting routines also allows you to keep your ears open for deviations in routine, which may constitute significant events.

Second, make sure your write-up includes significant events or statements that participants make. One good way to start is to note anything that a participant does or says that is surprising, confusing, or that seems to echo a statement you've heard multiple times before. Surprises open avenues for future inquiry. In a related manner, noting confusion gives you a base for clarifying questions later and indicates that you still have work to do to understand your scene. Keeping a record of what people say when it starts to fall into a pattern will help identify themes in your fieldwork. A second key aspect of writing down events that are "significant" is to observe how your fellow participants react. If other fans at a performance scream with excitement at a particular moment on stage or if an unusually large number of people in your social network share a fellow members' post, they are telling you that they find that moment or that comment important. Read your fellow members' cues for what is significant, and include these events and comments in your notes. When you move from jottings to a write-up, do your best to record these statements accurately, quoting directly when possible and making a note if you are paraphrasing. If instead of a verbal statement you heard in-person or online, these statements were shared as typed text, also take a screen shot or copy text with any special characters to record exactly how these were conveyed.

Finally, record your own reactions. This can be in the same dated file for the event or in a separate log that also carries the date and time on it, depending on your work style. If you are in the habit of keeping a separate field log for personal reflections, carry this practice over into your hybrid ethnography. I record my responses in the same files but use a visual marker [like square brackets] to indicate when I am moving from primarily describing events to primarily reporting how I am reacting to them. Are you feeling a sense of elation that your group finally got a piece to come together in rehearsal? Do you have an emotional response to a comment a group member makes about performance roles and gender? Do you experience concern because of a participant's aggressive body language at a public event? This is useful information to record in this third category.

Your jottings and subsequent write-up should include significant events. The definition of a significant event varies. Sometimes this is clear. For example, if you rehearse with a troupe two times a week, each rehearsal is a new event that warrants a fresh note entry. This is true also for the portion of your work that occurs online. For example, if you are researching how participants create music within a multiplayer online game, each gaming session you participate in is an "event" worth jottings and a subsequent write-up. If you are living and working in your field—for example, at a summer theater festival—your daily life interactions warrant notes, even if there is no specific "event." If you are spending time over the course of your day reading group members' posts on social media between when you see them in person or watching videos on a fan site, fit in time to record and reflect. In cases where you interact throughout your entire day, structure moments of your time at least daily to pause and do a write-up.

Try exploring digitally driven ways of organizing your data. Depending on your comfort with and affinity for computer-based data organization, you may want to try creating a private website that links your media to your fieldnotes (Barkin & Stone, 2000) or using software that facilitates data organization and storage, described in the following section.

DATA ORGANIZATION TOOLS

Multiple programs are available to organize your data. The most important aspect is not the specific mechanism you use but how you use it. As long as your information collection is structured, archived, reliable, and anchored, any tool from a simple word document to a comprehensive software program can serve your research project.

These types of programs can all be used with the method laid out above:

- Annotated documents created with a word processor
- Spreadsheets
- Notetaking software

- Qualitative analysis software
- Suite with data in one place
- File sharing service with searchability

Keeping in mind that researchers' needs determine the best tools for individual projects, here are some considerations for selecting the program that works for you. Specific program information is current at the time of writing. The general guidelines on how to select and use these tools provides useful support, even as new versions of programs emerge or are sunsetted.

One key way to organize offline and online fieldnotes together is to have a clear strategy for transferring your notes from physical fieldwork into the location where you store the rest of your information. Following a traditional fieldwork methodology is a solid option: Bring a notebook with you, and then make notes with pen and paper when time and social norms allow.[1]

If you find yourself taking notes on a phone or other handheld device in the field, consider using a program that lets you organize information across multiple devices. Notetaking apps like Google Keep, Simplenote, and Apple Notes (web/iOS/Mac only) facilitate syncing from your cell phone or tablet to your computer. These are useful for taking quick notes in the physical field on your handheld device. Working exclusively with text, a program like Scrivener allows you to compile and organize notes, write-ups, and other text documents together from your phone, tablet, or computer. More powerful programs like Evernote are also popular because they offer syncing between computers and mobile devices. Using more than two devices may add cost, as it does in Evernote, or may not be available, so compare program specifics with your own work needs.

A program designed to integrate notes, documents, and media can be a powerful data organization tool. Programs like OneNote, Evernote, and NixNote are designed to keep all of your information in one place. If you plan to collaborate with other researchers or participants at the data collection phase, there are also options to share and edit files together. Programs like TiddlyWiki are highly customizable and allow you to work with hypertext.

---

[1]Sanjek (1990) includes examples of handwritten and typed fieldnotes for reference on pages 124–135. His chapter "A Vocabulary for Fieldnotes" in the same volume is a useful reminder that the fieldnote is both a document itself and designed to help trigger the ethnographer's own recollections.

This can be a boon for both sequential and nonsequential writing (see Allen, 1994). Look for options that allow for the media you use most. Many tools allow for the integration of photos, video, audio, and text.

Qualitative research software may be useful, particularly if you are working with a large number of participants or media formats. These tend to offer clear ways to input documents and code for themes. NVivo allows for analysis of text, audio, and video, can be used for in-program transcription, and supports social media analysis. ATLAS.ti and MAXQDA are set up to work with multiple kinds of media, including audio and video. You can also incorporate survey data, which will be discussed in Chapter 7. Other options include DeDoose (mixed methods) and HyperRESEARCH (qualitative). These programs can be costly, and some of the features are less commonly used in ethnographic research than in other kinds of humanities or social science research. Depending on your particular project, specific features like the ability to hyperlink text, to transcribe and code, to share data between multiple ethnographers, or to import data directly from Twitter can make software worthwhile. If you plan to use research software, think ahead about how you plan to share your results: Some programs like ATLAS.ti come with integrated ways to share data through websites, which can save you time on the back end if this is a priority for your project.

Software that helps you document interactions on media platforms will have limits set by those private platforms. Programs that are capable of interacting with for-profit platforms like Facebook are subject to the limits on data recording and storage set by those platforms. For example, the program NVivo can capture web data, but Facebook allows only limited data capture on its own site: Users must be signed in, and private Facebook groups cannot be logged using the software. This reflects larger questions about working with data held on private sites or platforms.

BOX 4.4

Making careful records is crucial, as information on private sites may be deleted without warning. When investigating *American Idol* fan interactions on a Fox-owned website, Katherine Meizel found one day that the platform had changed and that she no longer had access to previous posts (Meizel, Cooley, & Syed, 2008). Contributing one's own work to privately held sites also carries some risk: Review user agreements as carefully as possible, given that they may change, for legal ownership ramifications of posting to private sites.

Practically, it means that even if you aim to use software to help organize your data, it is necessary to check what is and is not recorded on the sites you use and have backup strategies, such as screenshots and text capture, when you need to record information that your study deems ethically appropriate yet the software/private platform interaction disallows.

Cost is a factor. Some paid programs offer a free version, so consider the features of the version that fits your research budget to determine if it's a reasonable fit. Common limitations include amount of data (key if you are attaching video and audio to your notes) and offline accessibility. If you are interested in open-source options, try programs like NixNote and TiddlyWiki.

Take a look at privacy and data storage policies when making your choice. Consider the sensitivity of the information you are collecting and whether each platform can offer a reasonable standard of privacy for that information. Your own privacy as a researcher matters as well. For each app, look into what user information of yours is shared, whether you can opt out of certain kinds of sharing, and calibrate these options against your own online privacy preferences. This information can change quickly, so read the most up-to-date policies for the programs you prefer.

Look into where your data is stored. For example, Evernote stores data on servers in the United States, which means it is subject to U.S. policies, regardless of where the user is based. Try a program like TiddlyWiki if you want more control over where your data is stored. If you are collecting sensitive ethnographic data, you can choose to use a program that stores information only on your own device or server or one that uses SSL/https.

A notetaking program or qualitative research software might be right for you or you may prefer a program that simply allows you to access documents across your devices. A file sharing service, like Box Notes, DropBox, or Google Drive, can be set to automatically sync documents between different computers or mobile devices. If you are collaborating with a team, these are also helpful to allow for multiple contributors. Make sure to review current available options, including open source software, for possibilities as you draft a list of tools to consider.

EXERCISE 4.1

Take a few minutes to answer the following questions:

- Which devices do you use to collect or annotate information, and how many do you use?
    - *Tablet, phone, computer, watch, and so forth.*

- What platform(s) do you use?
  - *Windows, Mac, Linux, iOS, Android, and so forth.*
- What kind of media do you use most?
  - *Video, audio, images, PDFs, hyperlinked websites, and so forth.*
- Does your research project involve specific security or privacy concerns due to sensitive data?
  - *Consult with your institution's IRB/human subjects research office if you have questions about this.*
- What is your budget?
  - *Look into whether your university/institution has any subscriptions that would help defray cost and/or offer training on a program.*
- What is your level of skill and interest for customizing an app?
  - *Many open source programs have lots of options for user customization. This can be a boon if you will use them, and can streamline the data collection process. If you prefer something that is easy to use with no additional input from you, be realistic about this. In the next step, look for a program that is already streamlined in a way you could see yourself using immediately.*

Once you have completed the above questions, compare this basic inventory of your needs to the programs available. Take some time to play with various programs and see what feels comfortable to you. In addition to the programs listed in the discussion above, do a web search for the most up-to-date options. The goal is to pick something that streamlines your process. Set yourself a time limit to try different interfaces and settle on a program.

Pick a program with an initial learning curve that does not exceed your patience and one that offers the most features you actually plan to use. If you're excited about the program, all the better—use this enthusiasm to help motivate you if data organization ever feels less than thrilling.

Try it out first with sample ideas before inputting vital information. Give yourself several days of regular use to become comfortable with the interface. Then, you're ready to use the program to take notes and input media.

SUMMARY

Through this chapter, you begin the fieldwork stage of your hybrid ethnographic project. This chapter provides strategies for collecting and organizing data in the hybrid field. As in the physical field, a field log helps organize your time, and a regular notetaking strategy helps you create a useful record and make sense of your interactions. Documentation proceeds from jotting down details, expanding these into a fuller account—the fieldnote—organizing these alongside your own responses to the field, and encouraging collaborators to add their own ideas to the written notes. In the hybrid field, developing a social media profile, growing your network, and following a regular plan for online interaction help you integrate internet-based interactions into your inquiry. To face the potential problem of information overload, your hybrid field data collection should be structured, archived, reliable, and anchored. Finally, an exercise on research needs connects the individual researcher to data organization tools that are helpful for a specific project.

FURTHER READING

Allen, S. L. (Ed.). (1994). *Anthropology: Informing global citizens.* Westport, CT: Bergin & Garvey.

Barkin, G., & Stone, G. (2000). Anthropology: Blurring the lines and moving the camera: The beginning of web-based scholarship in anthropology. *Social Science Computer Review, 18*(2), 125–131.

Barz, G. (2008). Confronting the field(note): In and out of the field. In G. Barz & T. J. Cooley (Eds.), *Shadows in the field: New perspectives for fieldwork in ethnomusicology* (2nd ed., pp. 45–62). New York: Oxford University Press.

Buckland, T. (Ed.). (1999). *Dance in the field: Theory, method, and issues in dance ethnography.* New York: St. Martin's Press.

Clifford, J., & Marcus, G. E. (Eds.). (1986). *Writing culture: The poetics and politics of ethnography.* Berkeley: University of California Press.

Cox, J. (2015). I was taught to dox by a master [Blog post]. Retrieved from https://www.dailydot.com/layer8/dox-doxing-protection-how-to/

Dibbell, J. (2008, January). Mutilated furries, flying phalluses: Put the blame on griefers, the sociopaths of the virtual world. *Wired.* Retrieved from https://www.wired.com/2008/01/mf-goons/

Dicks, B., Mason, B., Coffey, A., & Atkinson, P. (2005). *Qualitative research and hypermedia: Ethnography for the digital age.* London: Sage.

Emerson, R. M., Fretz, R. I., & Shaw, L. L. (2011). *Writing ethnographic fieldnotes*. Chicago: University of Chicago Press.

Goodall, H. L. B. (2000). *Writing the new ethnography*. Lanham, MD: Alta Mira Press.

Green, K. (2014). Doing double Dutch methodology: Playing with the practice of participant observer. In D. Paris & M. T. Winn (Eds.), *Humanizing research* (pp. 147–160). Thousand Oaks, CA: Sage.

Jackson, J. E. (1990). "I am a fieldnote": Fieldnotes as a symbol of professional identity. In R. Sanjek (Ed.), *Fieldnotes: The makings of anthropology* (pp. 3–33). Ithaca, NY: Cornell University Press.

O'Reilly, K. (2005). *Ethnographic methods*. New York: Routledge.

Sanjek, R. (Ed.). (1990). *Fieldnotes: The makings of anthropology*. Ithaca, NY: Cornell University Press.

Schloss, J. (2009). *Foundation: B-boys, B-girls, and hip-hop culture in New York*. Oxford, UK: Oxford University Press.

5 PARTICIPATION, OBSERVATION, AND INTERPRETATION

Now that you have established your scene, started interacting, begun taking jottings on your experiences, and proceeded to write up notes about your experiences and responses to them, it is a good time to begin reflecting on what you are learning in the hybrid field. This reflection forms an initial interpretation. You will move back and forth between fieldwork, organizing information, and analysis. The initial research question will be inductively refined as you clarify ideas with fellow participants over time. This book's chapters outline a progression of activities, and you will likely move from initial interpretation to more detailed analysis and may even start writing to further process your ideas and then go back to more field experiences, extended interpretation, and additional analysis and writing. Your own experience and scene will determine this rhythm. This chapter invites you to ask and answer the following questions: How do I initially understand this field experience, and how do I interpret enough to ask more refined questions? As you interact and interpret, you will need to practically handle and productively conceptualize your ongoing ethnographic experience. Taking account of patterns of sociality in the hybrid field, the hybrid ethnographic approach includes documenting and interpreting texts that change over time, building capacity to understand and use scene-specific lexicon, and managing synchronous and asynchronous communication. You will reflect on what you learn from sensory details of your initial field experience. Finally, an exercise guides you through how to visually map relationships so as to make sense of emerging connections.

INITIAL INTERPRETATION ACROSS THE HYBRID SITE

Attitudes toward internet-based sociality have changed over time; they continue to shift. Because community has often been understood as physically fixed, some critics have questioned online community, arguing instead that "community is a local phenomenon, unmediated by technology, and bound by place" (Fernback, 1999, p. 212). Increasing access and utility of digital social tools has encouraged more expansive attitudes toward the kinds of connection that are possible online: 89% of American adults were online in 2018, and 77% of adults were using social media (Pew Research Center, 2019a). Internet use remains high across locations: In 2019, 94% of suburban, 91% of urban, and 85% of rural adult residents used the internet (Pew Research Center, 2019b). This ubiquity comes with a shift in how people use online social connectivity: As internet access and social media engagement have ballooned, being connected is not a special condition of the digitally literate but a common feature for increasing numbers of people.[1]

Initial work in online ethnography critiqued communications that happened via the internet as being flat. It is undeniable that humans are behind the content that we see on screens, and in the hybrid field, you encounter many of the same people across aspects of your scene. People create the programs we operate, and users transform the ways in which we employ them. Even if we'd rather not think of it, cell phones and computers were made with human hands, either directly or through machines people have made. Even bots are programmed by humans. Yet it's important not to dismiss critiques of flattened communication without considering them. While they may miss the point that humans are behind the images we see and sounds we hear online, these critics are expressing very real concerns: Online communication feels different from in-person communication, and these differences matter. Hybrid ethnography works with multiple mediums of transmission, and these have varied cues, tones and patterns that a researcher must interpret to understand the meaning participants convey. Of course, vocal inflections are missing in the written text of an email. You could say the same thing about the typewritten page in the books we have been reading for hundreds of years. Acknowledging this reality, researchers do the work of linking text and media encountered online with experiences in other parts of the hybrid field.

LANGUAGE AND PARTICIPANT OBSERVATION

What ethnographic texts say about "learning the language" (O'Reilly, 2005, p. 95) can just as easily apply to hybrid communication as to foreign languages. Colloquialisms, insider vocabulary, shorthand references, and situationally dependent taboos exist in communications across the fieldsite. In order to interpret multiple types of communications, it is crucial to learn platform-specific codes, apply them to your encounters, and remain open to subsequent reinterpretation as you place your interactions in context.

[1]Though this is U.S.-based data, the trend toward increased access and use is not unique to the United States.

In hybrid ethnography, you encounter the physical and digital presences associated with your same collaborators. Unlike online-only ethnography, in hybrid work you move along a continuum between face-to-face engagements with minimal mediation to online portions of your field that you engage from your computer, smartphone, or other device. This offers an advantage that you can leverage. Just as you learn to read the body language and vocal tone of people with whom you interact in physical space, you can learn the patterns and codes that people use online and connect the types of interaction with each other.

One of the rappers I've worked with sends very short emails. He does not sign them. He does not worry himself over capitalization or punctuation. He simply gets the message across. What might one read into text like this? Is this terseness an expression of disinterest? Anger? In person, he laughs easily, banters using complex ideas, and can talk for hours. Initially, this might seem like a strange contrast, but working with him across offline and online spaces helped me understand his online style and interpret it in the larger context of all our interactions. When he writes emails, he is quick and efficient, as if delivering a text message. It helps, too, that I've seen how he uses his phone. He does not agonize over specific words or include emojis or other special characters. He just gets the details to the person on the other end, sometimes while attending to another task. So when I interpret his emails, the context behind the words could be multitasking from a smartphone. His attitude is likely to be dedicated to delivering key details in a timely manner. Context helps to avoid the potential misreading of a message.

EXERCISE 5.1

Choose two platforms where you communicate online, and look at your last five messages on each one.

For example, look at the last five emails you have sent and your last five tweets.

Analyze them for the following:

Mechanics:

- Capitalization
- Spelling
- Punctuation
- Sentence length
- Abbreviations

- Colloquialisms
- Inclusion of links and/or special characters

Think about the following:

- Where were you when you sent each message?
- What device did you use for each message?
- How did you feel as you sent each message?
- What meaning did you hope to convey with each?
- Whom did you imagine reading each message?

When you consider the 10 messages together, what can you conclude about the following:

- How does platform influence the manner in which you write?
- What other aspects have the most impact on how you communicate (e.g., audience, device, location)?
- What meanings do you hope to convey based on the way you use mechanics?

Now, look through your recent exchanges on the platform(s) you are using for research. What patterns do you observe in mechanics? From yourself? From other users you know? From other users you only know online? Look for common abbreviations, insider terms, special characters, or grammar that mirrors physical feelings (e.g., text written in all capital letters showing extreme emotion).

When you begin to interpret your data, use your insider knowledge of common lexical patterns to identify what is typical—and atypical—in your venue. Because reading human communication is subjective, note which aspects of this lexicon are followed by most people most of the time and which are more open to interpretation. Spell out commonly used abbreviations and note when ambiguous terms or mechanics might carry multiple meanings or valences.

Just as a researcher works to understand patterns of language and behavior through written text, the researcher steadily observes how fellow participants convey meaning through bodily gesture and reflects on one's own bodily experience. The literal recording of verbal expressions is part of this process, as described in Chapter 6, as is the documentation of words and gesture, as described in Chapter 7. Before arriving at these stages, it is helpful to observe non-texted cues as well. For the hybrid sphere, connecting these ways of communicating to nonverbal gestures in written communication provides a fuller picture of meaning making.

MAKING SENSE OF HYPERTEXT AND MULTIMEDIA TEXTS

Hybrid fieldwork requires reading linear and nonlinear texts against each other. In online portions of your site, you will find some texts are made for networked reading through the use of hyperlinks and embedded multimedia. Hypertext allows for circular and other reading patterns, such as the "rabbit hole" phenomenon of losing one's self in time by following links to links to links. When starting to interpret information you read online, consult your fieldnotes (see Chapter 4) to help you recall how you encountered the text. Which links did you follow? With whom did you connect as a result? What media did you encounter along the way? Where did you end up when you stopped following the hyperlink trail? Read these notes from your own experience with hyperlinks. This provides an example of how these texts can be encountered. Communicate with other participants about what they take away from posts as well. Hypertext and multimedia links allow the person using a phone or computer to become an active reader and listener, making choices about which parts of the content to encounter and what to do with the material provided. For more on working with hypertext, research in online ethnography offers examples and strategies (Underberg & Zorn, 2013).

Special Considerations for Texts That Change Over Time

Many online texts are open to commenting or other kinds of interaction. This interactivity affects your interpretation in the following ways:

- Audiences, including yourself and your collaborators, have the ability to interact as creators of related content.
    - Read asynchronously posted remarks knowing that people have the ability to plan out what they would like to say and often edit it later.
    - Like a phone message sent after an initial encounter, respondents can carefully select word choice for a post. This does not necessarily make information any more or less reliable.
- Researchers are not the only participants who sometimes operate with imperfect information.
    - In person, you get other cues (blushing, winks, etc.) to contextualize information. Other commenters may not be doing the careful work you are doing to get a handle on codes, so may misinterpret written responses.

  - Read asynchronous comments knowing that writers might misunderstand each other, sometimes accidentally. What emerges from confusion?

- Content can change over time.
  - Refer back regularly to look for updates and new responses.
  - Make careful records because exchanges can be deleted.

When you interpret data, offer contextual information that illuminates the meaning of the phrases beyond the words on the page. For example, pay attention in your own analysis to uses of smiley faces in text and ask yourself where commenters are conveying humor or sarcasm. When you can include information about attitude, do so in order to clarify your reading.

As you take notes, include tone information. Whether on a videoconference call or at a café, note extra-verbal information in your interaction: Try writing [laughing], [winks], and so on. Flip forward to Chapter 7 for examples on how this can be done in interview settings, for in-person and internet-mediated interviews. Make note of ways that platform-specific tone alters literal meaning. In your notes, indicate tone information like [sarcastic], [kidding], or [with emphasis]. For an example of a researcher reading online text for tone, consult Kozinets (2006). In this article, the author describes how he reads *Star Trek* fan posts, pointing to insider styles of communication including acronyms, the use of uncited quotations from the show, how fans express criticism, and other aspects of writing style unique to the particular fan culture. The article has a commercial advertising focus, but the section on tone is still useful for ethnographic applications.

Connecting Bodily Gesture to Texted Gesture in the Hybrid Sphere

As you continue to work and interpret your experience in your field, paying attention to all of your senses helps you to participate immersively and reflect deeply. Much literature on fieldwork focuses on the auditory and visual, particularly around words people say and behaviors researchers observe. Hybrid ethnography adds attention to the words people type and images and sounds people share. In some scenes, other sensory information is also central to participation and analysis. The physical sensations involved in dancing with others, making music together, acting with a group, and other types of expression deserve to be recorded and reflected upon as much as words people say while engaged in these activities. In addition, your notes and self-reflections can include other sensory information as relevant to your scene. What does it feel like to transport yourself and your group's equipment across the city? What tastes do you experience when sharing a meal with fellow participants? What smells greet you when you enter your teacher's house? How does your body feel after spending hours watching your group's video footage on your computer?

Sensory information is part of the experience of the field. Further, it helps us to recall and even reexperience events later, when we encounter the same stimulus again. Start by paying attention to multiple senses and expand from there. When feeling the body in a new cultural space, the ethnographer learns to "interpret her or his embodied sensory experiences through other people's cultural categories and discourses, and as such to participate not only in their emplaced practices but in their wider ways of knowing" (Pink, 2009, p. 80). For hybrid fieldwork, even as you interact with digitally mediated aspects of your scene, you are still a body, as are your collaborators. The pinch of your back in a chair, a slurp of coffee at your computer, or the jolt of a bus as you read email on your phone are all kinds of sensory information worth paying attention to. You may be more deeply attending to your own cultural knowledge and discourses or learning ones that were less familiar to you as you process your bodily experience in your scene.

MAPPING THE RELATIONSHIPS THAT MAKE YOUR SCENE

To get a sense of the relationships that make up your scene during your initial experience in the field, it's helpful to create a map. The purpose of mapping at this stage is to identify key figures, start to explore how they relate to each other, and then develop questions for ongoing exploration. These three goals are tied to the three steps of the following mapping exercise.

EXERCISE 5.2

1. Draw up a map that clearly shows the key players in your scene. You may work exclusively with one platform (e.g., only presences on Facebook) or work across multiple spaces. If you are working with data organization software, use the program's features to code for individuals and organizations and refer to your growing list of these.

Regardless of the organizational strategy you chose, review your notes for players such as the following:

- Individuals, public figures
- Organizations
- Performance venues
- Schools and/or rehearsal spaces
- Social spaces, community venues, places of worship
- Businesses
- Ideas or concepts
- Web-only spaces

2. Identify how these people, groups, and locations relate to each other, as well as areas in which relative isolation exists. Strategies might include the following:
   - Colored or textured lines to show different kinds of connections
   - Layers or multiple maps that show various configurations of players
3. Use your map to identify the following:
   - What players did you learn about that you had not considered previously?
   - Which players emerge as central nodes in your map? Describe the multiple kinds of connections that exist around these nodes.
   - How do you fit into your map?
   - How might common or anomalous connections help identify the ways in which people, groups, and/or ideas are socially connected or isolated?

In Part 1 of the exercise, you identify key players and trace them across relevant platform(s). Part 2 begins your process of understanding relationships between them. For example, are most people in your scene affiliated with a particular organization? The questions you generate in Part 3 can feed back into questions you ask as you continue working in the field.

Visual and audio mapping helps you organize and understand information in more ways. Placing key players on a geographical map can reveal where different individuals and groups are located and trace movement. For example, W. F. Umi Hsu examined how a South Asian American punk band navigated its sense of national identity. She used data-mining to identify the location of fans on MySpace and then transformed the results into maps of fan activity. These showed how fans navigate a diasporic space that the band creates as it crosses

REFLECTION ON FIELD MAPPING: "THE ACCESS AXIS," BY KEVIN SLIWOSKI

Military bases are intentionally inaccessible and intimidating fieldsites for would-be ethnographers, especially non-military researchers. Every time I drive onto Marine Corps Base, Camp Pendleton, Marine guards hold their guns as they greet me at the gates; those guards then scan my military-issued identification card to verify whether I belong on base. I understand that my presence there is a privilege afforded to very few people, one that the military controls with weapons, gates, fences, walls, and computer systems. Even with my DoD identification card and military base access—my wife is an active-duty Marine officer—restrictions abound. In my research about the sounds of U.S. military bases in Southern California, my position as a researcher, writer, and military spouse provided me access to military bases, but not necessarily satisfying answers to my questions.

When I mapped out the three military bases I wanted to use as fieldsites, I found myself in a conceptual space I call the military "Access Axis," which represents the relationship between the extent of an ethnographer's acceptance within a fieldsite and their independent critical analysis. Although these variables trend upward together, cultural and legal variables inherent to military bases inevitably force outsider and insider ethnographers into an end point. My position as researcher is not at the center of the collective fieldsite. For example, my own name and position are small in this map, dominated by the many pieces of military base infrastructures in Southern California. Although my position occasionally intersected with parts or people of the three bases I investigated, my place was consistently to the side. This visual representation mirrors how I feel about my position within the U.S. military's bureaucracy and shows how bases dominate their surroundings. Furthermore, my official status is military *dependent*; spouses are supposed to be background figures. Military personnel often seemed unsure of how to answer my questions and interact with me as a researcher; they were used to spouses who did not ask difficult questions. In the scale of an individual military base, my questions about sound and militarization were tolerated but were not priority. Although I overcame methodological challenges of access, my critical engagement with military personnel and the base itself tapered off.

Since I started this project, as an ethnographer and a military spouse, I learned how to more successfully navigate my way through military bases and bureaucracy. Beginning as a military insider helped. That position offset some of the initial challenges of entering a base, like explaining your presence and justifying your plans. While a map like this one demonstrates scale and connections between different spaces and people, it also shows a series of research dead ends, where people and locations became insignificant either because they could not participate or because of institutional restrictions and issues of security. The process of creating a visual version of my fieldwork sites and research process helped me to

FIGURE 5.1 ■ Field Map Example, "The Access Axis"

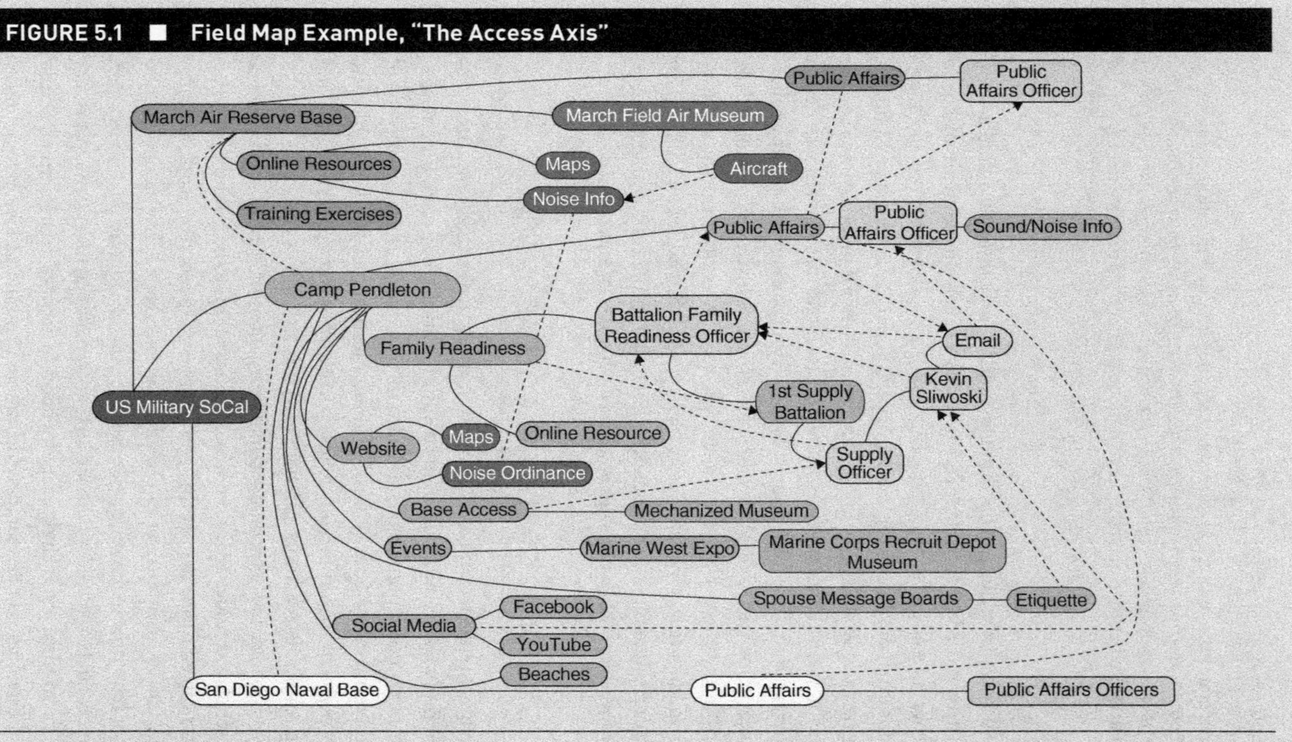

Created by Kevin Sliwoski

(Continued)

(Continued)

understand the military Access Axis. My sense is that all ethnographers encounter their own version of the Access Axis, and using methods like mind maps can equip ethnographers with a critical and self-reflexive perspective to better understand and approach their research and fieldsites.

national boundaries, in person through touring, and through online activity on Twitter and MySpace (Hsu, 2013). Hsu's work is one example of how a researcher uses advanced programming training in datamining to access relevant information. Interdisciplinary mapping applications are explored further in Dorrian and Rose (2003). GIS technologies allow for innovative storytelling with maps. Consult Adelusi-Adeluyi on how to curate maps for research design and presentation (Adelusi-Adeluyi, 2018). Try exploring web-based applications that allow you to organize and share your research visually. Knight Lab, out of Northwestern University, offers free tools for story mapping (https://storymap.knightlab.com) and, particularly useful for expressive culture, for integrating sound files (http://soundcite.knightlab.com). The learning curve on these tools is accessible; experiment and see what works for your project.

EXPECTATIONS FOR HYBRID COLLABORATION

The hybrid sphere encompasses communications across mediums. Being co-present online, asynchronous online communications, in-person experiences, and in-person communications that also involve online aspects are all part of hybrid ethnography. Some kinds of communication may feel less immediate or less personal to you or your fellow participants. Planning your time and setting realistic expectations can help with this part of the research.

Synchronous and asynchronous communications offer pitfalls and benefits. Some scholars consider asynchronous communications to be helpful in that participants can take time to offer thoughtful replies to questions you ask. Exchanging ideas in a written manner can be advantageous: Your fellow group members may not have time to answer questions while you are working on a project; performances can be too loud for sharing long or complicated ideas; participants may not want to share some kinds of information in front of a large group. Speaking and listening feel different in asynchronous communication. Asynchronicity removes the opportunity to ask for and offer clarifications in real time. Immediacy can be valuable. Would an online chat function offer continued one-on-one communication while you and your fellow group member act as sympathetic listeners and ask each other questions more directly? When switching from in-person, telephone, or videoconferencing communication to asynchronous text-based communication, pay attention to the real differences in how the medium fosters interactions. Maintain medium-specific protocols to keep up a good working rapport. Collaborating over email does not have the same feeling as sitting down for coffee in person, even with someone with whom you have a social relationship offline, but the communications you have across mediums inform each other. In the hybrid sphere, online and offline communications are not polar opposites. Rather, communicating across the hybrid space allows you to use the most relevant forms of communication for each purpose.

SUMMARY

Making sense of online connectivity as part of the research site is an important conceptual step that prepared you to take on immersive participation and reflection. This chapter's exercises, designed to move researchers from sensing to documenting to reflecting and back to sensing again, help you interpret your initial encounters. A visual map of spaces, players, and connections across your site provides images that convey a sense of where you are. These prompt your return to participation in a more focused way. This work prepares you for the next chapter, which will provide strategies for recording multiple kinds of media that are particularly relevant to fieldwork in expressive culture.

FURTHER READING

Adelusi-Adeluyi, A. (2018). *New maps of Old Lagos.* Retrieved from newmapsoldlagos.com

Hsu, W. F. (2013). Mapping the Kominas' sociomusical transnation: Punk, diaspora, and digital media. *Asian Journal of Communication, 23*(4), 386–402.

Kozinets, R. V. (2006). Click to connect: Netnography and tribal advertising. *Journal of Advertising Research, 46*(3), 279–288.

Pink, S. (2009). *Doing sensory ethnography.* Thousand Oaks, CA: Sage.

Stets, J. E., & Serpe, R. T. (Eds.). (2016). *New directions in identity, theory, and research.* New York: Oxford University Press.

Underberg, N., & Zorn, E. (2013). *Digital ethnography: Anthropology, narrative, and new media.* Austin: University of Texas Press.

6 PHOTOGRAPHY AND RECORDINGS IN THE HYBRID FIELD

Expressive culture research in the hybrid field entails making and using your own recordings as well as analyzing existing documentation created by participants. Audio recording, photography, and videography all play roles in ethnographic documentation and subsequent analysis. Creating an ethnographic record can be thought of as documentation; it may be cast as a form of artistic expression. This tension is depicted clearly in a conversation between anthropologists Margaret Mead and Gregory Bateson:

> Bateson: I think the photographic record should be an art form.
>
> Mead: Oh why? Why shouldn't you have some records that aren't art forms? Because if it's an art form, it has been altered.
>
> Bateson: It's undoubtedly been altered. I don't think it exists unaltered.
>
> Mead: I think it's very important . . . to give people access to the material, as comparable as possible to the access you had. (Mead & Bateson, 1977, p. 41)

In this excerpt, Mead and Bateson hit on key questions that inform the field worker's approach to documenting expression in audio and visual formats. First, what is the role of the ethnographic document? Mead suggests that the document allows those who were not in the field to experience central aspects through verisimilitude. Bateson offers that the document conveys artistic expression based on field experience.

This opens into a second question: Can the ethnographic document exist as an unaltered record from which multiple interpreters can glean meaning? This is an expansive question that cannot necessarily be answered. However, it invites researchers to consider the degree to which—and ways in which—our experience making recordings potentially becomes imprinted upon those recordings. How much is a photograph, sound recording, or video a document of what we saw or heard, and how much is it a record of us seeing and hearing the experience? Your own responses to these questions inform your strategy for making and interpreting recordings.

DOCUMENTATION IN THE HYBRID FIELD

Documentation cannot replace—and is not designed to replace—paying careful attention in the moment. Rather, photo, audio, video, and web documentation work together with careful notetaking and reflection. Recordings serve multiple functions. They act as documents for discussion with scene members. They log kinds of information (visual and auditory) in a way that augments written notes. Recordings can be shared with audiences, given permission, when you are ready to communicate findings from fieldwork.

A photograph, video, or audio recording does not depict what "is" but shows interpretive choices to present a partial sonic and/or visual impression of an event. Well-crafted documentation creates a feeling of immersion in a place and time, yet recordings fail to replicate the event. Brian O'Connor describes a dilemma he experienced attempting to photograph raindrops. Taking shelter during heavy rain, he observed, "There is no easy way to achieve the appearance of raindrops over the scene. The lower light levels in a severe storm mean that one has only a limited range of focus. One must settle for (delight in?) either the distant scene, distorted by out of focus drops and runs of water, or water in focus but the scene out of focus. In neither case is one likely to have a lovely spherical drop of water sitting quietly between the viewer and the background" (O'Connor & Wyatt, 2004, p. 36). Choices reflect the researcher's approach, and no choice precisely recreates the experience.[1]

Hybrid ethnographic projects draw from a variety of methods that are relevant to a particular scene and research question. This chapter synthesizes recording strategies with audio, video, and photography, including web-based applications of these methods. It details practical aspects of ethnographic documentation and suggests supplementary materials. The second half of the chapter describes how to document media made by other scene members and how to handle media responsibly. As is the case throughout this volume, the

[1]O'Connor and Wyatt (2004, p. 36) show a pair of images that illustrate this dilemma: one is the rain on the windshield distorting the view but allowing the viewer to see what is beyond it, and in the alternate, focused on the windshield, what is beyond it becomes blurry out of focus. Though the photographer feels the downpour, the raindrops of themselves evade straightforward documentary capture.

Further Reading section can direct you to resources that are applicable to your specific project.

Recording in the Hybrid Field: Changing Expectations and Needs

Guides for field recording often focus on creating products of publishable quality. This is why some people recommend not using a cell phone to make recordings. In hybrid work, this conventional wisdom does not hold. Given changes in technology and sharing practices, *purpose* determines the best tool for each task. A smartphone or tablet can be a practical instrument for hybrid ethnography.

First, as smartphone technology advances, the quality of recordings is increasing. If you have access to a sophisticated model, a smartphone or tablet can actually produce usable files. Adding attachments to a phone such as a compatible microphone makes a smartphone capable of even higher quality recordings. Be mindful of your storage capacity, as phones generally have less memory than dedicated recorders, and some, like iPhones, don't have expandable storage options. However, don't immediately discount the smartphone as a useful camera or recorder.

Second, in hybrid work, you will use multiple devices, depending on the area of your field in which you are working. Rather than asking, "Is this tool good?" it's useful to ask, "What is this tool good for?" Because fieldwork needs to nimbly adapt across portions of a site, researchers need a set of tools for different purposes. To record media from the web portions of your fieldsite, a laptop or desktop computer is advisable. Programs for recording and logging online media, which you read about in Chapter 5, work best from a computer. A smartphone or tablet is convenient for capturing screenshots, and this built-in functionality allows you to document as you interact. You can also pull media—directly or by copying links—to later explore in more detail on a computer. These devices are portable and connected to the internet. Use these features to fit the tool to the task.

Third, a smartphone fits in with ways other people in your scene are already documenting in a way that a professional recording device simply does not. Taking out a professional camera indicates to your interlocutor that, in your view, something special is happening. The "attention you pay to your recording machine" signals what matters to you and what does not (Jackson, 1987, p. 81). Of course, you will sometimes need to set up more professional equipment, and then it's helpful not to appear overly fixated on the machine so that people instead focus on the events. Yet sometimes using a recorder that blends in easily can minimize distraction. In hybrid fieldwork, participants are much less likely to get nervous around recorders than they once were. Because of the ubiquity of smartphones and other tools capable of recording, many people do not show the kind of wariness around technology that Jackson had to alert the fieldworker about in 1987. Yet this same ubiquity means that not all pieces of recording technology have the same effect. A performing group used to having fans take cell phone videos at shows can still feel extra pressure when professional video equipment is up and running. Smartphones might not provoke a strong reaction, which makes them great tools for documenting casual interactions.

Fourth, a smartphone is connected. This makes it a perfect device for sharing media immediately. Some media that you record will be for documentation, interaction, and drawing conclusions about your research question later. Other media will feed back into the hybrid field almost immediately. If you notice something intriguing, capture an image or file of what you've noticed. Share it with your fellow participants on the platform you are using. Recordings taken for this purpose don't have to be of publishable quality. They need to be legible for the audience you make them for and able to spark ongoing conversations. In this case, sharing your media in a timely manner matters more than getting a "perfect" recording.

A smartphone or connected tablet is one—and not the only—useful recording tool. Use a professional-quality camera, audio recorder, or video camera for recordings that you intend to share in publishable formats where file quality really matters. Making an audio or video documentary and printing photos require high resolution files. Chapter 9 details options for sharing media, but you can only take advantage of these if you have quality recordings to work with.

RECORDING STRATEGIES

Audio, video, and still image recording are all useful for expressive culture research. This section offers a process that you can follow to become more adept with photography, audio recording, and video recording. Each step offers specifics for still images, audio only, and video. Reread this section as you practice with the medium(s) that fits your scene. In the previous section, you had the opportunity to think through how your equipment maps to your engagement across your fieldsite. Now, you can start the work of making (and using) recordings.

1. Acquire a recording device and get to know how it works.

This basic first step is not quite as simple as it sounds. Try borrowing equipment from friends or colleagues if possible so you can get a sense of how different cameras, audio recorders, or video cameras work. Some universities and institutions lend out equipment. Learn about the settings on your specific device from the manual, user videos online, and experimentation. Practice with different settings to learn about your own documentation preferences.

Once you have one or more devices that you like, familiarize yourself with the kinds of shooting situations you are likely to encounter and prepare for these. For example, for photography, I often need to shoot in low light with no flash, in order to capture images at rehearsals and shows without disturbing performers. For audio and video, think about where you are likely to be recording. Location impacts the tools and settings you need here, too. One likely situational adaptation is for outdoor settings, in which you may need to use a microphone windscreen.

As you get to know your equipment, pay attention to practical aspects of your recorders. How long is the battery life? How many files can you fit on the memory card? What equipment do you need (extra lenses, microphones, back-up battery, a carrying case, etc.) for situations you may encounter? A note about storage: You can compress digital files later, but you cannot increase file quality. Be prepared with memory cards that allow for high-quality recording. Similarly, you can delete photos or edit down a video later, but once the event is over, your recording window is closed. Make sure you are equipped so you are not forced to record less than what you will need.

2. Look, watch, and listen to ethnographic recordings that are compelling to you.

Sources for these include professional photography, documentaries, and published research. What makes these recordings speak to you? What do you hope to emulate in your own work? For still photography, look at photo arrangement and captioning. Published photo books provide points of departure. Photo journalism, including slideshows on news websites, shows how web layout allows for narrative with images and captions. Online versions of the *New York Times* (www.nytimes.com) and *The Guardian* (www.theguardian.com) frequently publish examples. For expressive culture specifically, the *Japan Times* Culture section (https://www.japantimes.co.jp/culture) shares a wealth of still images and video with English-language captions and narration. Review images you find compelling, analyzing for angle of shot, headroom, and depth of field.

Podcasts and audio documentaries offer a variety of ways to showcase audio. Listen to podcasts or radio programs you already enjoy, focusing on the characteristics of included recordings. Try searching for audio on a site like Audio Documentary (http://audiodocumentary.org). Less processed ethnographic recordings are accessible through archives. Explore a global soundmap, like radio aporee (https://aporee.org/maps/), that plays snippets of field recordings. Listen for what sounds clear and compelling to you. Podcasts as a tool for research and sharing are further detailed in Chapter 9.

Documentary film can spark your imagination as you make decisions about how you record. Watch both public-facing documentaries and ethnographic films for inspiration on perspective. Try comparing films that use a camera placed on a tripod in a single location and those that use multiple cameras or angles to shift the audience's perspective between parts of a scene. For examples of ethnographic video, consult a database such as Ethnographic Video Online (https://search.alexanderstreet.com/anth). This source requires a subscription, but many libraries pay for access. It is searchable by ethnographer, cultural group, or theme. One of these themes, ethnographic methodologies, is of particular use for studying video techniques. Public sources for video documentaries include PBS and the BBC.

Archive.org is searchable by media, so you can use it to find images, audio recordings, and video. You can query the name of a photographer or filmmaker or browse collections. Peruse collections or set parameters to limit the vast quantities of results available. Chapter 9 delves further into making media as a way to share your results, but for now, let your reading of other recordings help you try out tactics for documentation.

BOX 6.1

As you look at sources for inspiration, pay attention to those that accept user submissions. Radio aporee is one of many online sources that also invites audience-contributed content. These venues will become relevant when you are at the sharing stage.

3. Composition matters.

Whatever your approach to the documentation/art tension described in the previous section, recordings must be legible in order for your ideas to get across to the audience. Bring your subject into focus, and pay attention to lighting. For stand-alone audio or that which accompanies video, pay attention to your levels and monitor with headphones when practical.

As you take pictures, best practice in photography can provide guidance, but feel free to bend or break rules as experience demands. For the rule of thirds, for example, imagine the image divided into three segments horizontally and three segments vertically. The key elements of the photo operate along one of these axes.

Here, the musician's face aligns with the left third of the image. The mirroring effect is shown along the right third. This adds visual interest and a sense of movement that a photo with a single subject in the center lacks. As you will see later in this chapter, positioning the image direct center in contradiction to this rule is effective for specialized purposes, such as Instagram.

Don't be afraid to get up close, and avoid potential graininess of zooming in from too far away. Take some detailed close shots, some contextual shots,

FIGURE 6.1 Field Photography and the Rule of Thirds

Photo by Jessica Margarita Gutierrez Masini, of musician Tremayne D. Majied Muhammad

and if relevant, some landscapes. A fieldwork project by Avalos and Blake demonstrates this variety. Their photo essay, available at ethnomusicfieldworkers.tumblr.com, includes pairs of crowd shots in which audience members and the performers on stage alternately take prominence. Try taking a photograph from the same location multiple times, focusing first on an item in the foreground and then on something in the background. Varying depth of field shots offers an opportunity to embrace the way in which the photographer influences a shot.

Consider how you appear in photographs as you proceed. In the image below, Nattapol Wisuttipat is doing fieldwork in a restaurant. The ethnographer's hand appears in the image, making his presence apparent. Simultaneously, a cook hands him a box of food and holds up two fingers, letting him know that this dish the kitchen prepared is a level two in spiciness. Nattapol reflected that his photos and videos both contain moments in which other members of the scene signal that they know he is capturing their images on film—they offer looks and gestures not shared off camera. Conscious that his presence as participant–ethnographer can alter the scene, Nattapol reflects, "While I was filming the cooks as they were interacting with one another with music being played in the background, a stir-fry cook suddenly handed me a freshly made *pad-see-ewe* (pan-fried fat rice noodle) in a to-go box" (Nattapol Wisuttipat, personal communication, March 11, 2019). Nattapol was surprised to have a cook interact with him directly while he was recording. She clearly saw him as a possible active participant in the scene, who could both take photos and

FIGURE 6.2 ■ A Stir-fry Cook Points up Two Fingers to Gesture The Spice Level as She Hands Nattapol a *Pad-see-ewe* in a *To-go* Box

Photo by Nattapol Wisuttipat

help with her tasks. He continues, "In addition to depicting myself, this very photo demonstrates the transient blurring of the participant-observer boundary, a liminal moment that caught me by surprise and unprepared" (Nattapol Wisuttipat, personal communication, March 11, 2019).

For audio, try allowing a range of sounds on the recording to capture perspective. For example, if you are walking through your site, let the sound of your footsteps stay in the recording, giving your listener clear information about how you are interacting with the space. Try juxtaposing this with an audio recorder set in place throughout the same event, and listen for what you pay attention to differently in these parallel recordings.

4. Careful documentation matters.

Keep a record of where you are shooting film. Make notes in your central document as you record. For audio and video, do a short verbal introduction to each shot naming the date, location, names of key participants, and event being recorded. Use this information to catalog images, audio, and video recordings, as described in Chapter 4. Use place and date details to tag your files as you import them into your computer, whether you are using a qualitative data management software program or simply placing your recordings into organized file folders. The information you take down about your recordings includes contextual detail about the vantage point of the recording. For example, note if you took a photo in an attempt to show a particular perspective or emotion. Back up all of your files. When deciding what to document, err on the side of more. With a careful file system (see Chapter 4), you can sort your media. You can't re-create an experience or easily unearth deleted online content, so document what might be relevant as it happens.

5. Review your recordings.

Look and listen through your recordings and examine them for what worked more and less well. Mark audio segments, videoclips, and shots that did not come out as anticipated. Review these for what happened. Was the shutter speed mismatched for motion? Is the lighting off? The focus? Were your levels set incorrectly? Diagnose for what you can try differently next time. Mark the pieces that accomplish something productive. Consider what worked well in those you keep, and emulate your successes in the next round.

As you go through your recordings, think about what you are trying to convey in your documentation. Some files may be particularly useful for your records, helping you recall sensory and factual information. These are also establishing and contextual recordings that can help another viewer or listener experience your fieldsite, in the manner described by Mead. Others might convey motion, emotion, and other forms of interaction. Recordings of this kind offer rich information for analysis, particularly around the way that participants feel and interact in your scene (see Pasqualino, 2007).

DIALOGIC PHOTOGRAPHY, VIDEOGRAPHY, AND AUDIO RECORDING

A powerful way to show multiple points of view in fieldwork is to collaborate with others. Working in a pair or team of ethnographers allows you to include images, sound, and video from everyone on the team. While one team member may have the most experience with photography, for example, including images captured by other researchers creates a more diverse set of perspectives in the documentation. Working with multiple people addresses the Mead/Bateson tension around how much the documenter imprints the recording in that the process invokes more than one perspective. Mead suggests setting up a camera on a tripod and letting it run. This can be yet another viewpoint in the mix.

Beyond the research team, it can be useful to work with other scene participants as documentarians. Strategies like photovoice incorporate dialogic photography into the research design. Also translatable for audio and video recording, this method incorporates documentation taken by participants. Photo elicitation strategies include multiple perspectives and include the actual documents made by participants in the research. Prompts might be as open as asking each participant to record what a space sounds like to them. Tailor your questions for the scene and research focus. This strategy can show variations not just in viewpoint but also in access to space and knowledge. After initial documentation by participants around the central theme, the recordings become springboards for further conversation and elaboration.

Dialogic recording creates a research environment in which multiple participants are all capturing sound, images, or video in ways they find meaningful. This is a useful strategy for incorporating multiple points of view. Additionally, it can offer insight into daily practices. For example, Linda Ikeda used the photovoice strategy to address how transgender individuals active in drag performances in Honolulu, Hawai'i, make family and community formations. She found that previous studies of female-identified transgender people, many of whom self-identify with the Hawaiian terminology *mahu* or *mahuwahine*, focused on public figures or sought novel aspects of transgender individuals' lives, so photovoice highlighted quotidian interactions that participants documented themselves (Ikeda, 2014, p. 136). Sixteen participants took photos of their own families and communities, which Ikeda used to collaboratively develop photographic or textual narratives about participants' lives.

Many people were motivated to take part in the study by the desire to share the normalcy of their lives (Ikeda, 2014, p. 139). Indeed, photovoice gave participants the means to share the regular aspects of their lives as performers, such as posed photos at drag pageants, as well as other aspects of their daily routines, like taking care of a grandmother.[2] Participants' photos of their families of origin and families of choice connect to descriptions of family ties that they discussed with the researcher. For example, close-up photos of smiling women and subsequent narration about these images show how many people had strong relationships with their grandmothers. This kind of emotional closeness is one Ikeda considers typical of people of all gender identities within many Polynesian societies (2014, p. 143). Using participants' voices and photos together, Ikeda identifies recurring themes that relate to the formation of *mahuwine* people's families, such as caring for family members and the creation of alternative family structures.

As photos become objects of mutual discussion, the dialogue continues. In interviews and focus groups, some people shared experiences of pain caused by distancing from families of origin, which emerged as a theme in Ikeda's study. She reflects, "Listening to recordings, one can hear (even more clearly than in the original narrations) the long pauses and attempts to regain composure, the faltering, the hurried tale, the subtle but perceptible changes in tone—so difficult to render on the page" (2014, p. 139). Here, Ikeda listens not just for the words that are being said, but for the meaning conveyed by tone and delivery.

In a hybrid fieldsite, a study like this one could productively expand. For example, it could be relevant to look at photos taken by participants for this research study and also those that the same photographers posted on a photo-sharing platform, such as Instagram, with a hashtag marking them as linked to the same research question. Both of these could then become touchstones for future discussions, and participants could be invited to elaborate on the individuals, actions, places, and emotional resonances of the photos in both sets. A researcher or research team might trace the same themes in all the photos, noting variation in content or affect across sets as relevant.

Some applications of a dialogic recording strategy rely on using participants' own recording devices. If participants already use smartphones, these

[2]For specific examples of photos, captions, and associated narrative, consult Ikeda (2014).

BOX 6.2

Photographs or recordings created by group members can form useful material that sparks further conversation. Denisha Jones' use of photo elicitation shows how the researcher can use participants' images as part of interviews. The photographs young people captured reveal the community through their eyes; subsequent conversations invite them to elaborate on how they see and understand their community (Jones, 2018). Autodriven photo elicitation can also reorient research questions to those considered most important to participants. Jeffrey Samuels uses this strategy to analyze how novices train in a Buddhist temple in Sri Lanka. This method expanded the researcher's understanding of which temple activities and qualities in a monk were most important to young participants (Samuels, 2007).

could record photo, audio, or video well enough to convey users' ideas. Providing devices ensures access, even for participants who do not own a recorder, and creates continuity across audio/video quality. If you do not already have a set of recording devices to lend out, select your equipment based on recording fidelity, price point, and ease of use. If your scene participants are already trained in recording or interested in learning, professional-level equipment can provide a breadth of choices for high quality sound and image. Otherwise, a user-friendly device without a steep learning curve is useful in dialogic recording settings.

DOCUMENTATION OF MEDIA BY OTHER PARTICIPANTS

As discussed in Chapter 1, researchers are no longer the only ones inscribing social discourse. In the hybrid research process, we encounter information created by a wide range of individuals and groups that circulates for multiple purposes. This adds a step to the process of documenting and interpreting media in hybrid research.

Following your documentation plan established in Chapter 4, access online aspects of your field in a manner that is structured, archived, reliable, and anchored. In your central document, keep track of online interactions and media you encounter. Qualitative data analysis programs allow for importation and coding of online content. Software such as NVivo and ATLAS.ti can import data from Facebook, Twitter, and web pages. An archivist–researcher collaboration, Documenting the Now offers tools for archiving social media data (http://www.docnow.io). The group produced an app for social media archiving and free tools that help researchers analyze Twitter data.

In addition to taking notes, save copies of significant audio and video that you encounter. To save media files, dedicated software programs are convenient. Debut Video Capture (http://www.nchsoftware.com/capture/index.html) offers video capture and editing. QuickTime (https://support.apple.com/quicktime) can record audio only or video and offers basic editing. OBS Studio (Windows, Mac, Linux) (https://obsproject.com/) can record video and audio and has a set of features for live streaming events. These programs can be used to compile a research archive, as well as to create media that can be shared back with scene members.

When you move toward analyzing media, described in Chapter 8, revisit your notes in order to account for how its provenance and purpose inflect its meaning.

EXERCISE 6.1

To contextualize photos, audio recordings, and video recordings in the hybrid site, identify and make notes on four key components:

1. Who is making the media?
    - This may have multiple levels of answers. If possible, identify the following:
        - The photographer/audio recorder/videographer
        - The group this person is associated with or organization they work for, if relevant
        - Secondary media makers—for example, a social media user who made a collage of previously taken photos or a group that posted a video that remixes existing sound with new photos
        - Organizations or groups associated with secondary makers, if relevant
2. How is it circulating?
    - Record where you encountered the media, and then identify other ways it circulates. These could include word-of-mouth, specific social media platforms, an official website, a video-sharing platform, text messaging, and so forth.
3. What reason(s) do the individuals or groups have for making and/or circulating the media?
    - These are likely multiple and may include education, event promotion, branding, social capital, financial gain, memory aids, or even humor.
4. Is it commercial, non-commercial, or somewhere in-between?
    - If someone is making money, who is it? How significant is it? And is it directly or indirectly related to the media circulation?

After recording, either at a live event or with media you encounter online, take time to listen or watch again. Pay attention to the ideas and themes in your central document or software. When you hear or see speech or visual cues that connect to these themes, make note of when they happen in the video. Write a description of gesture and transcribe relevant segments of video and audio. You may find yourself adding a new category to your central document if a new relevant theme is expressed consistently in this media. For detailed guidance on analyzing visual media online, including hypertext, consult Underberg and Zorn (2013). Chapters 1 and 2 detail the history of visual anthropology and apply it to web design. Analyzing visual data, including timecode logging, storing footage, transcribing video, analyzing footage, and coding footage, is detailed in Dicks, Mason, Coffey, and Atkinson (2005, pp. 148–156).

In hybrid research, some of your recordings can be shared immediately. Scene participants might regularly share photos, video, or audio of shows, gatherings, or social events. Your own strategy for social media may involve regular posts on a relevant theme or subtheme and dialogue about it. For example, Chun Chia Tai found that, though it was not her initial focus, the food shared in her scene was central to social activities, as in the dumpling party pictured in the following figure.

FIGURE 6.3 ■ Ethnographic Field Image

Photo by Chun Chia Tai

FIGURE 6.4 ■ Instagram Post

Photo by Chun Chia Tai

Her photograph gives a sense of the impressive variety and quantity of dumplings she made with her fellow participants. Throughout her interactions, she regularly posted images of food from shared meals to her Instagram page, which garnered interest from her fellow participants. This pairing demonstrates the unique constraints to which Tai adjusts her photography: Instagram uses a square frame and, contrary to traditional "best practice" photography, often features the subject in the direct center of the photograph. Tai's field image shows direction and expanse, and her Instagram image depicts the shared meal for the interest of others in her scene and followers.

ETHICS OF DOCUMENTATION IN THE HYBRID FIELD

Researchers have the ability—and in some cases the responsibility—to make our material available to people with whom we work. Particularly in research scenarios in which participants' voices are underrepresented or misrepresented in public discourse, documentation can provide needed accurate information. Counterbalancing the need to distribute material, sharing media and web data beyond the intended audience can have negative consequences, so appropriate safeguards should be put in place. Communicate clearly what information—visual, sonic, and otherwise—may be part of the research archive and put options in place for a range of preferences for privacy and sharing.

Records and Archiving

Where will your data be stored and with whom will it be shared? Privacy and appropriate sharing is crucial, as was outlined in Chapter 2. Ethics boards may dictate that research data can only be stored for a set amount of time and may guide the researcher in storing information on a password-protected computer or other safety measure. However, when it comes to audio/visual recordings of expressive culture practices, researchers are often asked to actively distribute information. That is, participants may choose to interact with researchers with the explicit purpose of making their stories and performances available to others. Always talk with participants before recording to learn about their expectations and preferences for the storing and/or sharing of recordings. This applies both to performances and to interviews, the latter of which will be further detailed in the next chapter.

When your collaborators agree, you can produce and distribute materials directly or contribute them to a relevant archive. Including participants' voices in their own words, dialects, or languages can create multivocal projects that sustain engagement. Researchers can plan ahead to share audio or video as part of public-facing research documentation (see Chapter 9). If there is a relevant local or online archive for storing and sharing information, contact an archivist to learn about how to contribute. Digital files, while convenient, can be vulnerable to loss of information through damage. Archival guidelines suggest storing at least two copies of digital media and storing them in different locations when practicable (IASA Technical Committee, 2017, p. 15). Whether or not this is practical for your data, this is a helpful reminder to back up your audio and video recordings, as you do with other information. If you share versions of your recordings through a public-facing format, like a blog post or website, you might use a compressed file format in order to make media accessible to users. However, preserve lossless copies in your own storage system in order to maintain high quality data that can be useful for community members and future researchers.

Media Distribution Ethics

Field recordings, including audio, video, and pictures, can help readers and viewers understand the scene in which you participate. They can bring wanted press and sales to performers or unwanted exposure for scene participants. When used without permission, this media can also become implicated in legally dubious sales of new media products. When you make recordings, you have an obligation to use them ethically. Ethnographic field recordings have been used for commercial purposes. Field recordings were infamously the means by which Eric Moquet and Michel Sanchez profited financially from sampling Afunakwa, a singer from the Solomon Islands, without her knowledge or permission (Zemp, 1996). Copyright law can feel ambiguous when it comes to expressive culture; it regulates sharing based only on majoritarian principles of ownership and sharing (Rees, 2003). Laws and related protections alone are not sufficient to protect the interests of individuals and groups who participate in field recordings, particularly when groups create collaboratively (Hill, 2007; Mills, 1996). Researchers must be cautious not to contribute to situations in which cultural knowledge may be appropriated. An acute concern for research with Indigenous cultural knowledge, this should also be in the forefront for all scenes in which researchers and co-participants navigate power imbalances with mainstream cultures. Major ethical pitfalls are circulating material without permission, denying financial profits to those who originally made the media, and facilitating misrepresentation of a group or practice. Anticipating these three areas of potential problems in the sharing of research media, proactively prevent similar problems in your own work. Recommended further reading on navigating these dynamics includes Seeger (1996) and Jaarsma (2002). Seek permission for any sharing, and work with your group to decide what limits you need to make on media distribution.

In hybrid research, the ethical responsibility to respectfully limit file sharing meets the research community's desire to have reasonable and sustained access to data. Recordings we make can have value to the people who participate in the recording. Files posted through streaming sites or on private websites or privately controlled social media platforms can be deleted, lost, or censored; their fate is uncertain as privately owned companies are bought out, merged, or change policies due to government regulation or revenue streams. Maintaining rich archives of notes and accurately tagged photos, videos, audio recordings, and web documentation can be a boon to your research community. Sharing digital research photos can present meaningful images to a community. Martin Slama shared photos with family members after some of his interlocutors had passed away, finding, "One might even argue that they have the moral right to receive these files, and it would be unethical not to share them" (Slama, 2016, p. 105). For well-documented case studies of how communities have used expressive culture archives for their own non-research purposes, consult also *Research, Records and Responsibility*, edited by Harris, Thieberger, and Barwick (2015), and "Repatriation as Reanimation Through Reciprocity" by Aaron Fox (2013), both in Further Reading.

Ethnographers are no longer the sole participants making and keeping recordings. This shift in the contemporary hybrid field contributes to a more equal balance of power, yet careful attention is still required. Communities have crafted creative solutions when an anthropologist, not those who performed, holds copyright to a field recording, yet an easier way to handle this problem is to avoid it from the beginning. Create a plan for how and where recordings will be stored. With fellow participants, determine who will require access. Use online and physical tools that allow you and group members to control who can use research materials. Communicate clearly about video, audio, images, and other media that will be posted publicly on the internet, as well as how social media data will be stored and accessed. A university ethics group or review board can provide additional advice on best practices for information sharing and storage of field recordings.

SUMMARY

Through this chapter, you have become familiar with the specifics of making and using documentation in the hybrid field. Changing expectations for photography and recording create unique needs for expressive culture research that incorporates all of the elements of the hybrid sphere. Interrelationships between participant–observers and scene participants make aspects of dialogic recording useful tools for the hybrid ethnographer. Due to the large amount of media created and distributed by participants, it is crucial to document and carefully interpret recordings by both the researcher and fellow scene members. Your own archive creates an opportunity to share relevant media in a focused and useful manner with scene members and relevant stakeholders. Documenting and sharing documentation requires careful attention to the privacy, expectations, and needs of fellow participants. In the next chapter, you continue the fieldwork process through interviews and surveys.

FURTHER READING

Fox, A. (2013). Repatriation as reanimation through reciprocity. In P. V. Bohlman (Ed.), *The Cambridge history of world music* (Vol. 1, pp. 522–554). Cambridge, UK: Cambridge University Press.

Harris, A., Thieberger, N., & Barwick, L. (Eds.). (2015). *Research, records, and responsibility*. Sydney, Australia: Sydney University Press.

IASA Technical Committee. (2017). *The safeguarding of the audiovisual heritage: Ethics, principles, and preservation strategy*. International Association of Sound and Audiovisual Archives. Retrieved from www.iasa-web.org/tc03/ethics-principles-preservation-strategy

Ikeda, L. L. (2014). Re-visioning family: Mahuwahine and male-to-female transgender in contemporary Hawai'i. In N. Besnier & K. Alexeyeff (Eds.), *Gender on the edge: Transgender, gay, and other Pacific Islanders* (pp. 135–161). Honolulu: University of Hawaii Press.

Jaarsma, S. R. (Ed.). (2002). *Handle with care: Ownership and control of ethnographic materials*. Pittsburgh, PA: University of Pittsburgh Press.

Jocson, K. (2014). Critical media ethnography: Youth media research. In D. Paris & M. T. Winn (Eds.), *Humanizing research* (pp. 105–123). Thousand Oaks, CA: Sage.

Jones, D. (2018) Friends, the club, and the housing authority: How youth define their community through auto-driven photo elicitation. In M. Boucher (Ed.), *Participant empowerment through photo-elicitation in ethnographic education research*. Heidelberg, Germany: Springer.

Mead, M., & Bateson, G. (1977). On the use of the camera in anthropology. *Studies in the Anthropology of Visual Communication*, *4*(2), 78–80.

O'Connor, B., & Wyatt, R (2004). *Photo provocations: Thinking in, with, and about photography*. Lanham, MD: Scarecrow Press.

Pasqualino, C. (2007). Filming emotion: The place of video in anthropology. *Visual Anthropology Review*, *23*(1), 84–91.

Rose, G. (2016). *Visual methodologies* (4th ed.). London: Sage.

Samuels, J. (2007). When words are not enough: Eliciting children's experiences of Buddhist monastic life through photographs. In G. Stanczak (Ed.), *Visual research methods: Image, society, and representation*. Thousand Oaks, CA: Sage.

Seeger, A. (1996). Ethnomusicologists, archives, professional organizations, and the shifting ethics of intellectual property. *Yearbook for Traditional Music*, *28*, 87–105.

Slama, M. (2016). File sharing and (im)mortality: From genealogical records to Facebook. In R. Sanjek & S. Tratner (Eds.), *eFieldnotes: The makings of anthropology in the digital world* (pp. 94–109). Philadelphia, PA: University of Pennsylvania Press.

Zimmer, M. (2010). "But the data is already public": On the ethics of research in Facebook. *Ethics and Information Technology*, *12*, 313–325.

7 INTERVIEWS AND SURVEYS

I stepped into the recording booth at the radio station, sat down, and started the familiar process of setting up the microphones. At the agreed-upon time, I placed a call to a rapper whom I had met for the first time several months earlier at an awards show. I patched him in. A sheet of prepared questions before me, I felt free to pause, listen, and improvise as we talked together. I monitored audio from both of us coming into the mixer, and for this interview, I was also working with a third audio source: the rapper's own music. During the conversation, I played a recording of one of his songs, and we stopped periodically to talk about it. I had prepared by listening for aspects that generated questions in my mind, including a moment when I heard an evocative sample that I thought I could identify and wanted to know more about. I also was poised to stop the playback when an idea struck him that he wanted to talk about. Sometimes we would listen to entire verses or choruses; other times we would stop multiple times in a single section. While we were ostensibly discussing one particular song, ideas bloomed outward: A question about a single sample led to a longer discussion about how lyrics inspire sampled sound and vice versa.

This conversation contributed to a research study, and it also provided the basis for an hour-long radio show and podcast in which I presented our conversation and the rapper's music to a wide audience. It demonstrates several key ideas in hybrid ethnographic research. First, the interview medium cannot be assumed. I recorded this interview at a radio station, but my collaborator was traveling, so he called in via telephone. Our previous formal and informal conversations had been in-person and through online messaging. This medium was chosen with logistics in mind for his travel plans, as well as to accommodate multitrack recording so that I could produce a listenable audio version afterwards, a format to which we had agreed together. Second, this is an example of an interview that uses an object, in this case a recording, to enhance formal conversation. It resulted in covering specific details and moving together toward more global concepts. Finally, this experience demonstrated the fluidity that makes for a productive semi-structured interview. I arrived prepared with specific questions and a recording, yet at times we needed to delve into details, and at others, new topics emerged. These moments were crucial to the interview. Preparation had made space for them, but it did not circumscribe their emergence.

The hybrid field offers many advantages for interviews and surveys. In-person communications are valid options that function well for some situations. Possibilities extend beyond in-person interviews and conversations that comprise typical topics in physical fieldwork manuals. Part two of Bruce Jackson's *Fieldwork* details rapport and interviewing in the offline field (Jackson, 1987). As is the case in physical fieldwork, moving to an interview in the hybrid field does involve a shift from casual interaction to semiformal communication. You arrive with questions, and your interviewee, too, has reasons for choosing to participate. An interview comprises a focused conversation that is structured to invite the interviewee to express opinions and ideas that relate to the overarching research question. Surveys are even more directed; questions can be open-ended but are predetermined in advance. An interview or survey is a shift in fieldwork interaction but need not feel like a radical departure from informal work. Starting with interviews and then proceeding to surveys, this chapter outlines strategies for successfully integrating these tools into an ethnographic study. You can draw from your own past experience and a wealth of literature on interviews and surveys in physical ethnography or in an online-only environment. This chapter complements existing resources and specifically focuses on adapting these tools for the hybrid field.

CHOOSING A MEDIUM

Choosing the medium for interviews involves weighing the pros and cons for each option. As discussed in Chapter 3, online communications offer possibilities for synchronous and asynchronous communications. A similar logic for your online interactions can extend to formal interviews: Pay attention to how discourse operates in your particular scene and select what works best for all parties.

Start with your typical forms of communication. For example, for people with whom you have a rapport in casual offline conversations, consider in-person interviews. Move to another format if you have questions that are not being adequately addressed. If typing in chat becomes too cumbersome, ask about a voice chat option. In-person conversations grow more naturally out of hanging out together in a studio. Chatting through a messaging app may well make sense if the app is embedded in the social media site in which you usually communicate. Choosing just one option is not necessary: It is entirely reasonable to communicate with the same person via multiple mediums over the course of a research project.

Interview location and activity are also part of this planning phase. In terms of activity, if you choose to sit down and stop doing other things in order to talk, you have the logistical benefit of being able to look at your notes, jot things down, and make a clear recording. You might alternatively have a rich conversation doing something you typically do with your interview participants, like warming up, walking together, paging through websites, or sharing a meal. I've had great conversations about research while watching powwow dances, having dinner, and, as in the introduction to this chapter, listening to music together. Pick a location that suits your activity and, when practicable, one that also helps create a conducive environment for the kind of notetaking or recording that you agree upon with interviewees.

Voice interviews (over the phone or through an app or online service) or videoconferencing provide additional options. These offer the ability to converse over a distance while still offering vocal inflection and other cues that add nuance to texted meaning. Videoconferencing also provides an additional layer, conveying facial expressions and some gestures as well. Texting, messaging apps, and social media platforms offer opportunities for real-time exchanges. When attention is paid to the conventions of the particular communication format, as described in Chapter 5, these can offer useful ways to interact. Asynchronous options are also possible and include email exchanges, texts, or comment threads. These provide you and your interviewees with time to carefully consider what you write and may result in well-crafted responses. This also works well for logistical reasons, particularly for busy participants who may not be easily able to carve out specific times in their schedules and wish to work on their posts or messages as time allows.

Technical concerns are relevant: Phones, especially cell phones, can cut out; video and voice chat services may be interrupted due to the quality of internet access (on your end or the other parties' end); and pauses in live chat may not actually result from your interviewee pausing but from a data or service interruption. I have conducted interviews via Skype and Google Voice, and communication on both platforms has been interrupted at key moments. Investigate what distance communication platform your university or organization uses for meetings. You may have access to a subscription service and/or advice about best practice given your location's specific technology needs.

This can be helpful, even if the platform is typically used for meetings and not interviews. Some platforms developed for remote business applications have integrated audio and video recording options that can be a boon for researchers as well. Just as you would practice with a physical recording device before doing an in-person interview, practice calls, videoconferencing, and chats in the location from which you plan to work. Choose a location with a reliable internet connection. You may well try multiple options before selecting one that allows for stable communication. Be prepared for interruptions, as there may be concerns on the other parties' ends that you cannot control.

Recording in the hybrid field comes with many advantages. Video, photography, and to a certain extent audio recording, are becoming increasingly common in daily interactions. This can help allay nervousness around technology that previous scholars have encountered in ethnographic research (Jackson, 1987, p. 87). Participants who are accustomed to recording are less likely to become nervous around recording devices, though even those who broadcast their own communications through social media may become more careful once you start recording. Many online tools come with built-in mechanisms for recording, or these can be added: Still screenshots and live capture make it possible to record sound and images online and can be used to create an archive when your fellow participants agree to this process.

In an atmosphere where smartphones are ubiquitous, it still makes sense to pay attention to the effect of professional-quality cameras and recorders. Putting a high-quality audio recorder on the table for an interview shows the seriousness of the interaction. Turning it on signals that what is happening is significant to you, and turning it off indicates that, in your view, the "important" part is over. Pay attention to the signals you give and opt for less disruptive practices when possible. Jackson's advice on when to record is still helpful: "Leave the recorder or camera at home or in the car or in the box or bag if you think the machine will alter the situation in ways you don't want or if you think it will cause harm. But don't suppress the machine because you assume people will automatically take fright when they see it. The fright is most often transmitted by you, not the inanimate box" (Jackson, 1987, pp. 87–88).

ETHICS FOR HYBRID RESEARCH SURVEYS AND INTERVIEWS

When conducting surveys and interviews, take time to look back at best practices that you learned at the design stage. This includes feedback from your IRB or research ethics panel and any additional guidance you received from your specialized field—for example, from a school if you are working with students. Refer to your professional organization's specific guidelines and those you developed for your own ethical standards in Chapter 2.

As online research has become more common, IRBs and ethics boards are more likely to understand issues relevant to this kind of interaction for interviews and surveys. Working across the digital divide may require some translation to make your research legible to your institution's oversight board; be prepared to separate out the "online" and "offline" portions into two categories if necessary to help your institution's reviewers understand your project in familiar terms. To this end, you may also need to adapt to an ethics board's distinction between written (e.g., email, chat) interactions and vocal interactions. Be ready to submit two lists of questions, one for written online interviews and the other for the in-person or phone/video chat (voice) interactions, if required by your board. It can also be helpful to have two separate consent forms—one that is designed to be physically signed in person and another designed for online use—so you can receive and document informed consent for interviews that begin offline and online. Surveys can be delineated very specifically, which makes them easily explicable for an ethics board. The clarity of steps also makes it possible for researchers to incorporate suggestions from these boards so that you proceed in a manner consistent with professional expectations. Even if a particular interview strategy or question might be approved by your research board, if it does not feel appropriate in the moment or with a particular participant, avoid it.

PREPARING INTERVIEWS AND SURVEYS

Interviews are a central part of ethnographic research. Hybrid fieldwork allows for an expansion of mediums of communication and provides opportunities for sharing media and results after completing interviews. Qualitative surveys are not always included in ethnographic project design, yet they have become more common with the advent of online ethnographies. You may be working with a relatively small set of participants who are active in your physical scene. It is not uncommon to primarily interview fellow group members or to interview a handful of key informants whose expertise is germane. Because at least some of the people with whom you interact face-to-face are also active in online portions of your fieldsite, the circles of connection do not end with your physical scene. Surveys, adopted from online qualitative inquiry methods, allow you to connect with and learn from participants who are active across the hybrid site. A focused survey enables participants to share information and anecdotes in a medium that is convenient for them—often through an online survey tool that can be accessed from a phone, tablet, or computer. It also helps you listen to a larger number of participants, including those people who might not have the time or inclination to also complete a traditional long-form interview with you. All projects will benefit from incorporating interviews into the design. Those projects that seek a combination of wide participation and relative depth of response, particularly from scene members who are active online, could benefit from integrating a survey as well.

Language

The language(s) in which you are speaking with your fellow participants carry history, political importance, and socially situated meanings. For her fieldwork in Bolivia, Kate Maclean navigated Aymara, Spanish, and English languages (2007). The researcher is responsible for communicating effectively with fellow participants, taking language into account for analysis, and making appropriate representational choices when presenting results, particularly when those results are in a different language than the one spoken in the scene. Maclean's article is a useful resource for thinking through how translation can pose a "problem" and also serve as the source of a solution: When done well, the process of translation can also become a process of critically engaging with meaning and value communicated through language use. If you work in a multilingual context, interview and survey design requires carefully choosing language(s) for communication, analysis, and sharing your results.

With your specific scene in mind, consider which of the following questions you will need to explore for your field. In what language(s) do you as researcher communicate with group members? When moving to formal interview settings, will you change languages from those of your regular interactions? Are there some scene members with whom you will work with a translator or interpreter, either formally or with another group member or community researcher? When might another member of the research team be the best person to conduct an interview, based on linguistic competence, social position, or both? What aspects of your interaction shift if, for example, you are speaking with scene participants in a common third language that is no one's primary language? When moving to analysis, a new layer of questions emerge: In your scene, what aspects of discourse are socially relevant in your language-specific context? Does code switching or situational language change emerge as a relevant category as part of interview analysis? Finally, for presenting results after your interviews and surveys, what are the benefits of presenting discourse as spoken or offering translated excerpts? How will you identify the language of communication in your write-up? If you present results in a language other than that of the research, will it also be useful for scene members if you produce a partner text in the language of the research?

Many researchers who conduct participant observation in a scene in which a minority language or multiple languages are used conduct interviews in the language or languages that they generally speak with scene participants. Littig and Pöchhacker (2014) outline the decision-making process for language choice in some detail and also describe the effects of using English (or we could extrapolate, another majority language) as a lingua franca. This article also offers suggestions on how to report multilingual data. Other resources on traditional ethnographic interviewing can be helpful for the hybrid ethnographer. Choi, Kushner, Mill, and Lai (2012) describe their process as a research team in which one of the primary researchers and participants speak one language (in this case, Korean) and other research team members analyze and present research in another language (here, English). This source navigates the logistics of working with translators and interpreters, as well as how the research accounted for ideas expressed verbally and nonverbally in a linguistic and cultural context that was not the same as the one in which the research was analyzed and presented. The authors provide examples from translation and retranslation, suggest when to keep original-language text, and provide a starting point for determining what kind of explanatory material is needed to help readers make sense of the dialogue.

Designing Questions

Interviews are about continuing relationships with people who share interests in some aspect of your scene. Questions are designed to reflect your specific approach and should be responsive to the scene in which you are working. Much best practice from face-to-face interviewing techniques applies to hybrid work. Interview questions provide scaffolding for a conversation that addresses topics of concern to the research project. At the same time, they need to be open enough to invite the interviewees to provide the narration they find most relevant, even if this covers topics that you as researcher have not yet considered. Specific question examples, tips, and common pitfalls for the novice interviewer can be found in Lichtman (2013). The sample questions in this source, primarily designed for face-to-face interviews, can be adapted for hybrid interview contexts. Chapter 10 provides examples for focus groups as well as online interview strategies (see also Spradley, 1979).

Hybrid research in expressive culture extends general best practice in a few key ways. Be sensitive to the way your chosen medium impacts responses. Online surveys generally require some multiple choice or yes/no questions to encourage completion, so be judicious about where to ask for descriptive responses. A one-on-one interview, be it in-person or using distance communication technology, allows for more descriptive questions, as well as follow-up and clarifying questions. Text-based chat interviews require medium-specific translation skills discussed in Chapter 5. Expressive culture researchers often interview artists who are public figures. This requires even more than the usual attention to asking informed questions. Avoid asking basic questions to which the answers are easily available, focusing your (possibly limited) time instead on the unique angle suggested by the research question. Researching with artists who work collaboratively also opens up the possibility of conducting interviews with multiple participants. These can be through a group conversation or by asking the same questions of multiple members of the same group. Ethics protocols can help with design, as some boards review questions ahead of time and expect consistency across interviewees.

Of course, your interview is about what people say. It's also much more: an opportunity to create and negotiate meanings through verbal and nonverbal interactions. Your conversation also entails other things that people do. In your notes and reflections, pay attention to kinds of communication that are not contained in the lexical meaning of words. First, this means noting how words are said—body language, tone, and volume all inform the meaning of the words that are expressed. The classic example of this is anthropologist Clifford Geertz's distinction between a twitch and a wink. Following Gilbert Ryle, he encourages the reader to imagine two children, both "rapidly contracting the eyelids of their right eyes. In one, this is an involuntary twitch; in the other a conspiratorial signal to a friend" (1973, p. 6). While the difference cannot be identified in a photograph, researchers' contextual knowledge allows us to determine when the behavior is an action undertaken as part of a social code and thereby transmitting an embedded meaning. Geertz goes on to describe many other layers—parody, rehearsal—that could be placed upon the twitch to give it extra meaning. In each case, additional signals are given off alongside a twitch to make it a more robust communicative gesture. In participant observation, all of these kinds of thick descriptive elements, as well as the larger social context in which they resonate, are part of gathering information. As was discussed in Chapter 5, spelling, capitalization, and speed of response all convey tone in digitally mediated contexts. What people do not say or do is also important. People might shy away from topics that are considered inappropriate for discussion, whether in general or in an interview setting with a particular researcher. These gaps convey information about social norms. Recall also that people are unlikely to verbalize information that they take for granted that you already know. Particularly when you are a participant, you might ask people to detail quotidian activities as relevant to your research question or let them know that, while a particular idea is understood in your scene, you would like to discuss it in detail. As much richness as there is that comes through the verbal aspect of an interview, regardless of medium, location, and activity, an interview is an experience that you have with your fellow participants. New meanings may be created; your interlocutors may come to new understandings as you dialogue; and you might find that you also come to see yourself and/or your research question differently through the course of the interactions.

Integrating Surveys

Surveys allow you to seek focused information about a subset of questions. These can be answered by your fellow group members, and you could also distribute these more widely through the sites or platforms on which you are active. Some survey participants may wish to complete an interview after the survey. The accessibility of a web-based survey can allow you to hear from scene members who would otherwise not be able to contribute. In hybrid research, consider the many possible applications for a survey, potentially in consort with or even during an in-person event in your scene. For example, you could provide a link for a web-based survey at a live event or integrate real-time feedback during a performance.

Entire books can—and have—been written on survey design for qualitative research. This section highlights key questions and points out specific concerns for expressive culture research. If you have less experience designing, implementing, and reporting on surveys, Fink (2017) provides a practical introduction. It details design choices such as question types and order, rating scales, and survey length. Concrete suggestions for online survey administration and strategies for reporting qualitative survey data are specifically relevant for hybrid research.

For expressive culture research, the following points are helpful. Offer a mix of question types to learn about the people who answer your survey, and make space for the stories and details they wish to share. Multiple-choice and yes/no questions are quick for survey takers to answer and deliver basic information. When designing general questions that prompt limited answers from a known set, consider the following: What kinds of information can you meaningfully elicit here? For expressive culture, these questions can deliver bare-bones biographical information, such as the number of months or years respondents have participated in a scene or the type of media in which they work.

Fitting qualitative responses into a form can feel limiting at first, but you have many tools available to assist with the process. Take advantage of software features that allow multiple responses on multiple-choice questions. For example, a menu of which instruments in a rock band participants have played allows respondents to check more than one box. Enable the option for an "other" category and allow for respondents to specify if they select this choice. This will alert you to answers you may not have considered and also relieves your respondents of the frustration of feeling like their answers cannot fit in your schema. Make sure to also include short answer questions, which allow your respondents more freedom. Finally, provide a text box for general comments and questions that are not restrained by a specific prompt.

Interpreting survey results requires knowing about the likely interpretive practices of your informants. A study of social media use by anthropologists across several continents demonstrated that ostensibly the "same" question is read and thus answered differently based on social context. Miller et al. (2016) detail the types of survey questions they asked, as well as how each scholar interpreted results contextually in Brazil, Chile, India, Trinidad, Turkey, England, and rural and industrial areas in China. This helpful resource on design and context-sensitive interpretation includes specific examples.

LOGISTICAL CONCERNS

Preparing for the interview necessitates getting a handle on recording technology that fits with your chosen interview medium. Pay attention to timing and other organizational logistics, which can necessitate careful planning in hybrid sites. Expressive culture research offers opportunities for interacting around an object or piece of media, which you will need to ready for discussion. Consent forms and any other relevant permission documents need to be prepared in advance of interviews and can be integrated into surveys directly.

General Communication

Because you are a known researcher talking with fellow participants in your scene, interviewees will already have some insight into your project. Still, they might want to know more about you or about the process.

Be ready to share the following:

- What the research is about
- More about your background and goals
- Why you are interested in talking with the specific interviewee
- Ideas you have so far
- What you are planning to do with the research

Recording

Before the interview, develop a plan for recording. A small handheld audio recorder is a typical choice for offline interviews, though you might opt to work with video. Using a telephone recording app or routing calls through your computer offers a way to record phone interviews. Online interviews can be recorded through some platforms or through a program that records audio or video on your computer. Practice with your recording device(s). When trying out a new recording strategy, especially for recording telephone audio or capturing media through my computer, I typically hold several short practice conversations. Contact a fellow researcher or generous friend who agrees to be recorded. Start the recording, set your audio levels, and chat back and forth to get a sense of how both ends of the conversation come across. Practice stopping the recording and then review your audio or video file. Listen for clarity and balance. Check in with your interviewees as well, to learn about any potential communication disruptions they experienced. Keep practicing until you have had time to troubleshoot these, and you end up with a smooth interviewee experience and a clear recording afterwards.

BOX 7.1

Recording a real-time interview that happens over distance requires extra steps. For privacy reasons, many programs do not make call recording functionality easily available, though they technically could. If you initiate the interview from your computer, there are direct and indirect ways to record. Google Voice currently allows the user to record incoming but not outgoing calls. You can work around limitations like these with a third-party program. A basic digital audio workstation (like the ubiquitous GarageBand on Mac) will record whatever comes through your sound-card—so if you are on Skype, FaceTime, or making a call through your

(Continued)

(Continued)

computer (like with Google Voice), you can record it as a sound file. Check your DAW for presets for voice recordings to streamline this option.

On a phone, investigate call-recording apps (generally paid), since phone manufacturers (like Apple) don't let you use the phone as-is to record calls easily. You can also invest in external technology if you're working with a wired landline.

Some paid platforms for video and audio offer in-call recording technology. Zoom, for example, offers the initiator of the call to record video from a call and also stores an audio recording separately, which is a boon for transcription. Meeting platforms like this one allow for multiple participants, and people can call in on the phone or join the call via audio/video or just audio online. For group conversations, participants can choose different options to connect. Of course, ask for and receive permission from all participants before making a recording.

If you are newer to interviewing, do a mock interview. Practice asking follow-up and clarifying questions. Try gentle and respectful redirects when your friend or colleague goes into a drastically different topic. Spend time getting used to *not* supplying words for your interviewees. Get used to pauses in conversation, and avoid rushing to fill them. Rather, let your interviewee insert more thoughts if they have them, as this can reveal important areas that you had not thought to ask about. Remember that an interview is a specialized kind of discourse that is different from daily conversation, and as such, it can take time to comfortably adapt to the process.

Timing

Getting on the calendar could be as straightforward as staying after an event to speak formally with a participant. It might take several attempts to figure out a mutually beneficial time. Suggest specific days and times. Go with what you know already about a person's schedule, and be flexible. Block extra time afterwards in your own schedule to allow for a possible long, productive talk. As you plan, be sensitive to work, family, and other concerns. This can be as simple as knowing if your interviewee has another appointment later in the afternoon or whether the person is blocking out a significant amount of time for your conversation. Finally, decide together how the interview will begin. Set a location or determine who will place the call or who will initiate the conversation online.

Hybrid work allows for distance communication, which comes with specific concerns. When speaking from a distance, pay attention to time zones. Think ahead about the interviewee's time zone, and request reasonable times for that schedule. Clarify with your interviewee the time zone in which you are setting your appointment—general best practice is the time zone of the interviewee. This puts the burden of time zone calculation on you, so double-check your math. If you are not meeting up in person, verify your communication details. Ask which phone number you should call, or agree on the online platform that you will use together.

Special Notes for Expressive Culture

For research in expressive culture, an object—like a recording, a website, or a photograph—or an activity—like a show—can provide a central point around which to scaffold a formal interview. I have had some of my most fascinating conversations with musicians as we listened to music together. We could talk specifics—like what lyrics in a particular verse meant to the rapper—and ground our conversation in them. Listening together also taught me about how an interviewee hears their own music, a topic to which I do not have access if we simply talk about music making after the fact. Asking a more general question, like asking an artist to describe their artistic process, may net general answers; working with an object adds useful nuance. Butler (2014) offers a model of how the researcher can use recordings—in this case, Butler's field recordings of artists' own performances—as a basis for discussion during interviews.

CONDUCTING SURVEYS

Surveys are useful tools for gaining qualitative information from a wide range of respondents. They can also serve as a springboard for future conversations. This section highlights aspects of survey collection that are useful in a hybrid context; it builds on existing best practices for surveys in fully offline and fully online research that are referenced in Further Reading. Surveys can be conducted in person. Surveys at performances are a classic example: Researchers ask tailored questions about audience members' reactions. Online tools bring this kind of survey in additional directions. An online survey can be conducted in person at an event by giving a prompt that can be answered on mobile phones. This generates immediate information and takes advantage of a hybrid space. Alternatively, a survey can

FIGURE 7.1 ■ Survey Question With Options for Multiple Responses and Text Entry

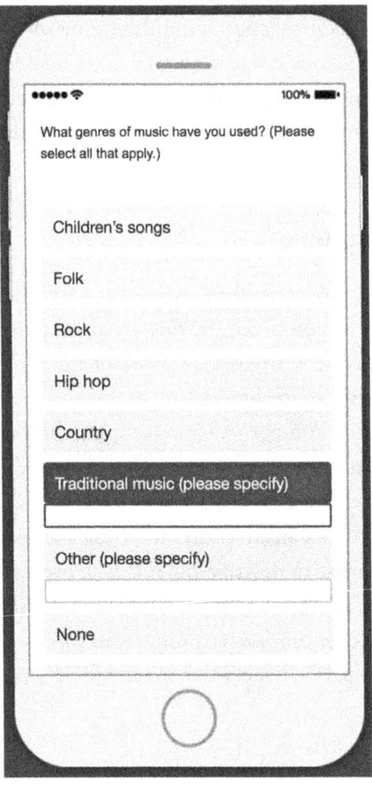

be conducted fully online. This allows for asynchronous participation and facilitates a wide circle of respondents.

Participant experience, data storage, and privacy are relevant for online survey techniques. Free accounts for survey tools, like SurveyMonkey, are ad supported. You may not want ads to intrude into your survey, or your review board may require avoiding ad-supported platforms. A paid service avoids this issue but increases researcher expense. Additionally, review how data is stored on your potential survey tools. Maintaining participant privacy to the greatest extent possible is key. Your university or organization may have subscriptions to tools, which can help reduce the costs to the individual researcher.

Once you have a set of questions, import them into the survey tool. When selecting a tool, match options available to your needs. Those with multiple question types and non-linear survey flow logic are practical. Google Forms, as well as costlier research-specific options, offer these functionalities. Align your question types with the tool's options, such as selecting more than one response to a multiple choice question or allowing additional text entry (Figure 7.1).

An online survey tool with skip logic shows only relevant questions to a respondent. Incorporate this design logic to produce a smooth participant experience. For example, your first question in the survey will be a question informing the respondent about your survey and asking for informed consent to participate. Using flow logic, trigger the survey to move to question 1 if the participant selects the answer indicating affirmative consent. If the respondent selects the answer indicating a lack of consent, direct the survey to an end page (Figure 7.2).

FIGURE 7.2 ■ Using Skip Logic

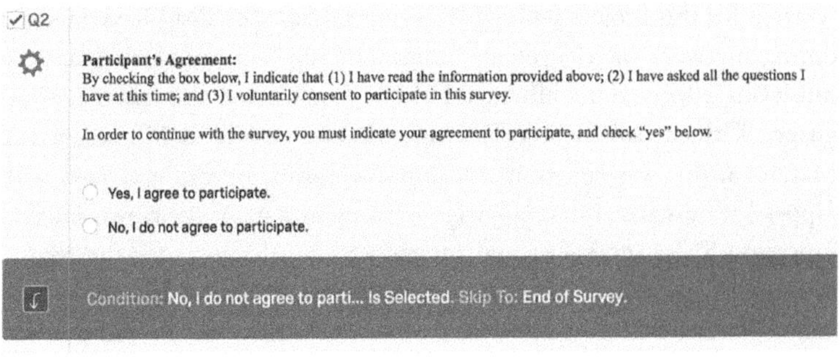

Q2

Participant's Agreement:
By checking the box below, I indicate that (1) I have read the information provided above; (2) I have asked all the questions I have at this time; and (3) I voluntarily consent to participate in this survey.

In order to continue with the survey, you must indicate your agreement to participate, and check "yes" below.

Yes, I agree to participate.

No, I do not agree to participate.

Condition: No, I do not agree to parti... Is Selected. Skip To: End of Survey.

Surveys provide feedback from individuals outside of your core group. As such, they also provide opportunities to connect with scene participants with whom you had not previously interacted. Giving survey participants the option to have a longer conversation provides the opportunity for interested participants to more fully explain their thoughts on the research topic and lets you as a researcher meet more people with relevant experience. At the end of the survey, include a question inviting participants to enter contact information—only if they wish to do so—to discuss the survey's ideas in greater depth. Collect emails, phone numbers, or handles of those interested, and then contact respondents to set up an interview. When you follow up with these respondents, use the strategies for interviewing to proceed.

Tools with options tailored for research, such as Qualtrics, provide tools to review and export results. Many services, including Google Forms, also offer easy ways to export your responses into a spreadsheet. Some research software connects directly to survey platforms, facilitating data importation. However you choose to collate your data afterwards, connect this information back to your central organizing document. Provide yourself with the list of questions, and file survey responses in the organization system that you chose in Chapter 4. Write a summary of your survey results, and maintain actual responses in searchable format.

INTERVIEWS AND SURVEYS TOGETHER IN A RESEARCH CONTEXT

Research I conducted on the role of music in language learning shows how it is possible to use interviews and surveys together strategically. Combining both methods and using in-person and distance communication technologies allowed me to connect with people I knew already, expand my research network, and learn from many people with relevant expertise. My research for this project proceeded in four phases. The first phase emerged during my work on citation in Indigenous hip hop, in which I noticed musicians' efforts to use bilingual lyrics in English and also a heritage language. With the subset of artists with whom I worked in Minnesota and Manitoba, this was largely in Anishinaabemowin. In my interviews with rappers, we discussed first language learning as part of their own musical processes. These interviews and interactions set the stage for the second phase of the project, in which I conducted semi-structured interviews with language teachers. Most interviews were conducted verbally, and one was conducted over email in a series of exchanges. Participant preference dictated the medium for each interview. For the third phase, I conducted an online survey with language teachers. Incorporating a survey allowed me to connect with friends and colleagues of people with whom I had worked directly. This strategy increased the number of people who were invested enough in the project to complete formal interviews: It reached people with expertise and interest who offered to be contacted for additional interviews, which was the last phase of the project. In this fourth phase, I conducted follow-up phone interviews with survey participants who wished to do so. At the first, second, and fourth phases, some interviews were conducted once, and other participants spoke with me multiple times. Each person was given a transcript of the interview, and some chose to give feedback or additional comments in response. I then collated my interviews, survey data, and analysis of heritage-language music (Przybylski, 2018).

I reviewed my interviews and surveys for repeated themes. Responses to open-ended questions in the survey offered additional perspectives that complemented my own fieldnotes, my readings of the musical performances, and interview transcriptions. I reread all my material, flagged passages that related to the main points, and jotted down additional observations. Then I revisited each thematic category. When I compared these central ideas to the ones I encountered in pedagogy literature, I found four major ways that popular music played a role in language learning: retention of words and phrases, inference of meaning based on context, development of linguistic flow, and creation of sustained self-motivated interest in learning. Listening to music in context and having ongoing dialogue with artists and teachers, I identified a fifth category: language revitalization. This information helped me refocus on my initial question, which asked how Anishinaabemowin hip hop lyrics were functioning for rappers. The project extended beyond these individual artists through the pedagogical expertise of many teachers and helped to show how, by supporting language revernacularization, hip hop music has a profound impact on cultural renewal.

CONDUCTING INTERVIEWS

By the time you conduct an interview, you will know some things about participants, and they about you. Before you begin, talk with interviewees about the process, and ask what questions they have. Go over consent documents as applicable. Ask whether or not you have permission to record, and remind your participant(s) that they may ask to stop the recording at any time. Creating a recording with a participant implicates professional obligations. The ethics of recording, as well as responsibilities for the researcher vis-à-vis recordings, are described in Chapter 6.

Start the recording when the person gives permission. Ask them to state their name and the date. This helps you set levels and also ensures that your audio or video file begins with the date and time and respondent's name, a boon for your organizational system. If not given permission to record, ask if they mind if you take notes. Use your skills from field jottings to write down details you may forget. Use abbreviations or shorthand, and be prepared to fill in your notes immediately after you complete the interview.

Keep in mind time restraints. Order your questions logically—for example, by theme or chronology. Make an additional inventory in which you order questions by priority. Introduce high priority topics earlier on, especially if you have time limitations. If you have three themes, for example, put the theme with the most high-priority questions first. Keep a list of lower-priority questions in the event that you have extra time. Refocus the conversation gently if it wanders while allowing for digressions your interviewee deems relevant. Always ask what else an interviewee wants to discuss. Let them tell you when the interview has been completed. Finally, invite interviewee to ask questions they have of you. It can be helpful to ask if there are other people that your interviewee recommends that you talk to about this topic.

End with next steps. Schedule a follow-up interview, when possible. Make a plan for how you will share the transcript with the interviewee, if they want to review it. Clarify together how the interviewee wants to be named. Let them specify their legal name, stage name, professional name, or other preferred name, or agree that you will use a pseudonym. Clarify whether or with whom transcription or audio may be shared. Discuss any other questions you have for each other.

Afterwards, write up any notes you have taken; make this write-up extremely detailed if you were not given permission to record. Take time to reflect in your field log, describing the interview as an experience and reflecting on your thoughts about the interaction. Log these notes in your central research document.

Follow-up interviews can flow from questions that arose during the first interview. Images or other documents provide objects for ongoing discussion with participants. Using a type of qualitative software outlined in Chapter 4, you could try putting together an image to help focus a conversation. For example, create and then discuss a word cloud generated from a set of content—say a group's website—with the people in your scene who made the site. Are there ideas that the website's authors would expect to see that are missing? What might be contributing to the centrality of specific words? You could alternately generate a visual using the transcript from the first interview as a source of discussion with your participant(s) in a subsequent interview. Word clouds and other research visualization tools are discussed in more detail in Chapter 8.

Despite the centrality of interviewing in expressive culture research, published texts typically only include excerpts that relate to the analysis or, less commonly, a partial set of interviews as an appendix. In addition to doing practice interviews, it's helpful to read interviews that others have conducted. Paying attention to how interviews are included in discipline-specific research is a useful step—you might even go back and reread articles or books you know well specifically to see how interviews are worked into the text. A few academic sources are actually primarily interviews, such as the Crafts, Cavicchi, and Keil (1993) listed in the chapter Further Reading.[1]

---

[1]This book presents transcriptions of open-ended interviews with interviewees aged 4 to 83. The interviews, on how people use music to make meaning in their lives, are presented individually, without intervening commentary. As such, this book offers a way to access interviews with many participants where the focus remains on the words of the interviewees. You can read for how people know themselves through the music they participate in, and it is possible to learn about individuals' musical perspectives in ways that transcend stereotypical expectations based on age, sex, class, or race. The editors have helpfully left in sections in which people contradict themselves, as humans tend to do. Also useful for presentational form, the volume demonstrates one-on-one interviews, models for self-reporting, and ways of including additional information, such as descriptions of non-verbal activity (in parentheses) as it accompanies what participants say. The appendix describes how this set of interviews was completed.

AFTER THE INTERVIEW

After your interview is completed, the immediate next step is transcription. Whether you spoke in person, on the phone, or through a computer program or app, approach your sound or video file as your first opportunity to review *what* was communicated and *how* it was communicated. As a general rule, transcribe interviews very shortly after they are conducted. Transcribing while a conversation is fresh in your mind can help increase accuracy and allows you to follow up with your participant soon after the conversation. Try playing back your sound at a slower speed so that you can type fluidly as the conversation moves forward. Introduce a new line for each speaker, and write out a timestamp that marks the point in the recording at which the speaker enters. This allows you to easily go back to the place in the recording and gives a sense of when in the conversation a certain thought emerged. For lengthy responses from a single person, it can be helpful to offer timestamps throughout, at about every 10 lines. Make notes for yourself about tone of voice and other non-literal meanings conveyed in the recording (Schegloff, 2007). As you jot down your reflections, recall that your interviewee is sharing their viewpoint; their opinions and recollections may vary from other participants' in the same scene. Hearing each person's situated perspective is precisely the point of conducting multiple interviews; review differences between interviewees' ideas as places to delve deeper into the material. Read more on balancing multiple opinions, forgetting, and misrepresentation (intentional and unintentional) in Atkinson, Coffey, and Delamont (2003).

Tag ideas that come to your mind as you transcribe, recording your reflections as comments to the main text. Transcription software can be helpful. These incorporate functionalities including playback speed controls, timestamps, and comment features within a single program. Examples include the free programs oTranscribe and Listen N Write (Windows) and the relatively low-cost F4 (Windows) or F5 (Mac). Much qualitative analysis software integrates the capacity to slow down audio so you can transcribe in-program. Ethnographers can use voice recognition programs to aid in transcription. With a smartphone, you can access voice recognition apps of varying quality, including voice memo features that may come standard on a device. If your workstyle and budget allow, you could try a more sophisticated voice recognition program, such as Dragon (PC/Mac, https://www.nuance.com/dragon.html), Dictanote (https://dictanote.co), or Dictandu (https://www.dictandu.com). Be aware that voice recognition software typically takes time to adapt to each voice and may not be optimal for multi-speaker scenarios. Always reread transcripts closely and bring an extra level of scrutiny to voice recognition documents, as misrecognition does happen. For multiple-ethnographer projects, the work can be spread across the team. Whether you work with a program, a team, or simply type what you hear, go through your transcription with your recording and check for accuracy. This is also a good moment to reflect in writing on the ideas that you encountered in the interview. Make a note of the transcription in your central research document and file the transcription into your organizational system.

Next, share the interview transcription in the manner that you agreed with the participant. For lengthy interviews, sharing sections can give participants a more reasonable amount of information to review. Having a conversation in person or remotely about the document allows for real-time interaction, in which a participant can offer clarifications, build on emerging thoughts, bring up potential inaccuracies, and ask questions. Sometimes it can be helpful to arrange for a conversation before you share the document. If sharing the complete document can feel too final, having a conversation midway through analysis can be useful. You could share the document and discuss it asynchronously through email or chat. Save any new information with the date of the conversation. Use the same archiving strategy you have been using for all of your materials, through your file system organization or software program, so that you have an easy-to-access and properly documented record of the interview, transcription, and follow-up.

While scholars may not talk about it, many worry that asking people to participate in ethnography could be an imposition. Some people enthusiastically come to the table. This can be the case for communities who are drawn into participation due to their enjoyment of the art form. Some people are engaged because of a shared love for the topic because they enjoy participating in the cultural practice or are invested in a place or cause.

Participants respond with varying degrees of engagement in the post-interview process. Asking for feedback with a typed document and asking for feedback without one can make a difference in whether or not a person responds and how much feedback she is willing to give. It's helpful to hold two things in mind: First, many people want to talk to you because you are taking seriously something that they care about and you care about. You are invested in this cultural practice, you are taking it seriously, and you are treating their thoughts with interest and respect. Some people will find it baffling that you worry about imposing a sense of obligation on them—after all, you too are invested in this topic.

Be realistic about different kinds of benefits that people seek in fieldwork situations. For artists, festival producers, directors, and other people who are looking for a public audience for their craft, working with an invested ethnographer can help the material reach new audiences. Presentations, publications, and sharing results through accessible media venues like online newspapers, podcasts, or blogs offer appealing ways to get the word out about work that participants take seriously.

SUMMARY

In this chapter, you planned, conducted, transcribed, and shared an interview. The chapter provided guidance on preparing, conducting, and collecting information from a survey that is directly related to your interview topics. Through continued interaction across your hybrid site, think about your formal conversations in the context of unfolding informal interactions. As you move toward written analysis, which is discussed in the following chapter, return to interviewees who were most active and consider offering to share a draft before publication. As the relationship allows, continue to be in touch after sharing the documents, whether socially, artistically, and/or as a researcher.

FURTHER READING

Atkinson, P., Coffey, A., & Delamont, S. (2003). *Key themes in qualitative research: Continuities and change.* Walnut Creek, CA: Alta Mira Press.

Briggs, C. L. (1986). *Learning how to ask: A sociolinguistic appraisal of the role of the interview in social science research.* Cambridge, UK: Cambridge University Press.

Buchanan, E. A., & Ess, C. (2008). Internet research ethics: The field and its critical issues. In K. E. Himma & H. T. Tavani (Eds.), *The handbook of information and computer ethics* (pp. 273–292). Hoboken, NJ: John Wiley and Sons.

Butler, M. J. (2014). *Playing with something that runs: Technology, improvisation, and composition.* New York: Oxford University Press.

Choi, J., Kushner, K. E., Mill, J., & Lai, D. W. L. (2012). Understanding the language, the culture, the experience: Translation in cross-cultural research. *International Journal of Qualitative Methods, 11*(5), 652–665.

Crafts, S. D., Cavicchi, D., Keil, C., & The Music in Daily Life Project. (1993). *My music: Explorations of music in daily life*. Middletown, CT: Wesleyan University Press.

Fink, A. (2017). *How to conduct surveys: A step-by-step guide* (6th ed.). Thousand Oaks, CA: Sage.

Geertz, C. (1973). *The interpretation of cultures*. New York: Basic Books.

Jackson, B. (1987). *Fieldwork*. Urbana: University of Illinois Press.

Lichtman, M. (2013). *Qualitative research in education: A user's guide* (3rd ed.). Thousand Oaks, CA: Sage.

Littig, B., & Pöchhacker, F. (2014). Socio-translational collaboration: The case of expert interviews. *Qualitative Inquiry, 20*(9), 1085–1095.

Maclean, K. (2007). Translation in cross-cultural research: An example from Bolivia. *Development in Practice, 17*(6), 784–790.

Miller, D., Costa, E., Haynes, N., McDonald, T., Nicolescu, R., Sinanan, J., . . . Wang, X. (2016). *How the world changed social media*. London: UCL Press.

Pasqualino, C. (2007). Filming emotion: The place of video in anthropology. *Visual Anthropology Review, 23*(1), 84–91.

Schegloff, E. (2007). *Sequence organization in interaction: A primer in conversation analysis*. Cambridge, UK: Cambridge University Press.

Society for Ethnomusicology. (2001). *A manual for documentation, fieldwork, and preservation for ethnomusicologists*. Bloomington, IN: Society for Ethnomusicology.

Spradley, J. (1979). *The ethnographic interview*. New York: Holt, Rhinehart, and Winston.

8 HYBRID FIELDWORK ANALYSIS

Hybrid ethnography entails months of interaction on social media, regular reading of relevant web pages, conducting interviews and surveys, participating in and documenting field experiences, and critically reading multiple kinds of media. How do all of these interrelated strategies add up to formal research findings? As discussed in previous chapters, hybrid ethnography involves updated strategies for interacting across a digital/physical divide and documenting large amounts of information gathered across the fieldsite. Moving through interpretation and into analysis, expressive culture research requires reading across multiple kinds of ethnographic data, accounting for the situated position of the researcher, and an ongoing commitment to dialogue with fellow participants. This chapter marks your pivot as ethnographer from in-field research to what comes afterward. This stage, covered in the next two chapters, comprises analysis, writing, and sharing findings of your ethnography with participants. You will continue to interact in the field, dialogue with fellow participants, and possibly conduct formal follow-up interviews, though you have moved into the analysis stage.

ANALYZING INFORMATION FROM FIELDWORK

Multiple tools are available for analyzing data. Many of the strategies used for either online or offline ethnography can be adapted here; your own research background and specific fieldsite will determine the most appropriate resources. Novice researchers can learn about content analysis of text and visuals, narrative analysis, conversation analysis, and discourse analysis in Grbich (2013). The synthesis offered here builds on either your past research experience or your reading on some relevant techniques.

This chapter will identify and then model how to apply a relevant analytical strategy to hybrid fieldwork information. First, **review documentation of your ethnographic experience and assess it for relevant, repeated themes.** Read over your central document that contains references to your jottings, write-ups, media, interviews, and surveys. As you reread your own fieldnotes, be open to the possibility that your understanding of what you wrote in your notes has changed over time. As you have learned more about your scene, are there earlier reflections that seem underinformed? Fellow participants and/or coresearchers may also have experienced changes of opinion or deepening of knowledge over time. Identify discrepancies and make additional notes with updated information. Refer to your codebook and observe the list of relevant themes you included. During this process, attune yourself to repeated themes. Some ethnographers prefer an informal approach: Read back, reflect, and write. Others opt to conduct a formalized coding process, particularly if using qualitative analysis software to help manage large volumes of data (see Bernard, 2011; Saldaña, 2016). Standardization is particularly helpful for processing information between multiple researchers. A middle ground involving structured visual organization leaves room for wild thoughts during the rereading process. I will describe this middle-ground approach.

Using your codebook (or your set of key terms from qualitative analysis software) as a start, determine if every concept listed is indeed relevant to the central document you just reread. It is possible that early on you thought certain themes might be important, but they have not emerged as such; remove these from your new list. You can always revisit these later and ask why their relevance changed over time. Keeping only the relevant concepts, write a new theme list. Then, reflect back on your read-through. Did you encounter repeated ideas that are not reflected in your new list? Add these in as necessary.

Visualization tools can help you sift through large amounts of data at this stage. If you are using a qualitative research software program, experiment with its capabilities for data visualization. Alternately, import your documents into a web-based tool that creates images. Visualization tools produce maps that outline terms that are repeated across your research documentation. Try using them to add recurring terms that are missing in your analysis and to further emphasize those concepts that appear frequently. One common example is a word cloud based on frequency. These images show which ideas appear the most in your documents. When you visualize information in word tree format, thick branches show ideas of importance based on repetition, and branching structures help you display how related ideas stem from each other logically. Hierarchy charts are useful if you want to get a sense of relative importance, based on guidelines you establish, of themes and subthemes in relation to each other. These tools are particularly helpful when you want to "read" large quantities of data—say months of multiple users' online interactions or social media data—that is impractical to analyze by rereading every word.

Next, mark where your key themes occur in your central document. This may involve hyperlinks, tags, or another tool relevant to your particular software or platform for data organization. Another strategy is to assign one color to each theme and to highlight or tag text and media annotations on your computer each time the theme occurs. If you work well with pen and paper, you could print out your central document and color it in with a set of highlighters. Many software programs allow you to accomplish this task through tagging. Use the search feature in your analysis software or word processing program to make sure you have not missed any iterations of key terms. However you choose to move forward, create a specific tag for each idea on your theme list and apply it to each relevant passage. Do not hesitate to identify one passage or interaction with more than one tag. Then, step back and look at your overall spread of information. Create a new document with everything of the same tag type, cut-and-paste your physical paper copy into multiple piles, or use your software to pull everything with the same tag into one area for you to read against each other.

Then, **take notes on your newly organized information.** In the notetaking phase, return to your new pages or documents organized thematically. Read each theme section as a whole, make note of what is consistent across dates, interviewees, and networked and face-to-face platforms, and write down any outliers you find. At this stage, reflect on how your themes relate to each other. These may be mutually influential; one may emerge as a subcategory of another. Rely on your experience with qualitative analysis from previous physical or online ethnographic work at this stage or read Saldaña, Leavy, and Beretvas (2011) for additional guidance.

As you reflect on themes in your rearranged material, questions may emerge. Why was a particular piece so popular? Was there a pattern to the moments in which you as a participant felt uncomfortable? Is it accurate that the majority of the performers expressed themselves in rehearsals in a way that was significantly different than their on-stage personas? These questions are part of what I think of as wild thoughts. Often, when engaged in a specific task, like observing information for repetition, other theories and questions show up. These ideas can be motivating, returning to why the researcher chose to formalize participant observation. They can also help refine or even point toward a direct answer for parts of the research question. Some may need to be saved for future research, as they point in new directions. Marking something as a useful idea for the future is helpful for the next project and a useful way to maintain pragmatic limits on the current one. Give yourself time to write down your ideas at this stage.

Third, **use the ideas that emerged from your thematic analysis to review relevant parts of your larger body of information.** Move from your central document to the media and notes to which it refers. For the wild thought that had you wondering about persona shifts, go back to each of your interviews for information and look at your notes on the shows in which each person took part. If one of your themes was changes in performance traditions, look back at your notes, photos, and videos to find instances of these. If other participants are helping you with notetaking (see Chapter 4) and recording (see Chapter 6) or you are part of a team of ethnographers, this also will be a collaborative process. Specific guidance on managing data together, collective analysis, and working productively with a team is found in Beebe (2014).

Fourth, **use the information to build toward general findings about your site.** Start with the specific social context for your field that you examined in Chapter 5. Look for patterns in the way events generally happen. As you describe norms for your hybrid field, pay attention to platform- and space-specific attitudes. Do behavioral patterns shift on different social media platforms? Do typical manners of communicating within your group alter when you talk in a meeting as opposed to via email? With these generalizations across or between aspects of your field in mind, keep your ears open for outliers. Some individuals or events may diverge from the general pattern; look into these more deeply.

In addition to looking back at your notes and media, keep checking in with your group members. Try sharing your ideas in casual conversations at events or arrange for a phone call, online chat, and/or in-person conversation with one or more group members who are likely to have input on a particular topic. What alternative explanations are possible? Ask how your provisional conclusion sounds to them and listen for potential additions, redirections, and nuancing.

Remember that the interpretive process is one in which you are producing meaning. Yes, you are reflecting in a grounded manner on what you have observed and done in your scene. As mentioned in Chapter 4, you aren't mining for facts. Your interpretation is situational and dependent upon who you are as a researcher. Some details of your field experience will not be able to be encompassed into larger generalities; this lack of a total neat resolution is instructive and should not be glossed over.

Fifth, **use theoretical models and previous research appropriate to your material to answer questions about your ethnographic experience that are yet unresolved.** Go back to the literature review you conducted before starting the ethnographic portion of your research and examine theoretical models that have been employed by other researchers working in similar scenes. Consider also more general theoretical literature that you have found helpful to explain internally complex aspects of cultural expression and interaction. Hybrid ethnography is useful in many interdisciplinary studies, so think widely about potential applicability.

Reading for ideas that come up over and over again in various ways offers a starting point, not an end, for thinking through how, why, and to whom they matter. Theoretical models—from your research community or reading—offer a variety of approaches for analysis (see Jackson & Mazzei, 2012). Look back at the new theme list you completed in Part 1 of this process. This can point you to relevant literature. For example, if expressions of masculinity is one of your themes, refer to your literature review and expand it if necessary to review scholarship in studies of masculinity that offer a model to help explain media and experiences you encountered in your scene. In addition to reviewing relevant scholarship for existing theoretical models, you may find that you need to adapt one model to your scene or synthesize two or more models in order to theorize your own experience. Generating a new theoretical approach might be the most helpful way to address those parts of your gathered information that cannot be explained by existing models. For more on building and synthesizing theoretical models, read Mason (2002); Chapters 8 and 9 are relevant here.

Finally, record questions that are yet unanswered. Identify irresolvable tensions. Make note of questions you have that you simply don't have enough information or experience yet to answer. Some of these will be areas for future study and research. Perhaps research needed to be conducted to even arrive at a particular question. Ideally, unanswered questions will now be articulated more productively than they were at the beginning.

INTEGRATING INFORMATION SPECIFIC TO EXPRESSIVE CULTURE

Hybrid research in expressive culture incorporates analysis of media, both the researcher's own recordings and those made and circulated by others. Data from websites and social media platforms offers relevant layers detailing how meaning is created and how ideas circulate in your scene. Interviews are a standard tool in research design, and, taking a cue from robust online ethnographies, surveys can provide relevant qualitative responses as well.

Interviews and Surveys

Carefully organizing information from interviews and surveys will help you make sense of this aspect of your field experience. Include both interview transcripts and your own notes about the interview in the information that you review as described in Part 1 above. This should be relatively seamless, as the descriptions are logged in your main document, and your transcriptions are saved in an associated location. For surveys, the information you have is slightly different: In your notes in the central document, you may have listed encounters you had about the survey, such as conversations or electronic communications you had with potential participants about survey participation. If the survey was asynchronous, you may have less direct information than you do for interviews. Use the notes you do have alongside survey responses in order to reflect on your results.

Collect your survey answers in a central location. Programs like Google Forms and Qualtrics facilitate extracting data as a spreadsheet, which provides a clear way to review multiple answers at once. Many survey tools, including both of these, also offer ways to visualize information for individual survey questions. Start with your general questions. How many people responded? Of these, what was your breakdown in terms of the categories you hoped to know more about? For example, how many people primarily work in performance, organization, management, fundraising, and communications? You then have the opportunity to look at similarities across all groups—how many people want to expand educational programming?—and in individual categories—how many performers want to expand educational programming? A variety of approaches are productive here, and you can choose models based on your experience with surveys or questionnaires in online-only or physical ethnography. If you are new to this process, one useful resource is Bernard (2011), particularly Chapter 9 on online questionnaires and surveys. Take time to reread your qualitative responses. As you would with comments on a social media page, review these answers for repeated themes, as well as anything that seems surprising or like an outlier. Make notes about what you observe, and log these into your central document. Refer out to the spreadsheet that encapsulates your data so that you can review this when you perform the holistic analysis described in this chapter.

Media and Web Data

Your analysis of video, audio, and other media you encounter or record yourself is a rich source that needs to be integrated into your analysis at this point in the process. Use the descriptions you wrote and segments of speech that you transcribed in Chapter 6 as material for your analysis. Reread your notes regarding websites and other online sources as well. Incorporate these documents into the first step of your analytical process described above. Refer back to Chapter 6 for details on transcription and documentation from your media. Note that some qualitative data analysis software allows you to search tags and comments on imported media, including images, audio, and video, as well as web data, such as web pages and social media data, to facilitate this process.

DIALOGUE

Continue conversations as you refine the ideas that emerge. Dialoguing throughout the process, whether informally in the fieldsite or formally over messaging or interviews, opens lines of communication and allows you to check in about your emerging ideas and keep the ideas of your research community at the center of your project. Based in dialogic ethnography, hybrid fieldwork incorporates a process in which the researcher shares sections of interview transcripts and provisional findings with participants regularly (Araújo, 2006). At each step, invite participants to comment on their own previous remarks, clarifying and updating as they see fit. This also makes space for participants to ask questions of the researcher(s) throughout the back-and-forth. Together, all participants, including the researcher, create living documents that the researcher can read alongside the central document when analyzing information and moving toward the study's findings. Dialogue is further explored in the context of sharing your findings in Chapter 9.

ANALYSIS: A FIELDWORK EXAMPLE

To provide a sense of how to review documentation from a hybrid fieldsite and move into analysis, I offer a snapshot of my process in a recent project. First, some context. I've had the opportunity to work as a researcher with a number of hip hop musicians as well as online and physical media distribution organizations over the past several years. Musicians, radio stations, web broadcasters, and others often use music as a medium to share a variety of messaging. This has been markedly clear when I've been interacting with artists who make music that speaks to their urban Indigenous identities. Fruitful discussions of politics often happen within hip hop circles; these are only sometimes present when larger publics discuss social issues. At moments of national crisis, governments and citizens frequently turn to public musical interventions, attempting to use artistic means to facilitate meaningful change that has not been accomplished through alternate means. With the ongoing rise of globalized Indigenous consciousness at the international level, nation states from the Americas to the Pacific are addressing their colonial pasts.

My research moves between the United States and Canada. Like many settler-colonial states, Canada is currently wrestling with the past, present, and future of relationships between Indigenous and non-Indigenous citizens. Children were required to attend Indian Residential Schools, where Indigenous language, music, and religion were barred. The Truth and Reconciliation Commission (TRC) investigated abuses children suffered when separated from their families and was charged with making recommendations for the future. As an American who lived in Canada while the TRC was conducting public events and formalizing its findings, I followed the process closely.

To start, I had conversations with friends and colleagues, particularly those active in the arts, about their thoughts on how the TRC used music to execute its mandate—and where this has fallen short of expectations. I participated in events by attending in person and by interacting with text and media shared online. Even as I heard people around me talk about how public programming could offer a point of departure for arts-based decolonial efforts around the world, I couldn't help but think—utopian visions for how music in the public sphere can combat oppressive forces and work on behalf of previously marginalized communities? I've heard this before. This sounds like some of the optimism that many hip hop heads have associated with the global spread of hip hop culture. Given what I heard around me, I focused my attention on where people were expressing optimism and also when reality stopped short of lofty expectations.

Looking back through my initial experiences, I did find that music had been central to official programming—but only certain genres of music and in some limited ways. I read web content and communicated with people about how the TRC has taken up its mandate to contribute to the reconciliation process in large part by hearing testimony and facilitating public events. I listened to and read about musical performances that were central to these events. I was part of the crowd when rock icon Buffy Sainte-Marie closed the four-day public programming in Ottawa. And I talked with other listeners and musicians about what they experienced and how they were moved to respond.

As a long-time hip hop listener and music researcher, I noticed a marked absence of hip hop in public forums. This stands in contrast to the high level of political engagement I've heard at hip hop-specific shows put on by Indigenous artists for Indigenous and non-Indigenous audiences. Given this discrepancy, my curiosity was piqued when a friend and fellow musician let me know of an upcoming collaboration between a new music group and a rapper that was designed to be part of the public conversation about reconciliation. This also gave me the chance to work with singers and other arts professionals I knew from my work as a musician. With this concert as a specific focus, I built on interactions and observations in which I had been participating. Zooming in on one collaborative performance that was inspired by TRC action steps, I started formal interviews. I observed rehearsals and reflected in writing on my own participation as a singer with these musicians on previous projects. I carried on with my web documentation and recording and added events and sites relevant to the new performances. I continued my media analysis and kept interacting with official websites and social media.

Moving From Fieldwork to Analysis

This section moves through the process outlined in the first half of the chapter. To begin the transition from fieldwork to analysis, **I review my ethnographic documentation. A handful of repeated themes emerge.** I further refine these for those that are relevant to the questions with which I approached this project. I reread my fieldwork notes and cross-reference these with my reflections of my own personal responses to the experience. As I go, I highlight passages related to specific themes and make annotations in the margins of my electronic document, keeping track of my responses to how iterations of each theme overlap with each other—and when they present variations on the theme.

Initially, I thought technologically facilitated distance collaboration might be important. Upon reviewing my archive, it seems clear that this is less widely talked about. It still could be relevant, but it's worth considering—do the other people with whom I am working think it is a useful focus? Does it bring me closer to answering a rich and interesting question that is still important to the research? In this case, I decide to nest distance collaboration under a larger collaboration theme. It seems important to one phase of the collaborative process, and though not always verbalized, distance technologies did play an important role in the creative process. At this point, however, it does not warrant a separate theme. Other options I could have taken in regard to a decrease in importance are (1) continuing to pursue the theme, (2) making note of the theme and saving related questions and observations for another project, or (3) refocusing away from the given theme.

As I reread, I'm also paying attention to new repeated themes as well as people and organizations that are emerging as more relevant. I find audience participation to be an emergent concept here. While not initially in my codebook, this is clearly important to my interlocutors and, as I read my own reflective notes and revisit conversations in my memory, increasingly important to me as well.

Adding Software to the Analysis

Because I'm analyzing a significant amount of web-based data, I also use a software program to help me read this information. I use a qualitative analysis program to help me search for repeated names and to flag each one. These end up being the names of my interlocutors and names of relevant arts groups. I also do a search of my saved webpage data, Twitter data, and Facebook data. Using the software, I highlight examples of the words and word stems associated with each theme. While this helps to comb through large data sets, it makes the most sense when read alongside my fieldnotes—here, I have written down responses to and thoughts about online interactions as they occurred. Using my notes and these data sets, I work to get a contextualized sense of what is important to revisit.

FIGURE 8.1 ■ This Image Shows the Key Terms in Large Text. Note That Proper Nouns Appear as Blank Spaces for Privacy.

To sift through my web data alongside my notes, interviews, and commentary on audio, video, and photographs, I also use a visualization tool. In this case, I find word clouds to be helpful. First, I run a word cloud using all of my documents. This suggests, by word frequency alone, that "composing," "audience," and "music" should be important here (Figure 8.1). The latter is too general to be of use, but the two former terms are indeed relevant. Next, I explore the data after excluding words that I know will appear frequently. In this case, I remove repeated proper nouns and the most prominent terms, which I have already noted. This leaves me more visual space to check for things for which I might not have been paying such close attention. When I do this, I see some new words crop up with relative frequency—"collaborative" and "sampling" (Figure 8.2). I can use the word frequency list to go back and look at where these terms have emerged across my archive. Rereading for contextualized information on these two ideas brings me to comments I've made on audio files, my own reflections on a rehearsal, and formal interviews, showing specifics of these ideas' relevance.

FIGURE 8.2 ■ With Proper Nouns Removed, New Key Terms Appear as the Largest Words.

I explore my larger data sets separately at this stage as well. I use visualizations for my web data to see relative frequency of participation on various platforms by the same people and groups. A hierarchy chart shows how often a given party contributes on different Facebook pages, which I compare to activity on Twitter. In my codebook, I have a list of people who are regular participants. I explore my online data to see if there are other people or groups who emerge as relevant—I look for people or groups who frequently retweet, comment on videos online, or post to pages. This can help identify if there are other names that need to be included in my set as I review how people and groups relate to each other.

My web-based archive shows similar repeated themes. Again, I flag repeated words that are not relevant and exclude them from the analysis. For example, in Twitter and Facebook data sets, the terms "http" and "www" appear repeatedly. These identify that users are frequently sharing links, but they do not help characterize the thematic content of communications. After noting the link-sharing frequency, I rerun my query without these terms. Without these high-frequency words, others come into focus. The word "missing" appears more often than I would have imagined. I review these instances. These iterations can have very different valences (e.g., social media posts encouraging audience members not to miss a show compared with those calling attention to the human rights crisis of missing and murdered women), so I carefully disaggregate these.

Reading Information From Multiple Angles

The way research themes interact with each other reveals more detail than frequency alone. My central themes and subthemes are mutually influential, and these interact with names in my codebook in multiple ways. To start to analyze these, I look for a visual sense of overlap. I search for instances in which I find a confluence of two interrelated themes. Software helps me find intersections between related terms: Matrix coding provides a list of locations of interaction, and a chart visualization shows where these occur. Without this tool, you could alternately do a text search or review your central document for color coding, looking for instances in which you have noted the emergence of both themes in close proximity.

I'm seeing clusters of words that link to themes on my list, so I review these alongside my related annotations. The data tools are just that—tools—and I use them as additional resources for my own guided reading. I pull together my annotations on interviews, notes, and media related to gender politics, my written reflections on these topics, and examples from my web data that reference women, men, rights, gender, and permutations of these words. I make note of where I see more in-depth conversations on these—in this case, more mentions on Twitter and with two particular interviewees than anywhere else—and I plan on bringing up what I've observed with participants in future online and face-to-face conversations.

Depending on your site, research question, and the kinds of interactions you are having, explore other tools for connecting important people and themes across parts of your field. For example, use a software program or online tool to group social media posts by number of responses. A list or visual image of these can help give you a sense of the kinds of posts, timing of posts, posters, and so forth that have received the most interaction and also invite you to revisit your own notes and experience with the on- and offline activity around the topic covered in popular threads. Create a visual mind map to show connections, a timeline to show spikes and lulls in activity, or revisit the image you created in Chapter 5 about the people and organizations that are central to your scene, adding additional players and kinds of connection as needed.

I now have a list of relevant people and groups. Largely, in this case, these are unchanged, but I do have some specific information about who is more—and less—active across web pages, social media, and in-person spaces. I can see when various people were more active and collate this with what I know about on-the-ground events in which I participated. This all contributes to my refined list of research themes: cross-genre collaboration, hip hop sampling practices, and protocol are central to the analysis.

Reflecting on Organized Data

Moving on to the next step, I can now **take new notes on my thematically organized information.** With my refined list of names (both people and organizations) and themes in my revised codebook, I examine them one by one. Starting with the theme of hip hop sampling practices, I use my software to generate a list of every iteration that I have flagged as being related to this theme. I chose to use NVivo for this process, but other qualitative data analysis programs, such as ATLAS.ti, offer a comparable set of tools. While I am using software, a comparable process could be used with color coding across documents or keyword tagging in a word processor. Now, when I read about sampling, I have excerpts from interviews, passages from fieldnotes, blog posts, Facebook comments, tweets, and my own tags from media I made as well as videos and photos posted by other people. Since I am only reading thematically relevant passages, I can read these across mediums and note what I observe. I read and make notes, finding additional depth and nuance as I work. Though my work is focused, as I read through thematically, other questions do emerge. I find repeated references to discomfort. My fellow participants talk about audience discomfort; I make notes about listeners seeming unsettled; and notes on my videos show moments of rupture. I'm not sure yet how I to address this, but it becomes clear that I need to keep revisiting it. How does discomfort relate to ideas of audience engagement or lack of engagement? With musicians' feelings of being heard? I move beyond the text. How did people say the words they shared about discomfort in interviews with me? What patterns can I see in how and when information was circulated online? This is unresolved and warrants more close attention.

After this, **I look and listen back at the notes and media** to which my thematic tags refer. I read for context beyond the paragraph I highlighted; I read the annotations I made in the first part of this analytical process; and I relisten to media segments that I flagged. I look back at the video, audio, and photos where I made annotations about each specific theme. I also generate follow-up questions—for example, to speak with a specific collaborator about a passage.

Generating Provisional Findings

This round of focused writing and reflection prepares me to **use the information to build provisional findings related to my research question.** After attuning to details, I zoom out. At this stage, I think back about what I know about the shape of my fieldsite and how people often work in it. For this research topic, it's helpful for me to consider moments when collaboration does not proceed in the expected manner. As I think about these divergences and what this implies for the idea of "collaboration" that participants talk about, I mentally move back to the granular level of my research data. I remember a comment the rapper made at one of the shows, about the audience moving around. I wrote about it in my fieldnotes because it stood out to me—I was seated in the audience at the time, as was everyone around me. I revisit this using my notes on the video. I zero in on a moment from one of the show videos and listen again as the rapper says, "Feel free to move around if you want. Let's get this element of hip hop going here." Why does this stand out to me? In this moment, the rapper articulates a norm in a hip hop setting. She brings an energy that is at home in that performance tradition, one that is at odds with new music performance traditions, which flow primarily from the staged presentational style of classical music. So I write about this moment of tension, think more about what happened in it, and frame it in context to put together what this incongruity indicates at a larger level.

This is a stage at which I check back in with participants. I share my thoughts about collaboration, ask questions about sampling, revisit discomfort, and ask for clarity around protocol. In general, this is a good time to update or amend conditional findings based on clarifications from participants. Checking in can happen over a variety of mediums, often phone calls, in-person conversations, emails, text messages, and posts. Posts and messages are typically shared with a closed group or small subset of participants at this stage. In these communications, I offer provisional findings and ask for feedback.

Positionality and Grounding the Analysis

Interpreting the information I have gathered, I realize that who I am as participant–observer informs the meaning that is created. At rehearsals and shows, I've been listening for what might translate—and not—between hip hop and new music. I knew the rapper's music before this, but since the rest of these compositions are new, I didn't know the rest of the music. I've long been fascinated by sampling practices in hip hop. I'm listening with a focused ear for how this concert showcases singers, who use their bodies to make the sounds of percussion, instruments, and samples without the help of machines. I'm also listening with my whole body, as a singer, knowing how it would feel to make various kinds of sounds with my own vocal instrument and what would be challenging or enjoyable for me. Yet for this specific case, I haven't been involved in the whole rehearsal process. Though I know many of the musicians as collaborators from previous projects, I participate in a way that is both outsider and insider. Writing about my role in my own notes helps me analyze the inflections of my interpretive approach.

As I work toward the study's findings, including aspects of fieldwork that are not easily resolvable, I connect back to related literature. There are two ways this generally proceeds. A researcher can reread to identify a theoretical model that accounts for questions that are otherwise unexplained. A model that can be adopted or adapted may well come from another area of study or an interdisciplinary field, as was mentioned in the first half of this chapter. Revisiting the closely related literature could instead offer an opportunity to review current lines of inquiry in your own academic field and to identify what existing approaches are relevant in the given scene. The bibliographic work mentioned in Chapter 1 is the starting point for this approach, and you can widen your circle of reading based on new information if applicable.

Tailored theoretical approaches and related literature are useful as far as they help address questions encountered in the field. I understand that the artists with whom I am working do their own theorizing; it isn't necessary to graft anything onto their work that doesn't help to productively analyze the fieldwork. For other parts of this study, I will revisit situated ideas of witnessing and applications of a theory of discomfort in theatrical and performative affect. For the more concrete question of sample usage, I've noticed tension around the ethics of sampling and what this implies about power dynamics in collaborations. Multiple artists have talked about this at length. I suspect that exploring this tension will help shed light on how power operates in collaborative music making. How sampling works in this case is reminiscent of—and markedly different in some ways from—instances of sampling that I am aware of from my own hip hop listening and from reading relevant literature. I look back at writing about cross-genre sampling in popular music. I read cases studies for their own specific contexts, examine the unique context of my fieldwork, and identify how published studies speak to my fieldwork.

After going through all these steps, I still have some questions that do not have definite answers. However, they have become more refined questions, and I have productive directions in which I could take them for future work.

SUMMARY

This chapter offers a model of how to generate productive findings from your research after completing the major portion of your fieldwork phase. You integrated ethnographic observations recorded in Chapter 5 and media analysis conducted in Chapter 6 alongside the interview and survey results collected in Chapter 7 to create a holistic analysis that responds to the research question. In the process, you refined your research themes, identified how these relate to each other, and clarified relationships between people and organizations. Dialogue with participants continues to be important, and it informs your progress, as you are now working toward productive answers to your research question. You will continue to refine your ideas as you write and create other forms of media to share your research, both of which are detailed in the following chapter.

FURTHER READING

Beebe, J. (2014). *Rapid qualitative inquiry: A field guide to team-based assessment*. Lanham, MD: Rowman & Littlefield.

Bernard, H. R. (2011). *Research methods in anthropology: Qualitative and quantitative approaches*. Lanham, MD: Alta Mira Press.

Grbich, C. (2013). *Qualitative data analysis* (2nd ed.). Thousand Oaks, CA: Sage.

Jackson, A. Y., & Mazzei, L. A. (2012). *Thinking with theory in qualitative research*. New York: Routledge.

Mason, J. (2002). *Qualitative researching*. Thousand Oaks, CA: Sage.

Saldaña, J. (2016). *The coding manual for qualitative researchers*. Thousand Oaks, CA: Sage.

Saldaña, J., Leavy, P., & Beretvas, N. (2011). *Fundamentals of qualitative research*. New York: Oxford University Press.

9 SHARING RESEARCH RESULTS

"We need more, not fewer, ways to tell of culture," explains John Van Maanen in *Tales of the Field* (1988, p. 140). His book identifies how ethnographic writing can adopt varied narrative strategies that attract different audiences. In the hybrid field, we can use not just varied rhetorical devices, as Van Maanen suggests, but also a plethora of mediums for conveying information. Researchers using a hybrid ethnographic methodology will produce results that can be shared in the form of an academic article or monograph. At the same time, integrating digital and physical spaces invites other formats for sharing information, including short films, radio broadcasts, podcasts, websites, and popular press articles. While highlighting the possibilities in disseminating results across multiple platforms, this chapter will help you prepare to share research findings in venues that fit your scene and goals.

A while ago, an academic journal published an article of mine on its free, open-source website. Because of this format, the article was easy to share on internet-based platforms. After the article was posted to social media, one of the first responses I received was from a friend and collaborator who had worked with me as a participant. I could not have been more pleased. Beyond the substance of the comment, which was generous, the fact of that response shows the benefits of open-source publishing: A musician I had worked with was able to access my published writing easily and early. Further, he could share thoughts about it online, immediately making his comments heard to a wide public.

PUBLICATION AND PARTICIPANT PRIVACY

When it comes to privacy, two principles are key: Respect participant preferences, and be realistic about how much privacy you can promise. Sharing results of qualitative research in expressive culture does not necessarily require anonymization of participant information. When I have worked with professional musicians, I have actually had specific requests that I make their names public as part of my research findings. Whether participants have a strong preference for or against anonymization or do not have a strong preference, always ask and respect their choices. If the choice is to release real participant names, work with your ethics body to make sure you have the appropriate steps in place: Boards may require additional information or escalate review level when participants' identities are shared.

For hybrid research, a new wrinkle in privacy emerges. In the event that some participants do not wish to be named, talk through options carefully. Researchers can follow best practices to offer participant privacy for information collected offline. Because hybrid ethnography also involves online participation, researchers can also follow current—and evolving—best practices in this sphere (Markham & Buchanan, 2012). When interacting with participants who contribute to public sites or platforms online, keep in mind that published comments become part of a searchable archive. That is, after you publish a quotation that a fellow participant made online, your reader could easily type the quotation into a search engine and locate the initial source. Even if you offer a pseudonym for an online handle in your publication, the original handle is thus easily discoverable. Because hybrid research works with the same community that exists across all parts of your scene, this original handle could be linked to the other portions of your research that took place with the same individual in other parts of your research field, including offline.

Recordings, too, must be used carefully. Some groups and individuals wish to be publicly named in photos, videos, and other circulated media. Indeed, the possibility to access new audiences may be one reason that artists wish to take part in research and can be part of research reciprocity. The informed consent process should identify which recordings participants are comfortable sharing and with whom. Photos and videos can include identifiable images and sounds, so think carefully about whether someone represented might be uncomfortable being recognized in the documentation. Recordings made at public events are held to less stringent privacy standards in terms of regulations, but as a researcher invested in your scene, you may need to use stricter community standards for which recordings can be distributed comfortably.

Several options are possible to address the realities of online distribution of expressive culture information. First, know that there are limits to what kind of privacy can be offered, and be candid about these limits with fellow participants. Second, should participants not wish to be named, adopt additional strategies to minimize how identifiable they are in the study. One is to quote directly only from information collected online that is not posted publicly—answers in an a survey you conduct using reputable software, for example. For material that is on public sites, describe interactions from your notes, paraphrase quotations in general terms, or offer data as an aggregate across several participants to avoid direct searchability. You may need to opt not to share some photographs or other recordings. Follow best practices for encryption and data protection for sensitive information, and let people know that even with best practices, there is still a small chance that data could be inadvertently accessed.

DECIDING HOW AND WHAT TO SHARE

Throughout hybrid ethnography, work in progress and results are shared with many stakeholders at multiple times. When and in what formats to share research are important considerations to make research useful, accessible, and productive. Increased interrelationship that is part of hybrid ethnography requires increased responsibility to the community. Consultation and clear communication are part of the process. When it comes time to share results at the writing-up stage, options emerge. What is it that you will share? Researchers publish articles or books or produce documentary film or audio. Focused pieces of documentation, such as images, maps, soundclips, or interviews, can be tailored for relevant audiences. Likely, these formats will be in addition to public presentations, either for a research audience, an artist or community audience, or all of these.

Before you start the initial polishing up of results, decide on a format or formats for making your work available to others. Sharing results makes content accessible to interested audiences that likely include fellow research participants. Multiple presentation formats may be optimal. Results from hybrid ethnographic research can be productively shared in academic publications, such as an article, chapter, or book. The publication of an article is a lengthy process; there are benefits to sharing material sooner and in other formats in addition to peer-reviewed publications. Popular press writing, such as for a print or online magazine or newspaper, offers shorter format options for sharing ideas that are of interest to a wider audience. While not peer reviewed, these offer a shorter timeline to publication for time-sensitive material and often have a larger readership. Publishing in multiple venues expands accessibility. Paid subscriptions, language differences, and academic writing style may each pose a barrier to some fellow participants. Research on expressive culture can be even more productively shared by incorporating relevant media. This is increasingly possible with online publishing of articles.

Where you have permission to do so, consider sharing other products in addition to your formal write-ups. Photos, maps, video clips, songs, or interview transcripts can be of interest to an audience. For example, you may choose to share your videos publicly or to a private group of users, both of which are possible on YouTube. Visual media can be shared in formats such as photo essays. For larger bodies of interactive media, a website offers a more robust opportunity to share material. You might take time to carefully edit video or audio for an audience, producing ethnographic or documentary film with your video or a radio show, podcast, or audio documentary with your audio materials.

EXERCISE 9.1

To decide how and where to share your research, think about the goals and potential reach of your project.

- What aspects of the research need to be shared widely, and what parts should not be?
- What elements of your research are potentially of interest to a wider community or general audience?
- How can you share your media in multiple manners for different audiences?
- What formats function best to reach researchers in the academy or industry?
- What formats are most accessible to members of your research community?

Most hybrid ethnographies will require more than one product to share research; your specific fieldsite will determine which mediums are most meaningful for you and your fellow participants.

Reciprocity and Multiple Venues for Sharing

As a researcher, there are many avenues open to you in terms of writing about your research. Rich descriptive writing has analytical value; it also emphasizes the real human interactions that are at the core of ethnographic research in a way that some researchers and participants appreciate for its warmth and nuance.

Sharing research is an important moment for reciprocity. Planning how best to share back with fellow participants draws on conversation and interaction throughout the hybrid fieldwork process. Typically, this is the moment for putting into action a plan for research sharing that emerged throughout the design stage. Documenting and carefully sharing information with relevant audiences can be one of the strongest benefits that researchers offer to communities. Sometimes, participants want and need to tell their stories and to have them heard by specific audiences. As Qwul'sih'yah'maht Thomas explains, when this is the case, the researcher has the responsibility to listen and document—especially when stories are challenging to witness—and then use the stories as agreed upon with their tellers (Thomas, 2005). When deciding how to share this information, assess the degree of overlap—including the possible extreme closeness or complete lack thereof—that exists between your audience of participants and your audience of fellow scholars. Then, consider the function that the research product needs to serve for each audience.

Reciprocal information sharing can take many forms. For hybrid work, this may include making information available on a website or other accessible networked presence for group members. You can make in-person participation available through talkbacks, workshops, or other group events. Data can also be shared usefully in a written format—for example, in segments suitable for grants or reports that are practical for an organization with which you have collaborated. For work with artists attempting to access wider audiences, popular press pieces, interviews, podcasts, or film segments can be appealing ways for the researcher to share the artists' work.

Contributing information in formats that are useful for invested audiences is a core outcome of research. Academic writing, academic talks, and university classroom teaching are the traditional homes for what some loftily term the advancement of knowledge. Public-facing writing, public presentations, other educational settings, and various media formats create spaces for people to use and dialogue with research results. Yet not all of the details from research are appropriate to share. Community norms and protocols may dictate that some information is only appropriate for certain audiences and that other information should not be shared at all. Erin Debenport's study *Fixing the Books* (2015), discussed in Chapter 2, provides an example of limiting what is shared based on community norms. Media, particularly when circulated online, can be copied and edited, so it should be shared with care and permission. Refer back to Chapter 6 for details.

WRITING

You have been writing throughout the research process. Writing has taken many forms and purposes: journaling before research began, jottings in the hybrid field, reflections as you work, messages to fellow participants, online posts, and many other iterations. Writing to share research is, in some ways, an extension of these. At this stage, the audience and purpose of your writing changes. You now have the opportunity to address a wider audience and to present concrete ideas—be these refined questions, provisional findings, or a newly emerging theory—to audience(s).

Writing is an interpretive process. And it is hard. Faculty members may not readily admit this to each other and to students, but perhaps we should. Ethnography presents challenges, which this book is designed to help you meet with skill. Those of us who choose to conduct ethnographic research often thrive in situations in which we are part of groups. We choose a research style in which we must be actively engaged in activities that fill our work days, and we are rarely at a desk alone for eight-hour stretches. Especially for researchers who flourish with this work style, transitioning to writing can be a challenge. When writing or other forms of research presentation feel challenging, keep the following in mind:

- Writing itself—or audio editing, or planning a community talkback, or creating a performance—can be a process of developing what you think and identifying how you know what you are learning.
- Critically reading—or listening, viewing, and so forth, for other media—is a productive strategy to make decisions about your own communicative goals and how you will structure and present your own communications.
- Consider your audience when writing or producing other media, performances, or events. Share relevant insights with specific listeners/viewers/readers in mind. Remember that you do not have to communicate every experience from the field: Choose what will be useful.

Writing style is an important option to consider, and it is a real choice. Even for academic publications, there is no one correct style or tone for presenting research. Write in a manner that feels authentic to you and that does the work you want your writing to do. Strategies such as performative writing allow a text to accomplish specific work (Wong, 2008). Develop your professional voice. Become familiar with how writing is typically done in your discipline. Allow yourself to learn new ways of expressing your ideas so that your intended audience can understand your ideas. But you do not have to put on one particular writing style like an off-the-rack garment. I once took an article draft to a group of fellow professors, and I told them that certain sections felt to me like a piece of ill-fitting clothing. We looked through those segments and decided together that there were specific points where my voice got swallowed up by the article's overall style. So I did a revision and wrote myself back in, and the article was stronger for it.

Where to Share

Think ahead about where you want to place your writing to identify factors that shape your written product. The venue you aim for informs your tone, article length, and imagined audience. To decide on these, peruse a variety of sources that are potentially relevant for your scene. For academic sources, look through recent issues of journals in your field. Consider journals in related fields, interdisciplinary journals, or journals on a geographic area or theoretical concern germane to your research. For each relevant area, get a sense of what is being published in different types of journals, from graduate student publications to the flagship journal in your field. Consult editorial policies or a "for authors" guide from each source to learn requirements for writers, such as article length and multimedia possibilities. Keep an eye out on listservs relevant to your area for announcements about calls for special issues or edited book collections that might be a good fit for your work.

For public-facing publishing, review sources that you and your collaborators talk about or share online. Websites, blogs, newspapers, magazines, and other print or online media sources that people in your scene use for information can be possibilities for placing your own writing because you know that people interested in your research's aspect of expressive culture already use them. Public-facing research opportunities for writing include op-eds, popular press articles, newsletters, and blog posts. Publishing in public-facing venues contributes to transparency and accessibility. If you have concerns about blinding or making sure that the double-blind peer review process is successful for an academic publication that you have under review, you can adjust the timing of an article aimed at the general public so that it does not interfere.

Online sources or those that publish both in print and online are particularly useful for expressive culture as they may offer opportunities for embedding video, audio, and color images that enrich your text and engage your readership. When writing regarding research communities that speak multiple languages or who do not speak the language in which your academic articles are published, translating or working with a translator to provide content in multiple languages promotes accessibility.

To select mediums for sharing your writing, consider the following:

- Does the medium allow for video, audio, or other relevant media?
- Does the medium allow for commenting or other interaction?
- In what language or languages is the writing published?
- How widely is it available? To whom is it available?
    - Is the journal available for free, or what is the cost to access content?
    - For subscription journals, is the journal available through a digital format to which many libraries subscribe?
    - Do you maintain copyright?
    - How many copies will be available to you in print or electronically to share with collaborators or community members?
- Is the journal or book peer reviewed?
- How highly do your peers respect the journal or press?
- How long will it take to get your material published?
    - What is the time to publication on your chosen source?
    - What is the acceptance rate?

Use your answers to these questions to help you decide which sources are worth pursuing. Keep a list of alternative sources in the event that you are not able to place your writing in your top choices.[1]

[1]If your material isn't accepted in your first choice venue, work with this list. If the editor offers feedback, read it, decide whether you agree with it, and revise your writing accordingly. When you then submit writing to a new venue, make sure to edit again for the new requirements, style, and audience. Keep streamlining your material, and remember that placement is about fit.

Writing as Guided by Research Design

Projects that involve collaborative research may be well suited for collaborative writing. Jointly written or multi authored texts, whether these be written articles or media products, provide viewpoints from more than one researcher. The process of producing such texts extends collaboration as participants shape the audience-facing product together. Collaboratively produced texts can be worked into the research plan and research outcomes for public scholarship. Eric Lassiter's writing describes some forms that these can take. At the writing stage, these can include inviting consultants to read and edit writing or ethnographer(s) and consultants coproducing texts (2005a). This article offers history and context for these strategies in the author's discipline of anthropology. Chapters 7 and 8 of his book, also cited in this chapter's Further Reading, specifically address writing.

Hybrid fieldwork makes space for, but does not require, collaborative production of texts. It does, however, invite thinking critically about the ways that we and our fellow participants could be involved with research products: We typically work with experiences that are cocreated, so the collaboration and conflict that are part of this coproduction may come out in our responses to the research. Think expansively about the form these responses can take: Cowritten articles, panel discussions with fellow participants, videos, photo essays, audio documentaries, blog posts, and public programs are but a few examples.

Producing texts together, writers come to realizations through dialogue. When I have cowritten articles, the writing actually began before we typed a single word into a draft: The research was the first phase of the writing. When we were ready to start sharing information with an outside audience, we had long conversations about what we would share and with whom. Later, my colleague and I drafted and redrafted outlines. For some sections, one of us took the lead on typing up a draft and then we shared the documents for online editing and real-time conversation. For others, we sat at the same table and talked about what we wanted to accomplish, one of us taking notes as we discussed. We generated a bibliography together and made suggestions on drafts, typically commenting directly on a document in a shared drive. The document we cocreated to share with readers was one expression of our ideas (Przybylski & Niknafs, 2015), but our dialogue pushed each of us into productive new areas and even opened space for future collaborations.

Style and Format

When presenting research as a finished product, many questions emerge for hybrid researchers: How much detail is necessary? What questions have finite answers? For written work, how much of the researcher's personal narrative ends up in the writing? You've read about alternative media formats earlier in this chapter. Ways to communicate ethnographic information in writing, too, are incredibly wide ranging. Personal narrative, novels, and short stories offer advantages for certain types of material; consult Clair (2003) for examples. Researchers newer to academic writing formats will find Chapter 12 of Tracy (2013) helpful for its introduction to types of qualitative narrative. This source also traces how to write titles, abstracts, literature reviews, conceptual frameworks, methodology sections, findings, and conclusions.

At analysis and sharing stages, research moves from the specific to the general.[2] Not all nuances are necessary in order to make the general points; some will be expressed in talks or other discussion forums but not in an article or dissertation chapter. Resist the urge to neatly tie up every loose end. Culture is complex. Human interactions are gloriously messy, and as participant–observers and participants, we are internally inconsistent. Studies where inconsistencies are not artificially smoothed out but rather included with the researcher's analysis are both realistic and convincing (James, 2001). The specifics of a particular scene are usually important insofar as they help answer the research question at hand or suggest ideas that are applicable to other scenes as well. If a particular nuance is very important to you and to your fellow participants, convey it in your writing. Do so even if it is not crucial for the understanding of your larger point. We are engaged in scholarly research, and we are also responsible to ourselves and our fellow participants.

Some studies begin and end with questions. The opening question is refined throughout, new information is shared, and in the course of the research, more productive questions and answers emerge. After doing research for a while, sometimes we forget that not every question will—or even can—end with a concrete and definitive reply. Would research be interesting if things always ended so squarely?

What you read—and who you read—impacts how you write. This straightforward point carries significant implications. It is an invitation to read

---

[2]Remaining with the specific—and resisting the generalizable—is a choice some researchers make. Anthropologist Lila Abu-Lughod's *Writing Women's Worlds: Bedouin Stories* (1993) shows how this type of feminist ethnography remains focused on individual women's lives as a strategic move.

widely, to diversify who we read, and then to select sources that speak to us for deep analytical reads and rereads. Other media to which we attend influences the kind of media we make, so a similar widening and deepening of listening, viewing, and interacting is useful in this realm when we prepare our ideas for audiences. As you consider format, read analyses that are written up with a variety of presentational strategies. Shawn Wilson organizes his book *Research Is Ceremony: Indigenous Research Methods* so that chapters have different audiences; he uses multiple authorial voices throughout. Some sections have a highly conversational tone. Certain chapters are addressed to his kids. Subsequent passages deliver academic references in sections of structured text. Each voice serves a purpose; the text reads like a whole (Wilson, 2008). Trinh T. Minh-ha's *Woman Native Other* presents images, film stills, and poetry in her writing, which is itself a form of analytical work about writing (Trinh, 1989).[3] Revisit other kinds of ethnographic writing to review how literature informed your research question and to reconnect with different strategies for presenting research. Consult Van Maanen (1988) and Goodall (2000) for more models of how one might read and interpret the writing styles in the ethnographies you encounter.

One productive way to hone in on a writing style and format is to review your research log for notes you have made about positionality, as discussed in Chapters 3 and 4. Reflect back on the section of your research log dedicated to your perceptions in the field. Your fieldwork notes offer cues for how you might present yourself and your collaborators based on the experiences you shared in the scene. Your place in the material you share will be guided by research design. Because of the multiple ways we interact with fellow participants, in hybrid ethnography, recognizing your role and the dynamics in your scene are crucial to the research. Yet your story is not necessarily the one that is showcased when you share your results. Critical dance scholar Jacqueline Shea Murphy identifies her position as a non-Indigenous dancer and scholar in her monograph *The People Have Never Stopped Dancing*. Because her project centers on Indigenous dancers and choreographers who have been peripheral in previous scholarship, it is not Shea Murphy's story but her collaborators' stories that take center stage in her written analysis (Shea Murphy, 2007). In contrast, a research design informed by autoethnography, discussed in Chapter 4, positions the researcher's personal experience at the

[3]Trinh's feminist analysis addresses expressive culture and models a presentational strategy that does not conform to a scholarly monograph mold. This strongly theoretical work does not fit into the box of ethnographic writing per se, but ethnographers can learn much from the volume.

center of the fieldwork and thus is expanded upon in detail in the write-up. Communications studies scholar Robin Boylorn uses an autoethnographic approach in her research on Black women's identities in the American South. As a result, her writing begins with detailed personal narrative. This leads the reader through her cultural critique, which incorporates prose crafted with academic citations. Centering on her own experience, she frequently writes in the first person and conveys first-hand experiences that relate to her research question. These writing strategies help Boylorn show how the Sapphire and Mammy stereotypes of Black women are used as tools of social control (Boylorn & Orbe, 2014). These two examples offer useful models for writing that reflect the researcher's choices in the design of the project.

There are multiple productive ways to present findings. As scholars and participants in expressive culture, we can continue to increase the discursive possibilities for ethnographic writing, locating work inside and outside of the existing repertoire (Pratt, 1986). Allow yourself to value your own knowledge and background, whether or not these fit into traditional research paradigms you have encountered in university. Do not force your own thinking into a linear narrative if this is not how you come to research and writing. Experiment with your writing style and use of media and seek a way to honor your own voice.

Writing as Thinking

You can and likely will move back and forth between writing up provisional ideas, asking more questions, revising your conclusions, and continuing to be involved in some way in your scene. To make your findings available to those who will find them useful, there is a time to shift a large portion of your energy to writing and editing. Invite feedback on your work throughout the drafting stage and incorporate ideas into your new draft. When you have a solid draft, one productive option is to send it to your fellow participants who are frequently quoted or whose interactions form the core of the specific argument. Ask questions like, how does this sound to you? Do you feel like the writing accurately conveys your words? Expect that some people might get back to you with requests to make small changes to more accurately convey meaning or tone and that others may not have any adjustments. During this process of dialogue, fellow participants can help check for accuracy overall and might comment on each other's words and experiences. This may point to places that require ongoing conversation. It gives scene members an opportunity to flag concepts of particular importance, show differing opinions on situations, and correct inaccuracies if needed.

Publishing some of your findings through media-rich or interactive formats presents a similar opportunity for inductive thinking. Like writing, this process necessitates structuring, refining, and editing your material. Expect to storyboard, select media, work on transitions, and create appropriate formatting for your video and audio pieces. For one of my projects, I decided to share a condensed version of an interview on the radio for a general audience. To produce a piece for broadcast and for podcasting, I spent hours in the editing studio. I storyboarded. I selected excerpts from the longer interview. I chose music excerpts from the artist's work. I set volume levels, adjusted transitions and fades, and listened repeatedly to ensure the final format sounded clean on air and online.

Sharing research presents challenges. The process of writing up or otherwise preparing your material for presentation may feel like an intensive process because it is one. Budget time for this step, consult the resources you need, and even if you get discouraged, keep going. Something that is involved is not by nature unpleasant. I have found concentrated calm in hours of audio editing; you may find your own groove in a particular aspect of the writing or editing process. Enjoy the flow of good writing when you hit your stride; persist when this is elusive. Goodall's *Writing the New Ethnography* (2000) provides writing prompts that are worth consulting if you are facing roadblocks with your prose. Exercises in John Freeman's *New Performance/New Writing* (2007) and Richardson and St. Pierre's "Writing: A Method of Inquiry" (2005) can also help you jump-start your creativity.

Writing as Collaborative Process

Collaborative writing, like collaborative research, can take a range of scene-specific forms. The voices that emerge in dialogue may weave together into shared ideas, yet sometimes, a coauthored text is particularly valuable when it maintains distinctions from person to person, refusing to offer a single authoritative interpretation. Writing together is a form of shared inquiry. Tools that allow for layered and simultaneous idea generation help a team navigate the mechanics of multiple people writing at the same time. For low-tech options, have multiple people write on a large surface, like a dry erase board, or distribute sticky notes to all participants and then group written responses based on theme. These tactics make the page as big as the room the cowriters inhabit. Online tools, like shared editable documents, mind maps, or for larger groups, live chart generation,[4] provide networked writing spaces. These tools make space for ideas from multiple scene members. However, not everyone needs to participate in exactly the same manner: Some people are more comfortable generating ideas in writing, others editing or compiling, and still others find oral or artistic response better suited to their skills than typing or handwriting ideas.

Dialogic writing mirrors the collaborative process of research. Thinking together does not end when participatory research transitions to writing but rather extends through the writing and results-sharing stages. For examples of a range of approaches to multiauthored writing, consult Graham and Vergunst (2019). Some chapters keep authorial voices separate, some present a single narrative that is multiauthored, and one includes voices from social media participants within the argument. In a chapter responding to group music making, coauthors write that, in order to produce a text, they "have come together to enact a process of co-writing that forms a kind of negotiated dialogic text-based equivalent of the co-production experiences" that were embedded in the research-performance project (p. 51). In the resulting text, block quotes from individual authors pepper the narrative that has a generally unified voice. In addition to the shared written text, the authors published a list of research outputs, including workshops, network days, audio recordings, and videos.

MEDIA

Protecting your collaborators is paramount for media sharing; protect yourself as well. Creating and editing media takes a significant amount of time and resources, so look into whether venues allow you and/or your group to maintain copyright. Creative control and rights to financial gains come with copyright. For publishing venues, determine whether your group maintains copyright in a manner that feels appropriate to the work. Learn about the formats in which you will be publishing. Some projects thrive on creative response media and ongoing circulation, but in other cases, ascertain whether the material will be distributed in a way that makes it highly vulnerable to being pirated or misused by others. The issue of pirating is especially relevant for cases in which material might be divorced from its original context in a way that is disrespectful to your group, as was discussed in Chapter 6.

[4]Software can help facilitate group idea visualization. Poll Everywhere and Mentimeter have free versions useful for asking questions and seeing answers for small to midsize groups.

Sharing media comes with responsibilities. These may be financial, as when your copyrighted material earns a profit. Working with your recordings offers possibilities for collaborative work. When these earn financial rewards, work with group members to allocate the gains appropriately. Your responsibilities are also representational. Be cognizant of the authority audiences are likely to invest in recordings as true representations and be explicit about how materials are edited or otherwise show particular points of view. Attending to these crucial details is worthwhile: Distributing your photos, videos, audio recordings, and other media productively expands the reach of your research beyond traditional publication venues.

Sharing Recordings

Typically, media sharing happens at the analysis stage and then offers a point of departure for analytical writing. It is also an opportunity for research reciprocity. Interacting with media helps clarify your own thoughts. The act of preparing, circulating, and discussing your media offers an opportunity to listen again to your fellow participants and continue your dialogue.

To prepare your media for sharing, edit your files. You have choices about how much to edit your documentation. Minimal editing involves minor changes for clarity. This can include cropping images to focus on the desired aspects of the shot or correcting an image to reduce glare or create clearer light balance. Clipping video or audio segments focuses the audience on crucial moments. Editing media clarifies your own thinking. What did you or your collaborators capture in the recordings? Are there things you wish you had focused on that you did not? As you edit, ask yourself, what are you keeping—and cutting—in your images or recordings and what does this tell you about what you value? Remember to keep unedited versions of your files for your records.

After considering your photos, audio, and video recordings in the larger context of your project, use these files to share information with your audience. If you are planning to use photographs or videos to share a narrative, consider image order and juxtaposition to convey information non-verbally. Write a caption for each photo or video. Captions convey basic information: who took the photo/video, where/when it was taken, and who/what is the subject. Subjects should be named according to the agreements you have with scene participants; images or videos are to be shared only with permission. You could include more detailed information about the context for the recording and connect the caption to the overall story of the photo essay or web post with video embeds. While this is often done with video and images, blog posts and web articles with audio embeds are effective for some projects.

Consider the format(s) that is(are) the most useful for your hybrid field. Sharing a photo album or set of recordings on social media offers participants in that platform immediate access. If you communicate via a platform that typically uses photo and video in posts, like Instagram or Snapchat, sharing media here is a useful choice. Digital storytelling platforms allow for creative interventions, such as the incorporation of audio recordings, audio narrative, still images, and video all in one project. Blogs associated with professional societies or researchers' professional blogs offer examples of how images, video, and/or audio can be curated for a public audience.

Finally, ask for and listen to feedback. Let shared documentation be a springboard for future conversations. Pay attention to responses on social media. What attracts likes or other forms of attention, and what is less engaging? Make note of participants' written comments. Discuss your documentation in person as well, if this makes sense for your scene. This can be accomplished either by sharing sound, video, or images with some participants face-to-face or by asking verbally about the material you shared online. As you contribute to the scene, your material becomes part of the dialogue.

The Authority of Recordings

As was discussed in Chapter 6, dialogic photo, audio, and video editing are well suited to some kinds of questions in expressive culture research. Field recordings document aspects of your experience in the field, show what you (or the collaborator[s] who recorded the media) find relevant, and give your audience a sense of immersion in your scene. Because media often feel more immediate than interpretive writing about the expressive culture you document, choose your media carefully. As Mike Ball and Greg Smith detail in their article "Technologies of Realism?," audiences tend to understand that writing is done from the perspective of the author, yet they may interpret field photos and recordings as unmediated (2001). This propensity places significant responsibility on the researcher. Your perspective and edits may not be immediately obvious to your audience, but the media you share tells a story about your scene that is filtered through your perspective. Offer captions and context. When practical, offer information about how the recording was made. Think carefully about how something like a photo essay, documentary film, or podcast portrays your scene. When in doubt, check back in with your collaborators about your material.

Photographs and recordings offer possibilities that written texts alone do not. This can be heard through dialogic recording, through which participants come into a form of conversation that is not limited to words. Steven

Feld and Nii Otoo Annan released two albums as part of a dialogic recording process.[5] When reflecting on this experience, Feld does attempt to put some of what he learned into words. The 2012 album included Annan's playing of "Africa Take Five," an instrumental track that riffs on "Take Five," which was popularized by the Dave Brubeck Quartet. Listening to Annan's musical citation, Feld hears "an African listening history and a new way of listening to and with the time experiment of swing in 5/4 offered in Brubeck's 'Take Five.' This is one way that listening to African histories of listening and engaging them through recording, opens us up to other ways of thinking about the play of time, groove and multiple metre" (Feld, 2015b, p. 100). Already an important opening into localized listening practices, this way of hearing also questions established narratives. As Feld explains, "One of those narratives is distinctly political, because 'Take Five' was, in its time, very much racialized as the cool jazz played and listened to by whites, Europeans and educated elites. Nii Otoo's creative Africanization of 'Take Five' opens up the possibility that the song was heard differently in Africa" (Feld, 2015b, p. 100). By making the album together, the musicians listened and then listened to their own listening in order to get a better sense of the social context for the music they made. Consent and participation among members of a scene determine what media can be shared and with whom. In this example, Feld and Nii Otoo communicated about what to record and how to process and distribute the audio. Feld's writing about making dialogic recordings reflects this collaboration.

OTHER FORMATS FOR SHARING

Aspects of your research project may lend themselves to being shared with invested parties. For example, a map that you created as part of a larger argument might be useful in and of itself for members of your scene, as was described for W. F. Hsu's research in Chapter 5 (Hsu, 2013). Formats for which you might edit parts of your results include the following:

- Websites
- Films
- Photo essays

[5]These albums are Nii Otoo Annan and Steven Feld, 2012. *Ghana Sea Blues* (Santa Fe: VoxLox), and Nii Otoo Annan and Steven Feld, 2008. *Bufo Variations* (Santa Fe: VoxLox).

- Video or audio documentaries
- Infographics
- Digital collections
- Electronic museums
- Podcasts
- Maps

The places you and your scene members interact are ideal places to start for sharing these research products. Some may be shared in person, such as in a guided small-group discussion with fellow participants. Selected recordings could be uploaded, with permission, on media-sharing sites, such as a SoundCloud page or curated YouTube channel. Photos and media clips could be shared on the same social media platforms in which you participate for your study. Adapting ethnographic information for some of these formats will require special training. Taking courses in documentary film and audio editing or securing a museum internship can be productive if you want to pursue these specialized and fruitful forms of distribution. Whole bodies of literature and practice have grown around using theatre and related presentational means to share ethnographic work. This endeavor also requires extensive study and practice (Jones, 2002). Tedlock describes examples of theatre that come from fieldwork. For example, farmers in Chiapas who began the theatre company *Lo'il Maxil* share their own Mayan history and culture with audiences, while a researcher, here an anthropologist, worked alongside the ensemble as its dramaturge (Tedlock, 2005).

Often embedded into multimedia websites or written articles, infographics visually convey trends or takeaways from large data sets. This is a common feature in public-facing research. Hybrid ethnographers may find images useful to communicate relevant subsets of social media data. For strategies on making and sharing infographics, consult Rose (2016), Chapter 13. This chapter also provides guidance on launching a research website to share findings.

An interactive format incorporating many kinds of media, virtual museums share curated material with a public audience online. One well-developed example is the Smithsonian Latino Center Virtual Museum, which offers digital collections, online games, immersive experiences, and lesson plans. This content is available thanks to the labor of scholars, community members, and museum curators. Trained in anthropology, Xóchitl Chávez distributes her research in multiple mediums. Chávez shares her research on women's participation in Zapotec bands in Oaxaca and California in scholarly forums and on a public-facing bilingual website (2017).[6] In 2016, she traveled throughout Southern California to record and broadcast interviews on cultural practices related to regional Día de los Muertos events. In this public-facing scholarship, Chávez used her ethnographic training to conduct interviews about food preparation, making altars, and other living traditions. She presented interviews live through the Smithsonian Latino Center's Ustream channel.[7] These broadcasts are archived and searchable for public viewing via the video-sharing website YouTube. This kind of public-facing work that incorporates text, image, audio, and video is an expanding edge of research publication. Some scholars curate material for physical museum spaces, wherein photos and recordings invite interaction so that audience members experience material relevant to their own lives. These kinds of shows are particularly useful for scenarios in which audience members do not have reliable access to telecommunications infrastructure that facilitates sharing of media-rich data files (Emberly, 2015). The next chapter concerns more ways to continue to adapt to changes in hybrid field research.

SUMMARY

Sharing research offers opportunities for reflection and reciprocity. Publications and media distribution also need to respect the protocols, privacy guidelines, and information-sharing limits established by your research design. Choosing multiple mediums is often productive for hybrid ethnography, as it allows you to reach scholars, fellow participants, and other overlapping interested audiences. Writing is an interpretive process—one that presents the researcher with many choices. Select styles and formats that reflect the material, the researcher(s), and the scene to convey ideas in a convincing and useful manner. Communicating results across the physical/digital divide will become even more useful as the field continues to change.

---

[6]English and Spanish versions are available at http://boomingbandas.com.

[7]Available at http://www.latino.si.edu. The mobile broadcasts are accessible at https://www.youtube.com/channel/UCzY4FzKJyXt_OJhU1MazVeA/videos?view_as=subscriber. On Google Arts and Culture, a collaborative piece with contributions and curation by Xánath Caraza, Stacey Fox, Melissa Carrillo, and Paola Ramirez is available at "La Catrina, Lady of the Dead," https://artsandculture.google.com/exhibit/la-catrina-lady-of-the-dead-smithsonian-latino-virtual-museum/ngKy6vigFS4BJw?hl=en.

FURTHER READING

Ball, M., & Smith, G. (2001). Technologies of realism? Ethnographic uses of photography and film. In P. Atkinson, A. Coffey, S. Delamont, J. Lofland, & L. Lofland (Eds.), *Handbook of ethnography* (pp. 302–319). London: Sage.

Chávez, X. C. (2017). Booming bands of Los Angeles: Gender and the practice of transnational Zapotec philharmonic brass bands. In J. Kun (Ed.), *The tide was always high: The music of Latin America in Los Angeles* (pp. 260–266). Oakland: University of California Press.

Clair, R. P. (2003). *Expressions of ethnography: Novel approaches to qualitative methods*. Albany: State University of New York Press.

Emberly, A. (2015). Repatriating childhood: Issues in the ethical return of Venda children's musical materials from the archival collection of John Blacking. In A. Harris, N. Thieberger, & L. Barwick (Eds.), *Research, records, and responsibility* (pp. 163–186). Sydney, Australia: Sydney University Press.

Freeman, J. (2007). *New performance/new writing: Texts and contexts in postmodern performance.* New York: Palgrave Macmillan.

Graham, H., & Vergunst, J. (2019). *Heritage as community research: Legacies of co-production.* Bristol, UK: Bristol University Press.

James, C. (2001). Cultural change in Mistissini: Implications for self determination and cultural survival. In C. H. Scott (Ed.), *Aboriginal autonomy and development in Northern Quebec and Labrador* (pp. 316–331). Vancouver, Canada: UBC Press.

Lassiter, L. (2005a). Collaborative ethnography and public anthropology. *Current Anthropology*, *46*(1), 83–106.

Lassiter, L. (2005b). *The Chicago guide to collaborative ethnography.* Chicago: University of Chicago Press.

Pratt, M. L. (1986). Fieldwork in common places. In J. Clifford & G. E. Marcus (Eds.), *Writing culture: The poetics and politics of ethnography* (pp. 27–50). Berkeley: University of California Press.

Przybylski, L., & Niknafs, N. (2015). Practice what you preach: Teaching and learning popular music in higher education through interdisciplinary collaboration. *Iaspm@journal*, *5*(1), 100–123.

Richardson, L., & St. Pierre, E. A. (2005). Writing: A method of inquiry. In N. K. Denzin & Y. S. Lincoln (Eds.), *The SAGE handbook of qualitative research* (pp. 959–978). Thousand Oaks, CA: Sage.

Rose, G. (2016). *Visual methodologies* (4th ed.). London: Sage.

Shea Murphy, J. (2007). *The people have never stopped dancing: Native American modern dance histories*. Minneapolis: University of Minnesota Press.

Tedlock, B. (2003). Ethnography and ethnographic representation. In N. K. Denzin & Y. S. Lincoln (Eds.), *Strategies of qualitative inquiry* (pp. 165–213). London: Sage.

Thomas, Q. R. A. (2005). Honoring the oral traditions of my ancestors through storytelling. In L. Brown & S. Strega (Eds.), *Research as resistance* (pp. 127–151). Toronto, Canada: Canadian Scholars' Press.

Tracy, S. (2013). *Qualitative research methods: Collecting evidence, crafting analysis, and communicating impact*. Malden, MA: Wiley-Blackwell.

Trinh, T. M. (1989). *Woman, native, other*. Bloomington: Indiana University Press.

Van Maanen, J. (1988). *Tales of the field: On writing ethnography*. Chicago: University of Chicago Press.

Wilson, S. (2008). *Research is ceremony: Indigenous research methods*. Black Point, NS, Canada: Fernwood Publications.

10 CONCLUSION

Remaining Nimble in the Changing Field

When I was teaching early in my career, I was sharing some songs by a relatively unknown artist with students in a popular music course. Her music was primarily available on her MySpace page. Just a few years later, a student of mine was surprised that people were still using MySpace, and not too long after that, none of my students were even aware of the platform. Social media platforms come and go as do media-sharing sites, and it is helpful to stay current with the specific avenues that collaborators find useful. At the same time, though details may change, certain elements remain consistent. The hybrid field is not going away. Despite initial enthusiasm around internet-based communities, people still connect in person; musicians, dancers, and other artists often choose to create and share projects together in real time. While computers, phones, and other devices change, they continue to allow users to bring internet-based communication into physical locations of exchange. And even if specific sites and platforms alter over time, there is a through line in the kinds of information shared online. Just as skills you gain in one physical field can inform future research in a new place, skills you gain as a researcher moving with your fellow participants between an on-the-ground rehearsal and an online-mediated dialogue are relevant, even if the specific platforms change.

The pace of change can feel dizzying. As researchers, many of us grew up without the social media sites or even regular web access that now make online activity part of regular interactions for significant numbers of people. Due to age, location, or access, we may have come later to the tablets and smartphones that have allowed online interactions to nearly seamlessly intersperse themselves into daily life. Even emerging researchers whose lives as students have always entailed online connectivity are coming into a networked way of being that is not yet fully understood. We do not yet know how the increasing integration of digital and physical fields will alter our social and cultural lives. Nor do we have a complete picture of the implications of how lack of access to affordable and reliable internet in some areas and increasing screen time in others will differently affect the futures of individuals and groups with varying levels of access. If the internet is a teenager, as it is commonly described to be, then the increasing permeation of digital and physical interactions is still a child.

Because of the pace of change, this book prepares you for conceptual shifts in the hybrid field and provides you with tools and resources to conduct integrated ethnography. Over the course of all of our careers, we can anticipate ongoing significant change. To prepare for some of these changes, we can listen closely so as to be ready to adopt platforms that become relevant to our communities. Friendster has been superseded by Facebook; groups that used to share media on MySpace have shifted to BandCamp and YouTube. To remain nimble in the changing field, take time to read and listen for changes in technology. Try out a new space or communication strategy if it is gaining traction in your scene. Also, remember that you may stay on a message board or "unhip" site if activity continues there. You may even try out these different strategies simultaneously. Depending on the community in which you do your research, you may or may not need to be an early adopter of all new devices and platforms: Take your cues from your collaborators, and meet them where they are.

We also need to be aware of how the social attitudes people have toward technology in our lives are changing and how these changes vary across scenes and individual participants. With increasing news coverage about how companies profit from consumer data, do people in your community interact differently with each other? Perhaps people put less personal information online, shift some conversations to phone calls or face-to-face interactions, or choose other mediums for sharing photos, videos, or other files. Perhaps people develop their technological savvy in order to use data to, say, target potential audience members or reach new people with similar interests.[1]

Access, cost, and social attitudes all impact the way in which each particular hybrid fieldsite is composed and potentially recomposed. Do your fellow participants begin to shy away from certain devices that bring online communities into offline life? Keep your ears open to hear if members are purchasing "dumb phones" designed not to make online apps and sites available and appealing. If you are working with people who never had smartphone access—by choice or by circumstance—how does their approach toward

[1] An interesting example comes with the revelation of the large numbers of bots on Twitter designed to masquerade as real people. This can spark reactions from abandoning the platform to treating it and its influencers with additional scrutiny to purchasing bot followers of one's own to potentially increase one's influence.

technology shift in potentially divergent ways? Keep updating your fieldnotes about your own attitudes as well. If media overload is bringing forth your luddite tendencies while other scene participants are embracing the integration of the home robot and smart watch to integrate online media more often in more places, this will affect what you see, hear, and don't hear.

As individuals change behaviors about how we integrate technology into our lives, tech companies alter some of their strategies, and it behooves us as researchers to learn what we can about how new algorithms, policies, and procedures affect communication. For proprietary algorithms on platforms like Facebook, the way Google uses data from home robots like Google Home, or decreases in net neutrality that alter the sites our fellow community members can access, we must also sit with the uncomfortable realization that some specific kinds of information are not accessible to researchers.

This book has focused on using tools that are currently common in the hybrid field. As mediascapes change, the kinds of devices and tools for circulating media will alter with them. Other devices, too, may become relevant or may peak in use and then subside. Keep listening to other participants, and be ready to adapt your tools as relevant.

The hybrid field incorporates the domain of traditional face-to-face ethnography. The direction of changes in hybrid work is not necessarily toward increasing use of networked technologies as part of daily life. Yes, we are in a time in which new technologies are emerging rapidly. Even so, cost, access, personal attitude shifts, and political climate all impact the adoption, rejection, or creative reuse of these technologies in the lives of researchers and fellow participants. Your scene members may move toward more face-to-face connection, physical written communication, telephone calls, or other offline forms of interaction. Be aware that "off-label" uses for new technologies emerge—you may observe or even take part in leading creative misuse of emergent technologies in ways that serve your group's needs.

Even among tech enthusiasts, people sometimes carve out moments that are not networked. I remember clearly being at a show in which the headliner asked us all to put away our phones, not to record or take photos but to just try to have an unmediated experience with the music and each other. I was surprised at first, but all around me in the venue, people put down their phones and kept them away for the show duration. Ask questions about moments like these that are offline by choice. What happens in those spaces of physical encounter that are marked by the specific absence of digital interactivity? What changes in the quality of the experience?

CHANGES IN TOOLS

Hybrid ethnography will change as new tools become available. It will be helpful to upgrade your research kit as recording devices improve in quality or decrease in cost and thus become available to you (see Chapter 6). As an example, photovoice-style projects (wherein multiple community members take photographs to contribute to the larger project) used to rely on technologies like disposable film cameras. Digital cameras of decent quality have become significantly cheaper and physical film development less common and more cumbersome, so multiple-photographer projects can now often rely on an all-digital set of cameras. As in this example, changes in technology sometimes present just a change in degree, not kind, so the procedures around communication and strategy to produce a multivocal research project remain consistent.

For both data collection and analysis, changes in software invite regular reevaluation. Some of these changes mean that programs increase in sophistication. For example, speech recognition tools, which can be used to help transcribe notes or interviews, have increased in fealty. Researchers who previously dismissed these as too error-prone might reconsider them now. Current limitations, like programs that cannot easily accommodate multiple speakers or languages, may be updated in the future. Other adaptations to be on the lookout for include availability on new operating systems or devices. For example, software for data collection and organizing (see Chapter 4) that begins on one operating system often expands to include others, and features only available for, say, Windows may later be available for Mac, Linux, and so forth. These programs can also add new features to make them practical for new devices. "Lite" versions for phones and tablets can increase in sophistication, making them more powerful and therefore more viable for research use.

Of course, some changes actually make software less viable. Old software stops being updated, companies are bought out, and some tools are phased out over time. You may find this obsolescence while using data capture programs, for example (see Chapter 6). Update your software when prudent, work on fixes for open-source programs if you have the inclination, and look around for new programs should a phase-out occur. For fieldsites where highly specific tools are required to gain and share the information you need, you may already be relying on tools you develop or amend yourself.

Not all changes in software move toward increased ease for data collection and analysis. Typically, for recording, storage capacity increases, image and sound quality increases, and cost decreases over time. Generally, analysis tools become more sophisticated and able to handle more types of data, even if cost does not decrease. Yet social attitudes change the way technology is available to us; we are not necessarily barreling toward sophisticated data collection. Rules and perceptions about privacy change the way tools are designed. For example, while smartphones and applications for them could have the capacity to easily record incoming and outgoing audio and video, many product companies and app developers have chosen to limit this capacity due to public standards of privacy. Of course, researchers are ethically obliged to obtain permission for any kind of recording, and we maintain clear communication about how recordings are to be used. Yet even when permission is granted, the tools we have available sometimes require work-arounds (see Chapter 7) to function as desired.

A NOTE ABOUT CONSISTENCY

For all this—useful and relevant—talk about changes in the field, do not lose sight of what is constant over time. In Chapter 1, you were introduced to key aspects of the hybrid field. Even as specific platforms or scenes shift, you can anticipate ongoing relevance of these strategies you have developed to address the features of the hybrid field. You continue to be one of many documenters; there is no indication that the volume of relevant data is likely to decrease. While new tools may become available and older ones emerge as relevant again, the method of purposefully using available data collection, organization, and analysis strategies remains consistent. As participants continue to creatively engage with media across the hybrid field, you continue to think situationally about how different participants contribute to your scene beyond a strict producer/consumer divide. You and your fellow participants continue to take on multiple roles across the fieldsite, and the strategies you use to understand your community members in their multiplicities will remain relevant. Now, as in the future, some nuances will remain that cannot be subsumed in generalities. The hybrid field continues to require synchronous and asynchronous communication and to encourage nimble movement among all of the places involved in the relevant fieldsite. Time management strategies and careful self-reflexivity about roles will continue to serve you well in a changing field.

The responsibilities and possibilities of hybrid ethnography, too, are stable. Because this kind of ethnography responds to multiple close connections between researcher and fellow participants, dialogue continues to be a central feature to the work. Decolonial and feminist methodologies are helpful; reciprocity is anticipated. Hybrid ethnography embraces emerging models for sharing research—what exactly these models are will change, but their networked, public-facing nature is ongoing.

THEORIZING CHANGE

Engage with theoretical literature appropriate to your scene and experience in it. Observing technology use in your changing field is part of, and not the end of, the way you conceptualize your hybrid research site. In an influential text, Donna Haraway uses the figure of the cyborg to theorize how society is changing as boundaries between human and nonhuman animal, organism and machine, and the physical and nonphysical are being eroded (Haraway, 1991). This fascinating example continues by probing what a hybrid human-machine figure could mean for social organization. As both-and, in-between and neither, the cyborg makes a case for the way a feminist political project is strategically enacted; Haraway's argument has been expanded upon in a variety of situations. Haraway calls attention to our intimate reliance upon electronics. Echoes of her conceptualization of the posthuman can be heard from daily conversations in blog responses to the most recent advances in wearable technology to conversations about smartphones and social media in which we hear anxieties, possibilities, and a wide range of potential implications of a convergence between our physical bodies and the technologies that we regularly employ.

Social formations that are emerging in the hybrid field involve a range of types of participation. We continue to interact directly with our fellow humans while also engaging on platforms guided by changing algorithms and logics whose effects are not yet fully known. We are experiencing increasing interpenetration of Artificial Intelligence into human social spheres. Thinking reflectively about the changing nature of the hybrid field means recognizing that changes in aspects of the field known to be impacted by digital technologies may even alter the way we operate in those that at first appear not to be networked at all. That is, as we shift our sociality in online networked aspects of the field, we may well take some of those attitudinal and behavioral shifts to aspects of the field that we conceptualize as fully offline.

Think carefully about conversations with fellow participants about technology in the hybrid scene, revisit your notes on your own reactions, and observe the role of physical space interactions. How do our experiences of materiality and our relationship to embodied knowledge alter as we have new opportunities for digitally mediated encounters? What happens if physical aspects of the fieldsite become inaccessible? How do conceptions of self- and group-making come into the fullness that exists between the purely digital and purely physical, and what other boundaries are questioned as these categorizations emerge? Listen across your scene for questions about the nature of the hybrid field itself, consult this chapter's Further Reading for models of how other researchers are theorizing change, and find what you need to adapt and extend to address your fieldsite.

SUMMARY

This book has guided you through ethnographic research in our contemporary world where the digital and the physical interact so deeply as to not be fully separable. By now, you have theorized how the hybrid field itself impacts your scene. This hybrid research landscape will continue to change over time. As the scenes in which people make and share expressive culture keep shifting, remain open to emerging technologies and continue to reflexively catalog your own attitudes toward these shifts. Dialogue with your fellow participants about their attitudes toward technology. Learn what you can about changes in platforms and devices, and recognize when transparency is not fully available. It is important to keep on-the-ground aspects of your site in focus and to recognize that changes in hybrid research may turn toward increasing use of some physical forms of communication. Finally, revisit previous chapters of this volume as needed, recognizing that ethnography is never a strictly linear process.

FURTHER READING

Haraway, D. (1991). *Simians, cyborgs, and women: The reinvention of nature.* New York: Routledge.

Haraway, D. (2016). *Staying with the trouble.* Durham, NC: Duke University Press.

Hayles, K. (2005). *My mother was a computer: Digital subjects and literary texts.* Chicago: University of Chicago Press.

Ihde, D. (2010). *Embodied technics.* Copenhagen, Denmark: Automatic Press Publishing.

James, J. (2013). "Concerning Violence": Frantz Fanon's rebel intellectual in search of a Black cyborg. *South Atlantic Quarterly, 112*(1), 57–70.

Miller, K. (2012). *Playing along: Digital games, YouTube, and virtual performance.* Oxford, UK: Oxford University Press.

Whitehead, N. L., & Wesch, M. (2012). *Human no more: Digital subjectivities, unhuman subjects, and the end of anthropology.* Boulder: University Press of Colorado.

BIBLIOGRAPHY

Abu-Lughod, L. (1993). *Writing women's worlds: Bedouin stories*. Berkeley, University of California Press.

Adelusi-Adeluyi, A. (2018). *New maps of Old Lagos*. Retrieved from newmapsold-lagos.com

Allen, S. L. (Ed.). (1994). *Anthropology: Informing Global citizens*. Westport, CT: Bergin & Garvey.

American Anthropological Association. (2007). Code of ethics. In A. C. G. M. Robben & J. A. Sluka (Eds.), *Ethnographic fieldwork: An anthropological reader* (pp. 325–330). Malden, MA: Blackwell Publishing.

American Anthropological Association. (2012). *Statement on ethics: Principles of professional responsibilities*. Arlington, VA: American Anthropological Association. Retrieved from www.aaanet.org/profdev/ethics/upload/Statement-on-Ethics-Principles-of-Professional-Responsibility.pdf

American Psychological Association. (2017). *Ethical principles of psychologists and code of conduct*. Retrieved from http://www.apa.org/ethics/code/

Araújo, S. (2006). Conflict and violence as theoretical tools in present-day ethnomusicology: Notes on a dialogic ethnography of sound practices in Rio de Janeiro. *Ethnomusicology, 50*(2), 287–313.

Atkinson, P., Coffey, A., & Delamont, S. (2003). *Key themes in qualitative research: Continuities and change*. Walnut Creek, CA: Alta Mira Press.

Ball, M., & Smith, G. (2001). Technologies of realism? Ethnographic uses of photography and film. In P. Atkinson, A. Coffey, S. Delamont, J. Lofland, & L. Lofland (Eds.), *Handbook of ethnography* (pp. 302–319). London: Sage.

Barkin, G., & Stone, G. (2000). Anthropology: Blurring the lines and moving the camera: The beginning of web-based scholarship in anthropology. *Social Science Computer Review, 18*(2), 125–131.

Barnhardt, R., & Kawagley, A. O. (2005). Indigenous knowledge systems and Alaska native ways of knowing. *Anthropology and Education Quarterly, 36*(1), 8–23.

Beebe, J. (2014). *Rapid qualitative inquiry: A field guide to team-based assessment*. Lanham, MD: Rowman & Littlefield.

Bernard, H. R. (2011). *Research methods in anthropology: Qualitative and quantitative approaches*. Lanham, MD: Alta Mira Press.

Berry, M. J., Argüelles, C. C. , Cordis, S., Ihmoud, S., & Velasquez Estrada, E. (2017). Toward a fugitive anthropology: Gender, race, and violence in the field. *Cultural Anthropology, 32*(4), 537–565.

Boellstorff, T., Nardi, B. A., Pearce, C., & Taylor, T. L. (2012). *Ethnography and virtual worlds: A handbook of method.* Princeton, NJ: Princeton University Press.

Boylorn, R. M., & Orbe, M. P. (Eds.). (2014). *Critical autoethnography: Intersecting cultural identities in everyday life.* Walnut Creek, CA: Left Coast Press.

Bruckman, A. (2002). Studying the amateur artist: A perspective on disguising data collected in human subjects research on the internet. *Ethics and Information Technology, 4*(3), 217–231.

Buchanan, E. A., & Ess, C. (2008). Internet research ethics: The field and its critical issues. In K. E. Himma & H. T. Tavani (Eds.), *The handbook of information and computer ethics* (pp. 273–292). Hoboken, NJ: John Wiley and Sons.

Buckland, T. (Ed.). (1999). *Dance in the field: Theory, method, and issues in dance ethnography.* New York: St. Martin's Press.

Burnim, M. (1985). Culture bearer and tradition bearer. *Ethnomusicology, 29*(3), 432–447.

Burrell, J. (2009). The field site as a network. *Field Methods, 21*(2), 181–199.

Butler, M. J. (2014). *Playing with something that runs: Technology, improvisation, and composition.* New York: Oxford University Press.

Cagle, M. (2016, October 11). *Facebook, Instagram, and Twitter provided data access for a surveillance product marketed to target activists of color* [ACLU of Northern California]. Retrieved from https://www.aclunc.org/blog/facebook-instagram-and-twitter-provided-data-access-surveillance-product-marketed-target

Chávez, X. C. (2017). Booming bands of Los Angeles: Gender and the practice of transnational Zapotec philharmonic brass bands. In J. Kun (Ed.), *The tide was always high: The music of Latin America in Los Angeles* (pp. 260–266). Oakland: University of California Press.

Cheek, J. (2005). The practice and politics of funded qualitative research. In N. K. Denzin & Y. S. Lincoln (Eds.), *The SAGE handbook of qualitative research* (3rd ed.). Thousand Oaks, CA: Sage.

Choi, J., Kushner, K. E., Mill, J., & Lai, D. W. L. (2012). Understanding the language, the culture, the experience: Translation in cross-cultural research. *International Journal of Qualitative Methods, 11*(5), 652–665.

Clair, R. P. (2003). *Expressions of ethnography: Novel approaches to qualitative methods.* Albany: State University of New York Press.

Clifford, J. (1988). *The predicament of culture.* Cambridge, MA: Harvard University Press.

Clifford, J., & Marcus, G. E. (Eds.). (1986). *Writing culture: The poetics and politics of ethnography.* Berkeley: University of California Press.

Collins, P. H., & Bilge, S. (2016). *Intersectionality.* Malden, MA: Polity Press.

Comaroff, J., & Comaroff, J. (1986). Christianity and colonialism in South Africa. *American Ethnologist, 13*(1), 1–22.

Conquergood, D. (1985). Performing as a moral act: Ethical dimensions of the ethnography of performance. *Literature in Performance, 5*, 1–13.

Conquergood, D. (1991). Rethinking Ethnography. *Communication Monographs, 58*, 179–194.

Cox, J. (2015, January 6). I was taught to dox by a master [Blog post]. Retrieved from https://www.dailydot.com/layer8/dox-doxing-protection-how-to/

Crafts, S. D., Cavicchi, D., Keil, C., & The Music in Daily Life Project. (1993). *My music: Explorations of music in daily life*. Middletown, CT: Wesleyan University Press.

Crenshaw, K. (1991). Mapping the margins: Intersectionality, identity politics, and violence against women of color. *Stanford Law Review, 43*(6), 1241–1299.

D'Amico-Samuels, D. (1991). Undoing fieldwork. In F. Harrison (Ed.), *Decolonizing anthropology*. Washington, DC: Association of Black Anthropologists and the American Anthropological Association.

Debenport, E. (2015). *Fixing the books: Secrecy, literacy, and perfectibility in Indigenous New Mexico*. Santa Fe, NM: School for Advanced Research Press.

Densmore, F. (1918). *Teton Sioux music*. Washington, DC: Government Printing Office.

Denzin, N. K. (2013). *Interpretive autoethnography*. Thousand Oaks, CA: Sage.

Dibbell, J. (2008, January 18). Mutilated furries, flying phalluses: Put the blame on griefers, the sociopaths of the virtual world. *Wired*. Retrieved from https://www.wired.com/2008/01/mf-goons/

Dicks, B., Mason, B., Coffey, A., & Atkinson, P. (2005). *Qualitative research and hypermedia: Ethnography for the digital age*. London: Sage.

Dorrian, M., & Rose, G. (Eds.). (2013). *Deterritorialisations: Revisioning landscape and politics*. London: Black Dog Publishing.

Driskill, Q.-L., Finley, C., Gilley, B. J., & Morgensen, S. L. (2011). *Queer Indigenous studies: Critical interventions in theory, politics, and literature*. Tucson University of Arizona Press.

Durham, A. (2014). *Home with hip hop feminism*. New York: Peter Lang.

Emberly, A. (2015). Repatriating childhood: Issues in the ethical return of Venda children's musical materials from the archival collection of John Blacking. In A. Harris, N. Thieberger, & L. Barwick (Eds.), *Research, records, and responsibility* (pp. 163–186). Sydney, Australia: Sydney University Press.

Emerson, R. M., Fretz, R. I., & Shaw, L. L. (2011). *Writing ethnographic fieldnotes*. Chicago: University of Chicago Press.

Ess, C., & AoIR Ethics Working Committee. (2002). *Ethical decision-making and internet research*. Approved by AoIR, November 27, 2002. Retrieved from http://aoir.org/reports/ethics.pdf

Evans-Cowley, J. S. (2010). Planning in the age of Facebook: The role of social networking in planning processes. *GeoJournal: Spatially integrated social sciences and humanities, 75*(5), 407–420.

Feld, S. (1987). Dialogic editing: Interpreting how Kaluli read sound and sentiment. *Cultural Anthropology, 2*(2), 190–210.

Feld, S. (2015a). Collaboration in/through ethnographic film: A conversation with Antonello Ricci. *VOCL, 12*.

Feld, S. (2015b). Listening to histories of listening: Collaborative experiments in acoustemology with Nii Otoo Annan. In G. Borio (Ed.), *Musical listening in an age of technological reproduction* (pp. 91–103). Farnham, UK; Burlington, VT: Ashgate Publishing.

Fernback, J. (1999). There is a there there. In S. Jones (Ed.), *Doing internet research* (pp. 203–220). Thousand Oaks, CA: Sage.

Fink, A. (2017). *How to conduct surveys: A step-by-step guide* (6th ed.). Thousand Oaks, CA: Sage.

Fox, A. (2013). Repatriation as reanimation through reciprocity. In P. V. Bohlman (Ed.), *The Cambridge history of world music* (Vol. 1, pp. 522–554). Cambridge, UK: Cambridge University Press.

Freeman, J. (2007). *New performance/new writing: Texts and contexts in postmodern performance.* New York: Palgrave Macmillan.

Geertz, C. (1973). *The interpretation of cultures.* New York: Basic Books.

Geertz, C. (1998, October 22). Deep hanging out. *New York Review of Books*, pp. 69–72.

Goodall, H. L. B. (2000). *Writing the new ethnography.* Lanham, MD: Alta Mira Press.

Graham, H., & Vergunst, J. (2019). *Heritage as community research: Legacies of co-production.* Bristol, UK: Bristol University Press.

Grbich, C. (2013). *Qualitative data analysis* (2nd ed.). Thousand Oaks, CA: Sage.

Green, K. (2014). Doing double Dutch methodology: Playing with the practice of participant observer. In D. Paris & M. T. Winn (Eds.), *Humanizing research* (pp. 147–160). Thousand Oaks, CA: Sage.

Gressgárd, R. (2008). Mind the gap: Intersectionality, complexity and "the event." *Theory and Science, 10*(1), 1–16.

Haraway, D. (1991). *Simians, cyborgs, and women: The reinvention of nature.* New York: Routledge.

Harris, A., Thieberger, N., & Barwick, L. (Eds.). (2015). *Research, records, and responsibility.* Sydney, Australia: Sydney University Press.

Harrison, K., Pettan, S., & Mackinlay, E. (Eds.). (2010). *Applied ethnomusicology: Historical and contemporary approaches.* Newcastle Upon Tyne, UK: Cambridge Scholars Publishing.

Herising, F. (2005). Interrupting positions: Critical thresholds and queer pro/positions. In L. Brown & S. Strega (Eds.), *Research as resistance* (pp. 127–151). Toronto, Canada: Canadian Scholars' Press.

Herndon, M., & McLeod, N. (1983). *Field manual for ethnomusicology.* Norwood, PA: Norwood Editions.

Hill, J. (2007). "Global Folk Music" fusions: The reification of transnational relationships and the ethics of cross-cultural appropriations in Finnish contemporary folk music. *Yearbook for Traditional Music, 39*, 50–83.

Hofman, A. (2010). Maintaining the distance, othering the subaltern: Rethinking ethnomusicologists' engagement in advocacy and social justice. In K. Harrison, E. Mackinlay, & S. Pettan (Eds.), *Applied Ethnomusicology: Historical and Contemporary Approaches* (pp. 22–35). Newcastle upon Tyne, UK: Cambridge Scholars Publishing.

Houtman, G., & Zeitlyn, D. (1996). Information technology and anthropology. *Anthropology Today, 12*(3), 1–3.

Hsu, W. F. (2013). Mapping the Kominas' sociomusical transnation: Punk, diaspora, and digital media. *Asian Journal of Communication, 23*(4), 386–402.

IASA Technical Committee. (2017). *The safeguarding of the audiovisual heritage: Ethics, principles, and preservations strategy* (W. Prentice & L. Gaustad, Eds.). International Association of Sound and Audiovisual Practices. Retrieved from www.iasa-web.org/tc03/ethics-principles-preservation-strategy

Ikeda, L. L. (2014). Re-visioning family: Mahuwahine and male-to-female Transgender in contemporary Hawai'i. In N. Besnier & K. Alexeyeff (Eds.), *Gender on the edge: Transgender, gay, and other Pacific Islanders* (pp. 135–161). Honolulu: University of Hawaii Press.

International Sociological Association. (2001). *Code of ethics.* Retrieved from https://www.isa-sociology.org/en/about-isa/code-of-ethics/_

Jaarsma, S. R. (Ed.). (2002). *Handle with care: Ownership and control of ethnographic materials.* Pittsburgh, PA: University of Pittsburgh Press.

Jackson, A. Y., & Mazzei, L. A. (2012). *Thinking with theory in qualitative research.* New York: Routledge.

Jackson, B. (1987). *Fieldwork.* Urbana University of Illinois Press.

Jackson, J. E. (1990). "I am a Fieldnote": Fieldnotes as a symbol of professional identity. In R. Sanjek (Ed.), *Fieldnotes: The makings of anthropology* (pp. 3–33). Ithaca, NY: Cornell University Press.

James, C. (2001). Cultural change in Mistissini: Implications for self determination and cultural survival. In C. H. Scott (Ed.), *Aboriginal autonomy and development in Northern Quebec and Labrador* (pp. 316–331). Vancouver, Canada: UBC Press.

Jones, D. (2018). Friends, the club, and the housing authority: How youth define their community through auto-driven photo elicitation. In M. Boucher (Ed.), *Participant empowerment through photo-elicitation in ethnographic education research.* Heidelberg, Germany: Springer.

Jones, J. L. (2002). Performance ethnography: The role of embodiment in cultural authenticity. *Theatre Topics, 12*(1), 1–15.

Kisliuk, M. R. (1998). *Seize the dance!: Baaka musical life and the ethnography of performance.* New York: Oxford University Press.

Koskoff, E. (2014). *A feminist ethnomusicology: Writings on music and gender.* Urbana: University of Illinois Press.

Kozinets, R. V. (2006). Click to connect: Netnography and tribal advertising. *Journal of Advertising Research, 46*(3), 279–288.

Kozinets, R. V. (2010). *Netnography: Doing ethnographic research online.* London: Sage.

Lassiter, L. (2005a). Collaborative ethnography and public anthropology. *Current Anthropology, 46*(1), 83–106.

Lassiter, L. (2005b). *The Chicago guide to collaborative ethnography.* Chicago: University of Chicago Press.

LeCompte, M. D., & Schensul, J. J. (2010). *Designing and conducting ethnographic research* (2nd ed.). Lanham, MD: Alta Mira Press.

Lichtman, M. (2013). *Qualitative research in education: A user's guide* (3rd ed.). Thousand Oaks, CA: Sage.

Lincoln, Y. S. (2005). Institutional review boards and methodological conservatism: The challenge to and from phenomenological paradigms. In N. K. Denzin & Y. S. Lincoln (Eds.), *The SAGE handbook of qualitative research* (3rd ed., pp. 165–181). Thousand Oaks, CA: Sage.

Littig, B., & Pöchhacker, F. (2014). Socio-translational collaboration: The case of expert interviews. Qualitative Inquiry, 20(9), 1085–1095.

Lysloff, R. (2003). Musical community on the internet: An on-line ethnography. *Cultural Anthropology, 18*(2), 233–263.

Lysloff, R. T. A. (1993). A wrinkle in time: The comic interlude in the Javanese puppet theater of Banyumas (West Central Java). *Asian Theatre Journal, 10*(1), 49–80.

Lysloff, R. T. A., & Gay, L. C. (Eds.). (2003). *Music and technoculture.* Middletown, CT: Wesleyan University Press.

Maclean, K. (2007). Translation in cross-cultural research: An example from Bolivia. *Development in Practice, 17*(6), 784–790.

Madison, D. S. (2005). *Critical ethnography: Method, ethics, and performance.* London: Sage.

Marcus, G. (1998). Ethnography in/of the world system: The emergence of multi-sited ethnography. In *Ethnography through thick & thin* (pp. 79–104). Princeton, NJ: Princeton University Press.

Markham, A. N. (2004). Representation in online ethnographies: A matter of context sensitivity. In M. D. Johns, S.-L. S. Chen, & G. J. Hall (Eds.), *Online social research: Methods, issues, & ethics* (pp. 141–155). New York: Peter Lang.

Markham, A., & Baym, N. (2009). *Internet inquiry.* Thousand Oaks, CA: Sage.

Markham, A. N., & Buchanan, E. A. (2012, December). *Ethical decision-making and internet research: Recommendations from the AoIR ethics and working committee* (Version 2.0). Approved by AoIR. Retrieved from http://aoir.org/reports/ethics2.pdf

Mason, J. (2002). *Qualitative researching.* Thousand Oaks, CA: Sage.

McCall, L. (2005). The complexity of intersectionality. *Signs, 30*(3), 1772–1800.

Mead, M., & Bateson, G. (1977). *On the use of the camera in anthropology. Studies in the anthropology of visual communication, 4*(2), 78–80.

Medicine, B. (2001). *Learning to be an anthropologist and remaining native* (S.-E. Jacobs, Ed.). Urbana University of Illinois Press.

Meizel, K., Cooley, T., & Syed, N. (2008). Virtual fieldwork: Three case studies. In G. Barz & T. J. Cooley (Eds.), *Shadows in the field: New perspectives for fieldwork in ethnomusicology* (2nd ed.). Oxford, UK: Oxford University Press.

Meredith, S. (2018, April 10). Facebook-Cambridge Analytica: A timeline of the data hijacking scandal. CNBC. Retrieved from https://www.cnbc.com/2018/04/10/facebook-cambridge-analytica-a-timeline-of-the-data-hijacking-scandal.html

Miller, D, Costa, E., Haynes, N., McDonald, T., Nicolescu, R., Sinanan, J., . . . Wang, X. (2016). *How the world changed social media.* London: UCL Press.

Miller, D., & Slater, D. (2000). *The internet: An ethnographic approach.* Oxford, UK: Berg.

Mills, S. (1996). Indigenous music and the law: An analysis of national and international legislation. *Yearbook for Traditional Music, 28.*

Murthy, D. (2008). Digital ethnography: An examination of the use of new technologies for social research. *Sociology, 42*(5), 837–855.

Mutua, K., & Swander, B. B. (Eds.). (2004). *Decolonial research in cross-cultural contexts: Critical personal narratives.* Albany: State University of New York Press.

Myers, H. (1992). *Ethnomusicology: An introduction.* New York: W. W. Norton & Company.

Nardi, B. A. (2010). *My life as a night elf priest: An anthropological account of world of warcraft.* Ann Arbor: University of Michigan Press.

Nettl, B. (1983). *The study of ethnomusicology: Thirty-one issues and concepts.* Champaign: University of Illinois Press.

Newsome, J. K. (2008). From researched to centrestage: A case study. Muzikoloski Zbornik *Musicological Annual, XLIV*(1), 31–49.

O'Connor, B., & R. Wyatt (2004). *Photo provocations: Thinking in, with, and about photography.* Lanham, MD: Scarecrow Press.

O'Reilly, K. (2005). *Ethnographic methods.* New York: Routledge.

Paris, D., & Winn, M. T. (Eds.). (2014). *Humanizing research.* Thousand Oaks, CA: Sage.

Pasqualino, C. (2007). Filming emotion: The place of video in anthropology. *Visual Anthropology Review, 23*(1), 84–91.

Pentzold, C. (2017). "What are these researchers doing in my Wikipedia?": Ethical premises and practical judgment in internet-based ethnography. *Ethics and Information Technology, 19*(2), 143–155.

Pew Research Center. (2019a). *Core trends survey.* Retrieved from https://www.pewresearch.org/internet/dataset/core-trends-survey/

Pew Research Center. (2019b). *Internet/broadband fact sheet.* Retrieved from https://www.pewresearch.org/internet/fact-sheet/internet-broadband/

Pink, S. (2009). *Doing sensory ethnography.* Thousand Oaks, CA: Sage.

Post, J. C. (Ed.). (2006). *Ethnomusicology: A contemporary reader.* New York: Routledge.

Pratt, M. L. (1986). Fieldwork in common places. In J. Clifford & G. E. Marcus (Eds.), *Writing culture: The poetics and politics of ethnography* (pp. 27–50). Berkeley: University of California Press.

Przybylski, L. (2018). Bilingual hip hop from community to classroom and back. *Ethnomusicology, 62*(4), 376–403.

Przybylski, L., & Niknafs, N. (2015). Practice what you preach: Teaching and learning popular music in higher education through interdisciplinary collaboration. *IASPM Journal, 5*(1), 100–123.

Rees, H. (2003). The age of consent: Traditional music, intellectual property and changing attitudes in the People's Republic of China. *British Journal of Ethnomusicology, 12*(1).

Reverby, S. M. (2009). *Examining Tuskegee: The infamous syphilis study and its legacy.* Chapel Hill: University of North Carolina Press.

Rheingold, H. (1998). The heart of the WELL. In *Composing cyberspace* (pp. 151–163). Boston: McGraw-Hill.

Richardson, L., & St. Pierre, E. A. (2005). Writing: A method of inquiry. In N. K. Denzin & Y. S. Lincoln (Eds.), *The SAGE handbook of qualitative research* (pp. 959–978). Thousand Oaks, CA: Sage.

Rose, G. (2016). *Visual methodologies* (4th ed.). London: Sage.

Saldaña, J. (2016). *The coding manual for qualitative researchers.* Los Angeles: Sage.

Saldaña, J., Leavy, P., & Beretvas, N. (2011). *Fundamentals of qualitative research.* New York: Oxford University Press.

Samuels, J. (2007). When words are not enough: Eliciting children's experiences of Buddhist monastic life through photographs. In Stanczak, G. (Ed.), *Visual research methods: image, society, and representation.* Thousand Oaks, CA: Sage.

Sanjek, R. (Ed.). (1990). *Fieldnotes: The makings of anthropology.* Ithaca, NY: Cornell University Press.

Schegloff, E. (2007). *Sequence organization in interaction: A primer in conversation analysis.* Cambridge, UK: Cambridge University Press.

Schloss, J. (2009). *Foundation: B-Boys, B-Girls, and hip-hop culture in New York.* Oxford, UK: Oxford University Press.

Seeger, A. (1996). Ethnomusicologists, archives, professional organizations, and the shifting ethics of intellectual property. *Yearbook for Traditional Music, 28*, 87–105.

Seeger, A. (2008). Theories forged in the crucible of action: The joys, dangers, and potentials of advocacy and fieldwork. In G. Barz & T. J. Cooley (Eds.), *Shadows in the field: New perspectives for fieldwork in ethnomusicology* (2nd ed., pp. 271–288). Oxford, UK: Oxford University Press.

Shea Murphy, J. (2007). *The people have never stopped dancing: Native American modern dance histories.* Minneapolis: University of Minnesota Press.

Sheehy, D. E. (1992). A few notions about philosophy and strategy in applied ethnomusicology. *Ethnomusicology, 36*(3), 323–336.

Slama, M. (2016). File sharing and (im)mortality: From genealogical records to Facebook. In R. Sanjek & S. Tratner (Eds.), *eFieldnotes: The makings of anthropology in the digital world* (pp. 94–109). Philadelphia: University of Pennsylvania Press.

Snodgrass, J. G. (2014). Ethnography of online cultures. In B. Russell & C. Gravlee (Eds.), *Handbook of methods in cultural anthropology* (pp. 437–466). Lanham, MD: Rowman & Littlefield.

Spradley, J. (1979). *The ethnographic interview.* New York: Holt, Rhinehart, and Winston.

Stets, J. E., & Serpe, R. T. (Eds.). (2016). *New directions in identity theory and research.* New York: Oxford University Press.

Stock, J. P. J. (2008). New directions in ethnomusicology: Seven themes toward disciplinary renewal. In H. Stobart (Ed.), *The new (ethno)musicologies* (pp. 188–206). Lanham, MD: Scarecrow Press.

Tedlock, B. (2005). The observation of participation and the emergence of public ethnography. In N. K. Denzin & Y. S. Lincoln (Eds.), *The SAGE handbook of qualitative research* (3rd ed., pp. 467–481). Thousand Oaks, CA: Sage.

Temple, B., & Young, A. (2004). Qualitative research and translation dilemmas. *Qualitative Research, 4*, 161–178.

Thomas, Q. R. A. (2005). Honoring the oral traditions of my ancestors through storytelling. In L. Brown & S. Strega (Eds.), *Research as resistance* (pp. 127–151). Toronto, Canada: Canadian Scholars' Press.

Thuiwai Smith, L. (2012). *Decolonizing methodologies* (2nd ed.). London: Zed Books.

Tracy, S. (2013). *Qualitative research methods: Collecting evidence, crafting analysis, and communicating impact.* Malden, MA: Wiley-Blackwell.

Trinh, T. M. (1989). *Woman, native, other.* Bloomington: Indiana University Press.

Turkle, S. (1997). *Life on the screen.* New York: Touchstone.

Underberg, N., & Zorn, E. (2013). *Digital ethnography: Anthropology, narrative, and New Media.* Austin: University of Texas Press.

Van Maanen, J. (1988). *Tales of the field: On writing ethnography.* Chicago: University of Chicago Press.

Walther, J. B. (2002). Research ethics in internet-enabled research: Human subjects issues and methodological myopia. *Ethics and Information Technology, 4*(3), 205–216.

Wilson, S. (2008). *Research is ceremony.* Black Point, NS, Canada: Fernwood Publications.

Wong, D. (2008). Moving from performance to performative ethnography and back again. In G. Barz & T. J. Cooley (Eds.), *Shadows in the field: New perspectives for fieldwork in ethnomusicology* (2nd ed., pp. 76–89). Oxford, UK: Oxford University Press.

Yuval-Davis, N. (2006). Intersectionality and feminist politics. *European Journal of Women's Studies, 13*(3), 193–209.

Zemp, H. (1996). The/an ethnomusicologist and the record business. *Yearbook for Traditional Music, 28,* 36–56.

Zimmer, M. (2010). "But the data is already public": On the ethics of research in Facebook. *Ethics and Information Technology, 12,* 313–325.

INDEX